Mariner's Menu
30 YEARS OF FRESH SEAFOOD IDEAS

BY JOYCE TAYLOR

EDITED BY SARAH FRIDAY PETERS • PUBLISHED BY NORTH CAROLINA SEA GRANT
PHOTOGRAPHS BY SCOTT D. TAYLOR • ILLUSTRATIONS BY CONNIE MASON

MARINER'S MENU: 30 YEARS OF FRESH SEAFOOD IDEAS
Copyright© 2003 by North Carolina Sea Grant
Printed and bound in the United States of America

Written and published by North Carolina Sea Grant
NC State University • Box 8605 • Raleigh, NC 27695-8605 • 919/515-2454 • www.ncseagrant.org
Ronald G. Hodson, Director • Katie Mosher, Communications Director • Linda Noble, Designer

Distributed by The University of North Carolina Press
PO Box 2288 • Chapel Hill, North Carolina 27515-2288
Additional copies of this publication may be ordered by calling 800/848-6224
or from the UNC Press Website, www.uncpress.unc.edu.

First Printing: 2003 • ISBN 0-8078-5513-8

TABLE OF
Contents

TABLE OF
Contents

Continued

What does a fresh fish look like? How long should clams cook? What species grill best? Chances are if you have a question about seafood, Mariner's Menu has the answer. Detailed descriptions, illustrations and tried-and-true recipes throughout the book make handling and cooking seafood simple — and delicious.

Three decades in the Seafood

Lab kitchen have proven to the

Carteret County Nutrition

Leaders that there are many

ways to prepare fresh seafood.

In this book, they share their

favorite cooking methods and

their best-tasting recipes

straight from the coast.

Mariner's
MENU

Mariner's
MENU

THANK YOU!

This book would not exist without the contributions of many people. Some are evident at first glance; others are unseen, yet equally significant. Heartfelt thanks to...

The Nutrition Leaders for all our seafood preparations and evaluations. You worked so faithfully for so long.

North Carolina Sea Grant for giving me such a fun job.

David Green for your constant support. Without your encouragement and persistence, I would never have completed this.

Lorraine DiBella for your day-to-day help and your patience with preparation of this manuscript. Also for writing the section on hybrid striped bass after my retirement.

Sarah Friday Peters for your beautiful depiction of our volunteers and for your editing. You have a way with words.

Connie Mason for your clear, precise illustrations that simplify the handling of fish and shellfish.

Scott Taylor for your photographs that bring this area and our volunteers to life.

Frank Thomas and *Ted Miller* for introducing me to the world of seafood.

Family and Consumer Science Extension Agents of the Cooperative Extension Service for inviting me to your communities and arranging my workshops.

The citizens of North Carolina for attending workshops and allowing me to share seafood information with you. You always inspired me.

The Seafood Marketing Division of the N.C. Department of Agriculture and Consumer Services for support of this publication.

— *Joyce Taylor*

For 30 years, a small group of gifted cooks has met in a Morehead City kitchen to develop and test seafood handling and preparation techniques using local seafood. The result is this one-of-a-kind book. Their commitment, and that of many others, provides an ongoing legacy of Tar Heel seafood traditions.

Home-grown and home-prepared. North Carolina seafood prepared by North Carolina people. The Nutrition Leaders have included many Carteret County cooks through years. Eleven of the most recent, active members are featured in Seafood Traditions, pp. 14-25.

ABOUT OUR NUTRITION LEADERS...

The current volunteers featured in this book have been active for quite a few years now. Most of them began in the 1980s and early 1990s. Their predecessors date back to the early 1970s.

We do not have complete records of the first years or of the period from 1986 until 1990, when we did not publish a newsletter. We place equal value on the work of those who participated during those times even though we do not have their names.

Following are the names of additional regular participants through the years:

- Claire Armstrong
- Vicki Austin
- Emma Avery
- Olene Blackburn
- Evelyn Callaway
- Edna Cannady
- Olivia Chadwick
- Clara Bell Daniels
- Julia Day
- Genette Dudley
- Sandra Ehrler
- Gertrude Fraenzel

- Janie Garner
- Julia Gillikin
- Sybil Godley
- Johnny Greene
- Helen Hayes
- Sarah Harris
- Emily Hrywny
- Nancy Kelly
- Kay Kerman
- Betty Lewis
- Edith Jarman
- Marty Jordan

- Louise McKamey
- Miriam Moore
- Jean Morrison
- Mary Jane Osborne
- Inez Parker
- Bea Phillips
- Lucy Piper
- Isabel Siglar
- Alice Spencer
- Janie Threatt
- Beulah Toll
- Hazel Weaver

Family and Consumer Science Extension Agents who have worked with the group are Floy Garner, Maurene Stewart, Lora Gray and Sarah Ann Sasser.

SEAFOOD
Traditions

In Eastern North Carolina, seafood means more than just food. The fresh clams, crabs, mackerels and other fish pulled from Crystal Coast waters are part of the region's history and heritage. They are part of the culture, too, woven into daily life like a tightly knit fish net, gathering in those who know and appreciate its extraordinary value.

SEAFOOD
Traditions

Written by
Sarah Friday Peters

In Eastern North Carolina, seafood means more than just food. The fresh clams, crabs, mackerels and other fish pulled from Crystal Coast waters are part of the region's history and heritage. They are part of the culture, too, woven into daily life like a tightly knit fish net, gathering in those who know and appreciate its extraordinary value.

Dolena Bell of Beaufort knows this just as well as anybody.

"My dad fished when I was a child," recalls the coastal native and long-time cook. "I helped pull the net and take the fish out. We sometimes had fish fries on the shoreline. I've helped pull hand nets for shrimp on the banks, too, clammed at Cape Lookout, and caught crabs from North River and other Down East areas," she adds. "We were blessed."

Blessed to grow up in a place where fresh air and sunshine seem as plentiful as the sand and shrimp. Where seagulls glide with the breeze. Where handmade boats and lifelike duck decoys are made with as much care and craftsmanship as homemade cornbread and a bowl of steaming hot stew. Blessed to know people who ply the waters for a living and farm the earth for potatoes and meat. And blessed to know that good food means good times — like oyster roasts and fish fries, clambakes and crab boils.

This book celebrates that heritage and the contributions of coastal cooks like Dolena Bell to the continuing Tar Heel seafood story. It combines the richness of a state known worldwide for its coastal harvests — clams, crabs, scallops, shrimp, oysters, bluefish, flounder and other fish — with 30 years of dedicated testing, and even more years of kitchen expertise. Mix the Atlantic Ocean's bounty with a dozen women who know it like their own names and you have *Mariner's Menu*.

Since 1973, representatives from each Carteret County home extension club have gathered monthly in a Morehead City kitchen to test new ways of handling, storing and preparing fish and shellfish caught off the North Carolina coast. First known as the "Health, Food and Nutrition Leaders," these cooks came, cooked, then shared what they learned with their own clubs back home in

Blessed to grow up in a place where fresh air and sunshine seem as plentiful as the sand and shrimp. ... Blessed to know people who ply the waters for a living and farm the earth for potatoes and meat. And blessed to know that good food means good times — like oyster roasts and fish fries, clambakes and crab boils.

Since 1973, representatives

from each Carteret County home

extension club have gathered

monthly in a Morehead City

kitchen to test new ways of

handling, storing and preparing

fish and shellfish caught off the

North Carolina coast.

Crab Point, Gloucester, Emerald Isle and other spots along the Crystal Coast.

The program started as a way to promote North Carolina seafood products through the North Carolina State University Seafood Laboratory. Since then it has sailed along as the Seafood Lab Nutrition Leaders, with now-retired Sea Grant seafood expert Joyce Taylor at the helm. The group's legacy continues with this one-of-a-kind book.

Mariner's Menu contains more than 160 easy and delicious seafood recipes tested and tasted by the Nutrition Leaders. Chapters cover various cooking methods such as broiling, grilling, frying and steaming and include such mouth-watering dishes as *Sautéed Soft Crabs with Fresh Lime*, *Carolina Shrimp Boil* and *Scallop Bisque*.

Many of the recipes use common ingredients and take little preparation time. As the recipes show, cooking fish doesn't have to be intimidating. Sometimes the simplest ones taste the best, Taylor says. In the lab she insists on the real, fresh ingredients — real lemon juice, fresh fish, fresh parsley, ground pepper — to get the most flavor out of each ingredient. "I even make them make their own bread crumbs," she adds. "You can really taste the difference."

Nutrition Leaders taste and rank each recipe on a scale of 1 to 5, with 5 as "excellent." Recipes in this book scored 4.5 or higher, making them the best of 30 years worth of cooking.

"I think the advantage we have is that if you use one of our recipes you can be sure it's going to be good," Taylor says. "We taste and we critique. We make comments. We go by taste, not preference."

Yet this book is more than a cookbook, as Taylor is quick to point out. It's a complete seafood resource book for cooks who want to know more than just how to bake or fry fish.

More than 50 detailed illustrations by Morehead City artist Connie Mason show how to debone fish, devein shrimp, crack a crab and all those other curiosities cooks have harbored about fish and shellfish. Plus *Mariner's Menu* includes information on seafood nutrition, health issues, handling and storage.

"It's almost everything you wanted to know about seafood but were afraid to ask," Taylor jokes.

Other local contributors who add to *Mariner's Menu*'s down-home flavor include photographer Scott Taylor, Sarah Ann Sasser and Lorraine DiBella. Sasser represented the Carteret County Extension Service at the monthly cooking sessions, carrying on a 30-year tradition and connection between the lab and the

Lorraine DiBella

service. DiBella, the lab's public information assistant, bought fish, scrubbed clams, peeled shrimp, read recipes and helped Taylor in innumerable ways.

At the heart of this book are the Nutrition Leaders themselves. People like Mary Dudley Price of Gloucester and Valaree Stanley of Morehead City who have made North Carolina seafood as much a part of their lives as family and friends. Many of these women grew up on the water with fathers, brothers, sisters and mothers who fished. They fished alongside, for finfish and blue crabs in the summer and oysters and scallops in the winter. Most grew up watching their mothers or big sisters frying up the catch. Back then the women, now mostly in their 70s and 80s, either fried fish, cooked it in stew or cooked seafood from cans, or corned or salt-preserved it.

About 40 Nutrition Leaders have passed through the Seafood Lab kitchen since its inception. (A complete list is on p. 4.) Eleven remained over the stove and by the sink to bring you *Mariner's Menu*. Here they all share what they have learned with you.

First known as the "Health,

Food and Nutrition Leaders,"

these cooks came, cooked, then

shared what they learned with

their own clubs back home in

Crab Point, Gloucester,

Emerald Isle and other spots

along the Crystal Coast.

NORTH CAROLINA SEAFOOD

As the Nutrition Leaders know first-hand, abundant fisheries have provided a healthy economic foundation for the North Carolina coast and boundless recreational fishing opportunities for generations, as well. With 4,000 miles of shoreline and 2.5 million acres of marine and estuarine waters where many species spawn, North Carolina hosts more than 65 fish and shellfish species. North Carolina consistently nets from $88 million to $100 million worth of seafood landed commercially each year, ranking it tenth or eleventh in the nation, according to 2001 North Carolina Fisheries Association data.

Each year, more than one million recreational fishermen and women flock to the Tar Heel coast to reel in sport fish and good-eating fish and shellfish. Shrimp, blue crabs, clams, oysters and sea and bay scallops remain popular shellfish. Yellowfin tuna, dolphin, king mackerel, shark, red drum, pompano, swordfish, wahoo, black sea bass and spot lure anglers to deeper waters. In 2001, recreational anglers reeled in their largest catch in 13 years with an estimated 23.9 million pounds of fish landed in North Carolina alone, according to the National Marine Fisheries Service (NMFS).

At the same time, North Carolina's 5,000-plus commercial fishermen landed 137 million pounds of fish and shellfish, NMFS reports. A harvest of

Sarah Ann Sasser

Anglers know, too, that fishing

along the Crystal Coast includes

some of the North Carolina's

best. Carteret County's 81 miles

of ocean coastline, plus miles of

waterways along Bogue and

Core sounds, and the area's

rivers, bays, inlets and creeks

provide endless places for

anglers to drop a line or

commercial fishermen to pull a

net or crab pot. Offshore, the

warm, southern Gulf Stream

meets the cooler, northern

Labrador Current creating

fine fishing beyond the

Crystal Coast shoreline.

nearly 30 million pounds of hard blue crabs made these shellfish North Carolina's top money fishery in 2001, and helped the state lead the nation in blue crab production. Other valuable fisheries include Atlantic croaker, bluefish, shrimp and summer flounder.

Anglers know, too, that fishing along the Crystal Coast includes some of North Carolina's best. Carteret County's 81 miles of ocean coastline, plus miles of waterways along Bogue and Core sounds, and the area's rivers, bays, inlets and creeks provide endless places for anglers to drop a line or commercial fishermen to pull a net or crab pot. Offshore, the warm, southern Gulf Stream meets the cooler, northern Labrador Current creating fine fishing beyond the Crystal Coast shoreline.

Year after year, Carteret County ranks No. 1 in commercial landings for the state, out of all coastal counties. In 2001, for instance, more than 66 million pounds of fish and shellfish such as menhaden, blue crabs and flounder were pulled from its waters, marking almost half of the state's total that year. The next highest county was Dare, with 31 million pounds.

With so many species, and many of them plentiful year-round, seafood markets, grocery stores and restaurants in North Carolina and beyond provide great variety with better availability to consumers. Such diversity and availability, coupled with consumers' needs for healthier, quicker meals make seafood education an ongoing need, says Seafood Lab Director David Green. People want to know about seafood safety, handling and preparation. But while most of us have readily ordered fresh flounder in parchment with dill sauce in a restaurant, we haven't been willing to try such adventurous recipes at home yet. Until now. ...

HOW IT ALL BEGAN

Around the time of shrimp cocktails and tuna casseroles with potato chips on top, sport fishermen and women in North Carolina wanted to know better ways to use their catch. In the early 1970s, the Morehead Yacht Club and other sportfishing clubs requested help from North Carolina State University. The plan for a place where good cooks could test seafood-related research and translate it to the public followed.

Spawned right in Carteret County, the project carried a two-fold purpose, according to a Coastal Seafood Laboratory history. The first was to "conduct and use applied research" and to "complement the seafood research work of the Raleigh (State University) laboratories." This meant food scientists such as

Steve J. Stokes, Frank Thomas and Neil Webb conducted valuable research on topics such as seafood safety, quality assurance and better processing techniques.

Back then, not too many sport or commercial fishers carried ice on their boats, for instance. NCSU researchers helped them and local processors find better ways to preserve a healthy catch.

Secondly, the Seafood Lab was charged with providing seafood education and training through statewide workshops and county extension programs. Food Science Extension Specialist Ted Miller started seafood extension with a business that wanted a better crab cake in 1973. For help, he tapped into the national network of "Health, Food and Nutrition Leaders." Beginning that year, representatives from each Carteret County home extension club came to the Seafood Lab to lend a hand and learn. From the group's inception until 2002, the Nutrition Leaders at the lab continued to support a primary advisory service sponsored by North Carolina Sea Grant, a federal/state program highlighting coastal research, education and extension.

"Carteret Extension Homemakers have assumed a scientific role as they work in the Seafood Laboratory," reads an 1970s public relations newsletter called "Scientists and Homemakers Research Together."

"The food scientist has a vast storehouse of information about seafoods, the changes which occur as a result of storage, aging and application of heat," the newsletter continues. "Homemakers, on the other hand, have a great deal of kitchen expertise of their own gained from experience. By working together, they hope to come up with some findings that will be mutually beneficial."

One of the Nutrition Leaders' first assignments was to find ways to use the "waste" from filleting fish. "The homemakers suggested that the heads and backbones, which are usually thrown away, could be boiled to extract the gelatin," the newsletter says. "Fish to be frozen could be dipped in the gelatin solution as a possible protection from freezer burn. This could mean better quality in frozen fish for the consumer."

Other tasks early on included finding new uses for shrimp heads and for clam, scallop and oyster shells. The group tested different recipes and ways for preserving seafood's flavor and nutrients. They tried out recipes for underutilized fish like eels and sea robin. And they developed their own new ways to prepare and use fresh flaked fish rather than canned options. Then, as now, Nutrition Leader members served as taste panels.

For three decades, the Nutrition Leaders kept their charge, providing quality seafood recipes and information to Carteret County and around the world, including through their former newsletter *Mariner's Menu*, which was

Other tasks early on included finding new uses for shrimp heads and for clam, scallop and oyster shells. The group tested different recipes and ways for preserving seafood's flavor and nutrients. They tried out recipes for underutilized fish like eels and sea robin. And they developed their own new ways to prepare and use fresh flaked fish rather than canned options. Then, as now, Nutrition Leader members served as taste panels.

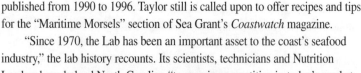

The beauty of such a program, says David Green, director of the Seafood Lab, is that it's "home-grown and home-prepared — North Carolina seafood products prepared by North Carolina people."

published from 1990 to 1996. Taylor still is called upon to offer recipes and tips for the "Maritime Morsels" section of Sea Grant's *Coastwatch* magazine.

"Since 1970, the Lab has been an important asset to the coast's seafood industry," the lab history recounts. Its scientists, technicians and Nutrition Leaders have helped North Carolina "to remain competitive in today's market, to promote, maintain and improve the standards and quality of North Carolina seafood products, and to support, through education and training, the general growth and success of North Carolina's seafood industry."

The beauty of such a program, says David Green, director of the Seafood Lab, is that it's "home-grown and home-prepared — North Carolina seafood products prepared by North Carolina people." North Carolina has one of the healthiest fisheries economies in the nation, and these women are helping to positively advance its vast resources.

What makes the Nutrition Leaders' program even richer, he adds, is that some of the volunteers have been involved for more than 20 years. "This is really amazing how long people have been in it. The people who joined in 1989 are the 'newcomers,'" Green says.

"This is a unique Carteret County thing we've created here," Taylor says. "I'm almost certain there's nothing else like this anywhere," she notes of the Nutrition Leaders. "Their contributions are remarkable. The work, the book would not exist without the Nutrition Leaders."

JOYCE TAYLOR ON BOARD

Nor would the Nutrition Leaders have existed without Joyce Taylor.

"As long as I live, I will be indebted to Joyce Taylor and her leadership at the lab for introducing me to the bounty of our coast and teaching me how to put it on my table in a wholesome and delicious fashion," says Mary Dudley Price, a Nutrition Leader since 1978.

"Joyce is just great," adds fellow cook Valaree Stanley of Morehead City. "She's real nice to work with. She has everything planned and ready by the time we get here. ... She's an expert in seafood. She knows everything about it. I've learned a lot from her."

One of the best decisions Seafood Lab administrators ever made, in fact, was to hire the Carteret County teacher in 1974. Taylor's first job at the Seafood Lab was taste-testing Carolina-caught croaker and gray trout part-time that year. The job soon worked into a full-time position writing newsletters,

Joyce Taylor

answering seafood queries and conducting workshops across the state on cooking, nutrition and handling fresh fish.

In 1989 Taylor wrote *No-Salt Seafood*, a health-conscious cookbook published by North Carolina Sea Grant. Her quarterly newsletter, *Mariner's Menu*, reported the Nutrition Leaders' best recipes to 3,000 subscribers around the world. She also wrote six seafood pamphlets like *Breaking into Bivalves* and *Bringing the Catch Home* for Sea Grant, and devised a seafood availability poster for seafood restaurants, markets and consumers. Then in the early 1990s, she cooked up a seafood safety and sanitation course for inspectors to use when combing local restaurants, seafood markets and grocery store seafood counters. Clearly, she and the Nutrition Leaders have influenced a generation of seafood cooks.

Not bad for an Asheville native who came east.

Taylor grew up in the Blue Ridge Mountains and graduated from the University of North Carolina in Greensboro in 1954. With a hankering for the water and sea air, she moved to the coast, working for two years before taking a fourth-grade teaching job in Carteret County in 1956. She taught in various grades for 17 more years before taking the job at the Seafood Lab, all the while slipping out in her boat and casting a line when she could.

With almost 30 years experience under her cooking mitt now, Taylor has become North Carolina's "guru of seafood," as a 1995 article in *Wildlife in North Carolina* called her. "For 30 years, Joyce has spread the word on fresh North Carolina seafood — the distinct flavors, the nutritional value," says Ronald G. Hodson, director of North Carolina Sea Grant. "With her dedicated group of Nutrition Leaders, she offers traditional and nontraditional fare that consumers trust they can make and enjoy at home."

In all that time, Taylor has seen seafood's popularity grow immensely.

Back in the 1970s, people didn't eat seafood at home much, except maybe along the coast and they were mainly frying fish like croaker, gray trout, spot, hogfish and mullet, she recalls. "People around here grew up on fried fish." Around the 1980s, seafood's popularity surged with more information on its value as a high-protein and low-fat meat, and more readily available species such as red snapper, grouper, mahi-mahi, salmon and fresh tuna.

"People have not been comfortable cooking seafood," she says. But after she demonstrates or shares a recipe from *Mariner's Menu*, people say, "It looks so easy, I think I can do it."

Taylor has a knack for blending flavors and fresh ingredients that enhance seafood instead of smothering it. Plus she's known for making the cooking fun with her quick wit and a wry sense of humor.

Back in the 1970s, people didn't eat seafood at home much, except maybe along the coast and they were mainly frying fish like croaker, gray trout, spot, hogfish and mullet, she recalls. "People around here grew up on fried fish." Around the 1980s, seafood's popularity surged with more information on its value as a high-protein and low-fat meat, and more readily available species such as red snapper, grouper, mahi-mahi, salmon and fresh tuna.

Workshop participants constantly told her she should be a stand-up comic, as they watched her juggle three pans of simmering fish and toss out funny retorts at the same time.

It comes from her experience teaching, Taylor says. "I don't think learning should be tedious. I have a good time."

Yes, says Nutrition Leader Judy Blessing, grinning. "If it wasn't for her personality, we wouldn't have stayed here this long."

IN THE LAB

Long before live cooking shows, the Nutrition Leaders served up the real thing each month in the Seafood Lab. Imagine a camera taking you inside...

As the Seafood Lab clock's hands inch toward 9 a.m., Joyce Taylor bustles around the well-stocked kitchen checking last-minute details before a new Nutrition Leader session begins. Before she hands out the six recipes they'll test today, she checks in with the women who, over the years, have become more than co-workers. They are close friends.

"We've got handouts. Remember I used to be a teacher," Taylor jokes, passing out the day's recipes and rating sheets. The list includes two sautéed items and some fried items.

For 26 years, Taylor urged seafood lovers to veer away from frying. "I preached it for years," she says, mainly for nutritional reasons. "But a book like this would be incomplete if it told you how to do everything but fry."

Like a well-trained team, the women, donned in "Eat More Seafood" aprons, divide the recipes from their coach and begin pulling ingredients out of large wooden cabinets and packed refrigerators. Taylor selects the recipes ahead of time, gathers ingredients and buys the fish. Today, it's 12 pounds — as always, bought the day before from a local fish market.

The women work steadily in pairs. Some have kept the same pair for more than a decade: Mary Dudley with Lissie, Vera with Martha, Betty and Dolena. ... The women consider it an honor to be here. That's why they don't leave. Some waited for years for an open slot and a chance to get to cook here.

A few minutes into the marathon cooking session, Taylor runs her finger lightly over a large, white grouper fillet and knows instantly there are no bones.

"I know the mahi mahi, snapper and flounder don't have bones today," today she yells over the rising din. She demonstrates how to cut grouper, reminding them it takes longer to cook if the fillet's thicker.

Recipes are timed so that dishes come out of the oven at different times.

Like a well-trained team, the women, donned in "Eat More Seafood" aprons, divide the recipes from their coach and begin pulling ingredients out of large wooden cabinets and packed refrigerators. Taylor selects the recipes ahead of time, gathers ingredients and buys the fish. Today, it's 12 pounds — as always, bought the day before from a local fish market.

Taylor leaves notes on most of the recipes, like "Check the amounts of oil, butter." Or "Check the amount of butter needed for sauteing."

"We've got to measure everything," Dolena Bell says. "She likes us to be absolutely correct in our measuring."

As the pairs cook away, Taylor checks in, offering suggestions, tasting, urging them to write down any important information. At one point she asks everybody to stop and taste. Part science class, part cooking show, the women work with a relaxed precision that only comes from time together in the kitchen.

By 10:45, Betty Motes and Dolena Bell start to cook their flounder for *Crispy Flounder Fillets*. Judy Blessing drops four snapper fillets in a pan of sizzling butter at the same time for her *Snapper Fillets Sautéed with Mushrooms*. Taylor gives a short lesson on clarifying butter.

Fifteen minutes later, Taylor and most of the Nutrition Leaders begin tasting *Deep-Fried Shrimp*. Dolena and Betty don't have time, yet.

By 11:15, the third dish is up — piping hot *Mahi-Mahi Sautéed in Butter*. The room falls silent as the group, now burgeoned with co-workers from down the hall, savors the dish.

"Well it's cooked to perfection. It's as moist as it can be," Taylor comments. "We should have used skinless fillets."

Within minutes, Valeree and Vera are back at work, dredging and draining firm white triggerfish fillets. "Let me tell you children something, look for bones," Vera cautions.

"I'll be one of your children anytime, Madam Mayor," jokes Judy to the former Emerald Isle mayor.

Next comes *Grouper Fillet in Beer Batter*. Again a hush fills the room, and the Nutrition Leaders fill out their rating sheets.

Just before noon, Valaree presents a platter of steaming hot, golden-fried triggerfish like a proud chef offering a succulent Thanksgiving turkey. Tasters in the now-crowded room line up with paper plates and plastic forks waiting for a bite and a dollop of homemade tartar sauce.

No one's disappointed.

Within minutes, countertops shine, the spices line up on the shelves again, the dishes are washed and put away. And the Nutrition Leaders chalk up another successful session.

"I believe I've eaten about a pound of fish today," Vera says.

Yes, adds Lissie, "We eat and go home happy."

Like a hearty stew or marinade, something happens when individual ingredients come together and meld over time. So it has been with the Nutrition Leaders, too. Separate women with separate lives, coming together once a month for a decade or two. Over the years they became seafood experts. And also they became friends.

SEAFOOD NUTRITION LEADERS

Like a hearty stew or marinade, something happens when individual ingredients come together and meld over time. So it has been with the Nutrition Leaders, too. Separate women with separate lives, coming together once a month for a decade or two. Over the years they became seafood experts. And also they became friends.

Honestly, says Lissie McNamee, "The ladies have meant more to me than the cooking."

Separately, some grew up in the city, in the North; others right nearby off the Newport River in Carteret County. Some have families; some, many friends. Some fished and crabbed before they could tell time. Others knew just canned salmon or codfish on Fridays.

Together, they laughed a lot in the lab and brought each other little gifts, like Vera Gaskins' crocheted items or Taylor's angel pins. Every Christmas, they threw an enviable covered dish and exchanged simple presents. They knew who needed a ride and who had grandchildren in town. And together they made donations to family scholarships.

Through it all, the Nutrition Leaders worked as one to continue to provide consistently high-quality recipes and seafood information to consumers. Here are their stories.

Dolena "Dolly" Bell

The youngest of five Gillikins, Bell grew up on a farm eight miles east of Beaufort in a little community called "Bettie." Back then, everybody worked. Her father and brothers worked the farm by day, then often her father fished at night to support the family. They raised hogs and chickens, butchering and curing them themselves as there were no refrigerators or freezers then, she recalls. On Saturdays, her mother took fresh vegetables to the Morehead City market. "Sunday was a free day. Sunday we went to church."

"I was always in the way, they told me," Bell says. "But at the same time, I was being taught how to pick the berries, beans, tomatoes and dig potatoes back on the farm. I helped my mom with the cooking and cleaning, especially the dish washing. She would prepare the food for our noontime meal before going to the fields.

I was sent to the kitchen to cook, to set the table and wash the dishes from breakfast, then to clean the kitchen after the meal — then back to the fields at age 10 or 11.

"I learned to cook vegetables, chicken, pork and seafood," she adds. "We were blessed with having fish, oysters, scallops, clams and crabs. Shrimp came later." The fish were salted, dried and smoked. The pork was smoked and salted. They made scrapple and hogshead cheese with the remaining parts. "I hated hog killing time. Also, we had mullet roe — salted and dried. Shad roe was fried or cooked with eggs. Seafood was fried, baked or stewed."

When her father fished, she sometimes helped pull in the net and take out the fish. "I've helped pull hand nets for shrimp on the banks, clammed at Cape Lookout, dug for oysters by the North River bridge and crabbed from the North River and Down East areas," Bell recalls.

Some of her favorite memories are going "down at the shore" for oyster roasts and fish fries. Each fall when the crops were in and the mullet were running, all the neighbors would tie their nets together and pull in fish all afternoon. Then they built a fire in the sand and had a fish fry. "It was kind of like a beach party for the neighborhood," she says.

In winter, she and her mother would often go down to the water when the tide pulled out and gather oysters, then roast them on the shore or back home. She remembers gathering and shucking scallops, too, then selling them by the bucket in her side yard. Later on, two brothers, Bell's son and a grandson carried on the Gillikin commercial fishing tradition.

Yet even with all she knew about fish, Bell says she's learned much at the Seafood Lab since joining in the early 1980s. Tips such as new ways to prepare fish and shellfish, how to use herbs and proper measuring. "Joyce likes us to be absolutely correct in our measuring," she tells.

A few of her favorite recipes from the Seafood Lab are flounder with herbs in parchment, crab Savannah, soft crabs golden-fried, oysters fried, scallops baked in a casserole, and shrimp "any way!"

"North Carolina seafood is hard to beat," she says. "It's the freshness of it. If you've got something fresh from the water, it has a definite, different flavor to it."

Judy Blessing

Cod and canned tuna were about the only fish dishes on Judy Blessing's menus before moving South. "Being from a Catholic family, I can remember eating fish every Friday," recalls the Athol, Mass. native. "We only had cod with tartar sauce or tuna casserole. Nothing fancy." Plus, she wasn't allowed in the kitchen, either, except to do the dishes.

All that changed when she married her husband, Frank, in 1977, and moved on board a 32-foot sailboat dubbed "Moon Mist." For six years, the newlyweds toured the world, sailing to the Caribbean, Ireland, England, the Mediterranean and finally the South. In 1983, they docked their boat in Beaufort, becoming the first to tie up at the new downtown dock. They started a farm and settled into the county where they knew they could farm *and* fish.

"Sailing for six years we caught lots of different fish" like lobster and squirrelfish. "But we only had a gas stove, so most of the fish were fried."

Along with farming vegetables and growing flowers such as gladiolas, daisies and zinnias, Frank became a commercial crabber, then signed on with a commercial fishing boat for another five years.

"Since Frank was bringing home all this good stuff fresh, we needed to learn how to cook it," she says.

So Blessing joined the Russell Creek Extension Club, then in 1985 became its representative to the Nutrition Leaders. Finally here she began to learn to cook seafood in a variety of ways.

"I learned more in the Seafood Lab than I ever could by myself," says the vivacious cook. For example, Taylor introduced her to fresh herbs and spices. "Once you taste the fresh herbs, it really makes a difference." Two favorite dishes she recalls are the mahi-mahi with lemon mayonnaise and the salmon with sour cream and dill sauce.

"It's been one-of-a-kind," she says of working with the Nutrition Leaders. "It's a unique experience that we shared. Something we'll never forget."

Vera Gaskins

Marrying a weekend angler in 1961 brought Vera Gaskins abruptly, but willingly, into the world of cooking seafood. A New Bern native, her husband, Walter, grew up by the water and fished every chance he got. He once even made the local paper Down East for reeling in two tarpon one year, as well as king mackerels and trout, his favorite.

"He loves the sport and I have always tried to use his catches to feed our family," says Gaskins, a native of Alabama. Her sister-in-law passed along a few tips on frying oysters and fish, but for years Gaskins relied solely on the book *The Art of Fish Cookery* by Milo Miloradorvich for help and ideas. When she and her family moved to Carteret County in 1978, she came across a copy of *Seafood Cookery*, published by the Carteret County Home Extension office. "These two books were my only sources until I agreed to represent our local homemaker club as a Nutrition Leader" in 1982.

Before then, Gaskins fried 90 percent of the seafood she cooked. Now she bakes, grills, microwaves, stews, steams and fries. "I'm not afraid to experiment and alter recipes, and I no longer shy away from cooking seafood for a crowd — or opening freshly caught bay scallops and clams."

Being a Nutrition Leader taught the former Emerald Isle mayor other valuable cooking lessons, too. Like keeping fish refrigerated before time to cook; pulling small bones out of fillets with pliers before cooking; baking fish only until it flakes; and using glass or non-metallic cookware for seafood. She notes she uses a lot less oil these days, too.

Mostly, Gaskins is grateful for the freshness and variety of seafood available right at her door in Carteret County. "It's part of our county's image — like Bogue Sound melons and vegetables," and oyster dressing and fish stew.

She saves the oyster dressing recipe she learned to cook at the Seafood Lab for special occasions like Christmas. A few other favorites include fresh corn and shrimp chowder, and oyster patties using crushed crackers.

Retired now, Walter still casts a line in the surf now and then. And the Gaskins are thankful for plenty of friends who keep them supplied in fresh fish.

Martha Giles

"I don't really remember 'learning' to cook," Martha Giles says. "We just did it, I guess, from helping Mother," back in her Chadbourne kitchen in Columbus County. "I do remember as a teenager baking on Saturday afternoons — homemade yeast rolls for hamburger buns for small family gatherings, lemon pies and cream puffs."

Growing up close to the ocean, "We cooked a goodly amount of seafood, especially fish and oysters," Giles recalls. "Our fish was usually fried or baked. But oysters — they were the best. I remember my mother bringing home quarts of shucked oysters that she bought from fishermen for about a dollar a quart. They were fried, stewed or, my favorite, scalloped. Many were eaten raw."

Marrying a fisherman — and a good cook himself — kept Giles close to the bounty of the sea. Often her husband, Thad, slipped down from Raleigh to Core Banks to fish for flounder,

pompanos, bluefish and spots. Then they bought a little house near the water so he could stay a couple days at a time. In 1982 the Giles retired to Davis for good. Now they could fish whenever they wanted. Surf fishing mostly, for flounder, blues and spots. She remembers one trip, especially, when the fish were coming in so fast she recalls telling them to wait!

The Giles ate or froze their catch most of the time, or shared it with friends back in Raleigh. They baked or fried fish at first. Thad could make a mean tempura. And "I still can't cook clam chowder (Manhattan-style) like he does. He likes to use the calico clams for this."

Joining the Nutrition Leaders from the Gloucester Extension Club around 1985 opened Giles' eyes to the possibilities and potential of seafood.

"First is fresh, fresh, fresh," she says. Fresh ingredients and fresh fish and shellfish taste better. "Also, that seafood can be cooked many different ways, not just fried." She especially liked learning how to flake fish for salads and how to grill. "I can't believe the difference between fresh tuna salad and canned tuna salad," she remarks.

Taylor and the group taught her the importance of measuring ingredients accurately, how to use herbs and spices with fish, and not to wash shrimp too much as it washes away the flavor.

"I've always loved fish," Giles says with a smile. "I don't fry as much as I used to, although my husband still wants me to."

Kay Holm

Squid. That was the first seafood ingredient Kay Holm was introduced to as the newest Nutrition Leader one day at the Seafood Lab in the early 1980s. "I looked at it and thought, ooooooh. But it was darned good!" says the long-time Merrimon resident. "We cleaned them. We fried them. Those things were buggers. But they were very, very good." The group even served the recipe at Carteret County's Strange Seafood Festival the following year, and she remembers people coming back for seconds.

In almost 20 years with Taylor and the Nutrition Leaders, Holm has learned a lot more, too, about other species, ways to cook seafood, herb and spice use and entertaining with seafood.

"I learned a great deal about cooking fish," she says. "I can look at a fish that comes out of the sea and say 'I think I know what I can do with it.'"

The Los Angeles native has always loved seafood and loved

to cook. She grew up by the apron of her Armenian mother and sister, Kron, both talented cooks, she recalls. She watched as her mother made stuffed grape leaves, pilafs, stuffed meatballs, and of course, baklava — the light, sweet pastry made with sheets of paper-thin dough.

"She used to make the dough, roll it out real thin," Holm remembers. "Mine looked like a stack of newspapers."

She married her husband, Richard, in 1952, and moved to Gloucester in 1975, then a few years later to Merrimon.

"Back then, I cooked seafood the way everybody did — I fried it." But after joining the Travelers Home Extension Club, then the Nutrition Leaders, her repertoire widened. "There are so many things you can do with fish now it's amazing. ... Although if you ask me, there's nothing like fried fish."

Over the years, she's enjoyed the dishes with shrimp and scallops, and can't recall a recipe she didn't like. "Some things were a flop, let's face it." But the group just said, "We'll do it again" and did.

Anne Lawton

When it comes to creating things, Anne Lawton's hands could work magic. Whether working behind a kitchen counter or a craft table, Lawton could turn a few scraps of cloth into a pretty quilt or a handful of ingredients into a mouth-watering dish.

"She was an excellent cook, no matter what she made," says her daughter, Anne Lawton of Morehead City. "She made a rice pilaf that you just made a pig out of yourself eating." It wasn't unusual to go back four or five times for "seconds" of her mom's sumptuous shrimp, rice and bacon dish. Then there were the crab cakes in the shell, her homemade bread, her caramel cake and fruitcake, too.

"She had this big metal tin that she mixed the fruitcake in," her daughter recalls. "I can just see her elbow-deep in the batter, stirring it with her hands." Those fruitcakes tasted unlike any you could buy.

One of five children to grow up on a farm outside Summerville, S.C., Anne Smith married Elmore Lawton, an Army man, in 1939. The couple moved from station to station in Louisiana, California, Virginia, Austria, Japan and Pennsylvania, and raised five children before retiring to Carteret County in 1968.

"Mom said when she married Dad that he knew more about cooking than she did," her daughter says, with a laugh. But with five children (four boys) and a job as a school cafeteria manager in Virginia, Lawton learned quickly and well.

"I used to love it when I was home sick when she worked in the cafeteria because she would bring home these wonderful home-cooked meals for me," young Anne recalls, especially the yeast rolls.

In Carteret, Lawton joined two home extension clubs and the Nutrition Leaders, becoming a sought-after expert in cooking and crafts, even demonstrating craft making for Belk's department store for a time.

Two decades as a Nutrition Leader led Lawton to cook more seafood for friends, family and her home extension club, her daughter says. "Everything she made was delicious."

Lissie McNamee

Living on the coast has its advantages.

"I have my own gill net — 50 feet long — three crab pots and a row boat," says Lissie McNamee of Merrimon. "It's just enough for me to go out there and catch a few mullet when I can on Cedar Creek off the Intercoastal Waterway. I do it right from my yard." She can dip her crab pots off the pier jutting from her house, too, for a few fresh blue crabs for dinner. "If you've got it right there in your front yard, you might as well learn how to harvest it," she says.

McNamee has learned more than how to catch a crab in her 20-year tenure with the Nutrition Leaders. Before joining the group, McNamee had never cleaned a crab or filleted a fish. "I really only knew frying," she recalls.

She grew up on a farm near Wilson's Mills, the sixth of seven children, and learned basic cooking skills helping out in the kitchen.

"We had lots of vegetables. We grew our own," she says. "And we raised our own beef and pork. Plus we had sheep, chickens and goats."

Then in 1963 she had the good fortune to marry a man who caught, cleaned and cooked his own catch. For 16 years, her husband, Wayne, a commercial fisherman, brought home fresh snapper, shark, grouper and the likes straight from the sea.

Joining the Nutrition Leaders in the late 1980s taught McNamee even more ways to prepare their fresh-caught fare. Plus she learned how seafood helps fight fat.

When the cheery woman with long wavy hair joined the Nutrition Leaders, she worked for the civil service in Cherry Point, taking off work to attend her home extension club meetings with the South River/Merrimon Club, but leaving on more pounds that she would have liked. Then she became the club's Nutrition Leader and very conscious of what good nutrition meant. She lost 50 pounds and gained good friends, loads of tasty recipes and good health. "I think I know more than doctors now," she jokes.

Wayne's retired now, but the Merrimon couple still finds time to sail out the creek or throw out a net between April and October for flounder, puppy drum, pinfish and speckled trout.

Yes, living on the coast has its benefits.

Betty Motes

A love of food and family run so deep in Betty Motes' life that no line can divide them. Like many coastal North Carolina families, Motes' mother and father farmed and fished, grew vegetables and raised hogs and chickens to make a living.

"I grew up an only child in a home where good food was a way of showing love," Motes says. "I didn't learn to cook while growing up because the kitchen was my mother's sanctuary." But she watched, carefully, and learned the ways of the farm and food.

"My mother cooked fish at least once or twice a week, but they were always fried except for a baked flounder with bacon, potatoes and onions once in awhile," she recalls. "We went clamming in the summer and bought oysters in the winter. We caught our own hard crabs in the summer. ... My daddy loved soft crabs.

"We also canned fish roe, which we ate with eggs from our own chickens, for breakfast. My daddy went down to the menhaden fish boats in Beaufort and broke the fish to get the roe. Many in Carteret County did this."

Her father worked for the state highway department for $75 a month. Right after payday, he drove his family into Beaufort so he could buy a western round steak. "So once a month for Sunday dinner we had country steak with lots of gravy, mashed potatoes and other vegetables," Motes recalls.

Fitting then, that the first meal she prepared for her husband-to-be in 1948 was country steak and mashed potatoes.

"I married a Yankee from Rhode Island, so I learned to cook some foods that were different from what I had growing up," Motes says. Foods like creamed codfish with mashed potatoes on toast, and corned beef and cabbage. Funny thing, though, she and her new mother-in-law made clam chowder the same way: fry fat pork, brown onions in the grease, chop clams, add potatoes, pork, onion, clams, water and cook.

As the Motes' family grew, Betty began her own cooking traditions like conch stew, fresh-cooked hard crabs and an oyster roast to savor all year long.

"Frying is still my family's favorite way to cook fish," she adds, "but they have learned to eat many of the recipes from the Seafood Lab."

But the ritual the Motes family will remember most is the annual holiday oyster roast.

"The day after Christmas, all the guys go oystering over at Middle Marsh, Harkers Island," tells Motes, a retired civil servant. "They get 18 to 22 bushels of oysters. ... We have 40 to 45 people come over. The boys cook the oysters outside and bring them into the garage and spread them on a long table. Everyone brings their own oyster knife. ... Everyone usually enjoys the oysters after all the turkey and ham." And there are usually enough oysters left over for her sons to take a couple bushels and have a party back home, too.

Cooking with the Nutrition Leaders for 20 years has helped Motes find new ways of cooking seafood without all the fat and calories she'd known growing up. With a summer home on Harkers Island, the Motes still harvest plenty of fresh fish and shellfish and think North Carolina seafood is the best in the world.

"I don't order seafood at restaurants that don't use local seafood," she explains. "And when I am away from Carteret County I don't order seafood." Even on a trip to Australia and New Zealand she opted out. "Yes, I am spoiled."

Mary Dudley Price

The seafood Mary Dudley Price remembers from her childhood in Tarboro and Raleigh came in cans or was salt-preserved. "Only oysters could be had fresh, and they were ladled out from large tins into quart and pint cardboard containers such as were used later to haul goldfish home from the store," says Price. Every now and then when her family got hungry for oyster soup, she and her sister, Josephine, would head from their Oakwood home down New Bern Avenue in Raleigh to a little "mom-and-pop" grocery for the fresh, juicy shellfish.

Her mother used the canned salmon for croquettes during the winter. And the salted fish (mostly mackerel, cod or herring) was soaked overnight and broiled in milk for family breakfasts. Too, "Mother often made fish cakes by combining canned fish with mashed potatoes.

"The only fresh fish I can recall from my early days were the result of my father's once-every-two or three-years going with a group of friends to fish out of Morehead," Price says. A school administrator, her father and about 11 other "school people" who called themselves "The Dizzy Dozen" headed offshore for a few days with Captain Tony Seamon. "My father's comments about such trips were mostly about the delicious cornbread the captain would provide," Price recalls. The year was around 1915 — way before Seamon began his now-famous Sanitary Fish Market in Morehead City. "I cannot help but believe this was the forerunner to his Sanitary restaurant and its hushpuppies!"

On August 31, 1940, Mary Dudley married Woodrow Price, a newspaperman and avid outdoorsman. For a while her husband worked nights at the Raleigh *News and Observer*, then headed east on the weekends to fish or hunt. "If there was anything to be caught, he could catch it," says the easy-going and jovial cook.

A journalist herself, Price somehow fit cooking in between writing and editing for N.C. newspapers and magazines and rearing four children.

Then in 1976, the Prices moved to Gloucester for good. "We could scallop or clam right out in the front yard," she says. She even manned a few crab pots close to shore, pulling in 50 to 60 crabs per pot.

Over time, Price learned how to cook blue crabs, scallops, clams and even the shad her husband of 60 years caught. Joining the Nutrition Leaders in 1978 helped. As one of the first on board with Taylor, Price and the group tested recipes for underutilized species and tried out new cooking techniques. She's learned how to pickle fish, can fish and smoke fish. How to skin eels and shuck a clam. And generally, how to make the most of the water's bounty.

Favorites recipes include those for stuffing and baking the large fish that came their way like puppy drum, bluefish and trout. And she loves the steamed clambake reminiscent of those from the past in Carteret County. "It is a delectable combination of seafood, poultry and vegetables," she says.

"As long as I live I will be indebted to Joyce Taylor and her leadership at the lab for introducing me to the bounty of our coast and teaching me how to put it on my table in a wholesome and delicious fashion."

Valaree Stanley

Yes, Valaree Stanley knows seafood, after growing up on the Newport River and cooking the catch for more than 80 years in Carteret County. But she knows what tastes good after a hearty seafood meal, too. Cake.

The baby of 13 children, Stanley got her start in the kitchen at about age 7 or 8 by watching her mother and older sisters, especially Alice. Alice loved to bake cakes from scratch, even making her own butter, and to sell them at the Morehead City curb market, which opened in 1935.

"Some weeks we sold as many as 125 cakes," Stanley recalls. Cottagers and locals alike clamored each week for their cakes — chocolate, lemon, jelly, coconut, pineapple, German chocolate, devil's food with white caramel icing and more. Stanley and her sister, who became known as "The Cake Lady in Carteret County," sold their mouth-watering goods at the market for almost 60 years, until Alice was in her nineties. "I got three children through college with money making cakes," Stanley notes.

Today, the vivacious cook still manages the local curb market, the longest continuously operating one in the state. She also volunteers in countless other endeavors. But as in the past, there's always time for seafood and her beloved Nutrition Leaders, which she joined in 1985.

Growing up by the river, seafood was plentiful, she recalls. "We caught oysters, clams, fish, crabs and also shrimp. We didn't think shrimp were edible so we threw them back in the water. When I later learned shrimp were good to eat, they became one of my favorite foods.

"We had seafood two or three times a week... fish, crabs, shrimp in summer, and oysters, clams and corned fish in winter," she continues. "Daddy salted the fish in summer in a wooden barrel. We would soak them in cold water and either broil or boil them." Clambakes, fish fries and oyster roasts added to the fun.

The family farm produced plenty of meat and vegetables to feed the family, too. "My mother cooked. She had to, she had 13 children," Stanley says with a laugh. She particularly remembers cooking collards — washing the leaves then breaking them into small pieces, adding water and a little steak or salt pork and simmering two hours in the summer and about 40 minutes in the winter. "They cook quicker after the frost falls on them."

She credits Taylor and the Nutrition Leaders for teaching her healthier and better ways to cook seafood, such as using herbs and spices, little salt and proper cooking times to avoid overcooking. Still, fried oysters and shrimp remain favorites, as well as the lab's baked flounder with onions, potatoes and a little bacon or salt pork slipped in for flavor... and a memory or two.

Dorothy "Dot" Whitley-Overton

"Daddy was a fishing and hunting man," recalls Dorothy "Dot" Whitley-Overton. "Mother canned fish and anything else that we could use. My bedroom looked like a grocery store" with Mason jars full of meats, fish, beans, potatoes and other vegetables from the family farm lining her shelves. "I was 16 before I knew what a hamburger was. Back then life was hard and you had to eat what you had."

But life near Havelock was good. As the oldest of five children, Whitley-Overton learned to cook by her mother's and grandmother's sides without benefit of measuring utensils or temperature gauges. "Cooking on a wood stove? What was 350 F?" she asks. "Somehow you learned. We never were hungry."

She remembers feasting on stew fish and fish cakes, and getting to go crabbing with her daddy on Saturday if she and her brothers and sisters had finished their chores.

Then, "I married a man who was part cat," she adds. "Fried fish one day. Two days later it was stewed fish. Fried or stewed was the only way I knew to cook seafood, until I was lucky enough to be Nutrition Leader for our home extension club." The Wildwood Home Extension Club, that is, from Morehead City, Newport and Pine Knoll Shores.

"I learned to cook at the Seafood Lab," she states. In the 24 years she's been with the Nutrition Leaders, she's learned how to cook crab meat and other kinds of fish, the importance of safe handling in seafood, and that freshness is the key. "Joyce would never allow us to take our seafood off ice until we were ready to cook."

Today, she and her husband, Tom, live on Harkers Island in the view of the Cape Lookout Light. They keep two boats and like to fish for whiting, flounder, bluefish and just about anything that will bite their hooks. Then she comes home and often flips through the notebook she keeps with recipes collected from the lab to find a favorite. When anyone asks her how to cook or eat any kind of seafood, she pulls out the same trusty notebook, too.

"Joyce has been the best teacher," Whitley-Overton says. "It has been a joy."

SEAFOOD IS
Health Food

Down East, we've always known seafood tastes good — like a platter

of fresh flounder, hot crab cakes or steamed shrimp right off the boat.

And now, everyone from seafood scientists to television chefs knows

SEAFOOD IS
Health Food

Down East, we've always known seafood tastes good — like a platter of fresh flounder, hot crab cakes or steamed shrimp right off the boat. And now, everyone from seafood scientists to television chefs knows seafood as one of the best sources of good nutrition, as well.

Fish and shellfish pack healthy amounts of protein, polyunsaturated fat and omega-3 fatty acids. At the same time, they are low in total fat, saturated fat, sodium, calories and cholesterol. To add to their appeal, they are naturally rich in vitamins and minerals such as iron and the B-vitamins, too.

Seafood provides one of the highest-quality sources of protein on the market. An average 3.5-ounce serving of yellowfin tuna, for example, contains 23.8 grams of protein — more than half the daily requirement for women (44) and close to half for men (56). Seafood also contains less connective tissue, which makes it easier to digest than other protein meats.

Seafood contains less fat, too. Most species of finfish, like hybrid striped bass and red snapper, contain less than 5 percent fat; and shellfish generally contains less than 2 percent. Any fat present is unsaturated, making seafood rich in polyunsaturated fat — which helps in reducing blood cholesterol. Beef, pork and lamb, by comparison, contain higher amounts of fat, which is saturated.

Seafood generally contain small amounts of cholesterol, too. A 3.5-ounce serving of tuna, for example, has 45 milligrams; and grouper, 37. In all, most finfish have fewer than 100 milligrams of cholesterol per serving.

Most shellfish contain low amounts of cholesterol, contrary to popular belief. Clams, oysters, scallops and mussels average about 30 to 50 milligrams per 3.5-ounce serving. Squid poses the exception, with 235 milligrams per serving.

Crustaceans — shrimp, crab, lobster, and crawfish — contain somewhat higher levels of cholesterol, ranging from about 55 to 150 milligrams per 3.5-ounce serving. According to many nutritionists, shrimp with 150 milligrams, and crawfish with 135, are still acceptable because they are extremely low in saturated fat.

Fish and shellfish pack healthy amounts of protein, polyunsaturated fat and omega-3 fatty acids. At the same time, they are low in total fat, saturated fat, sodium, calories, cholesterol and sodium. To add to their appeal, they are naturally rich in vitamins and minerals such as iron and the B-vitamins, too.

The American Heart

Association, in its October

2001 journal, recommended at

least two servings of fatty fish,

such as tuna or salmon,

weekly. This comes in addition

to the AHA's recommended

diet rich in fruits and

vegetables, legumes, whole

grains, low-fat dairy products,

lean meats and poultry.

Saturated fat is the chief culprit in raising levels of blood cholesterol. Cholesterol contained in foods plays a less significant role.

The nation's longest-running heart study, the Framingham Heart Study, has been ongoing in Framingham, Mass. for more more than 50 years. It is currently under the National Heart, Lung and Blood Institute. William Castelli, the study's former director, says, "I always say that if you can't be a vegetarian, then eat a vegetarian from the sea — namely oysters, clams, mussels and scallops. And no, I don't think you have to be concerned about lobster or shrimp. You can have them all."

Keep in mind that cooking methods can add fat, cholesterol and calories. Baking, broiling, steaming, poaching and grilling usually add little fat. Frying is out of favor with most nutrition guidelines. However, you can lightly sauté seafood without adding much fat. And since considerable controversy brews about the harmful effects of trans fatty acids found in margarine, some people have begun to use a little butter instead.

The American Heart Association, in its October 2001 journal, recommended at least two servings of fatty fish, such as tuna or salmon, weekly. This comes in addition to the AHA's recommended diet rich in fruits and vegetables, legumes, whole grains, low-fat dairy products, lean meats and poultry.

Why seafood? Research in the 1970s revealed a direct relationship between the consumption of seafood and the low incidence of coronary heart disease in Greenland's Eskimos. Highly polyunsaturated fat called "omega-3 fatty acids" in their diet proved to be the heart guard. Omega-3s are found primarily in seafood. Continuing studies confirm the benefits of eating fish to cardiovascular health.

In 1985, the prestigious *New England Journal of Medicine* echoed these findings saying, "The consumption of as little as one to two fish dishes per week may be preventive in relation to coronary heart disease."

For years physicians have recommended low-fat fish as part of a healthy diet. Now we know that seafood with higher fat content can also benefit health.

The adult daily requirement for omega-3 fatty acid is estimated to be 300 to 400 milligrams a day. So how can you know the omega-3 content of seafood? Generally speaking, the higher the fat content in fish and shellfish, the higher the omega-3s *(see charts p. 30).* Nutritional charts usually divide omega-3 content into three groups: 0.5 grams and under, 0.6 to 1.0 grams, and more than 1.0 grams.

Additional studies indicate potential benefits between omega-3s and other diseases such as cancer and some inflammatory diseases such as arthritis. Other research continues to look into the connection between omega-3s and various health problems.

 Low sodium and calories add to the list of seafood's health benefits. Most fish contain fewer than 100 calories and 100 milligrams of sodium per 3.5-ounce serving. Shellfish counts are similar, with about 100 calories per serving and between 150 to 300 milligrams of sodium. Much of the time, though, seafood tastes salty because of added table salt, not because it comes from salty water — as some people think.

Fish, especially dark-fleshed species, provide a good source of the B-vitamins pyridoxine, niacin, and B-12. Many seafoods contain some of the other B-vitamins, too.

The minerals potassium and phosphorus are found in abundance in seafood; and dark-fleshed fish, oysters, clams and mussels are good sources of iron. Others supply trace minerals.

The nutritional makeup of many popular finfish and shellfish follows. Remember that the listed composition values are averages. These amounts may vary due to the fish or shellfish's age, food sources, gender, geographical location and the time of year harvested.

There are many reasons to include seafood as part of your regular diet. Isn't it good to know that this great-tasting food is also good for your health?

Fish, especially dark-fleshed species, provide a good source of the B-vitamins pyridoxine, niacin, and B-12. Many seafoods contain some of the other B-vitamins, too.

COMPOSITION OF SELECTED FINFISH (PER 3.5 OUNCES)

Species	Calories	Protein (grams)	Total Fat (grams)	Saturated Fat (grams)	Cholesterol (mg)	Omega 3 (mg)
• bass, hybrid striped	97	17.7	2.3	0.5	80	0.7
• bluefish	124	20	4.2	0.9	59	1.2
• croaker, Atlantic	104	17.8	3.2	1.1	61	0.2
• grouper, red	91	20.4	1.0	0.3	37	0.3
• mullet, striped	115	19.2	3.7	1.1	35	0.4
• salmon, Atlantic	129	18.4	5.6	0.9	55	1.4
• sea trout, gray	106	17.5	3.5	1.1	*	0.5
• snapper, red	110	20.2	2.6	0.5	40	0.6
• spot	135	18.8	6.1	1.8	*	0.8
• tuna, yellowfin	124	23.8	2.5	0.6	45	0.6

* not available

Sources: Seafood Business, *Seafood Handbook*, 1999. Seafood Business, *The Complete Seafood Handbook*, 1995. Seafood Business, *The Advanced Seafood Handbook*, 1992. Nettleton, *Seafood and Health*, 1987. Nettleton, *Seafood Nutrition*, 1985. Exler, *Composition of Foods*, USDA, Agriculture Handbook No. 8-15, 1987.

COMPOSITION OF SELECTED SHELLFISH (PER 3.5 OUNCES RAW)

Species	Calories	Protein (grams)	Total Fat (grams)	Saturated Fat (grams)	Cholesterol (mg)	Omega 3 (mg)
• clams, hard	60	9.2	1	0.2	40	0.2
• crab, blue	81	16.2	1.0	0.2	76	0.3
• crawfish	90	19.0	1.0	0	135	0.2
• lobster, American	90	19	1.0	0	95	*
• mussels, blue	89	12.0	2.2	0.4	63	0.4
• oysters, Eastern	74	8.2	2.2	0.4	56	0.5
• scallops, bay	80	14.8	0.6	0.1	*	0.1
• scallops, sea	87	16.2	0.8	0.1	36	0.2
• shrimp, Gulf	90	19.4	0.8	0.2	96	0.3
• squid, long-finned	90	1.6	1.0	*	23.5	0.5

* not available

Sources: Seafood Business, *Seafood Handbook*, 1999. Seafood Business, *The Complete Seafood Handbook*, 1995. Seafood Business, *The Advanced Seafood Handbook*, 1992. Nettleton, *Seafood and Health*, 1987. Nettleton, *Seafood Nutrition*, 1985. Exler, *Composition of Foods*, USDA, Agriculture Handbook No. 8-15, 1987.

SEAFOOD IS
Safe to Eat

In the past few years,
concerns about food safety
have increased with media
scrutiny — seafood included.
Some reports proved true,
but others were sensational
such as two urging consumers
never to eat fresh tuna or
any fish found near reefs,
such as snapper.

SEAFOOD IS
Safe to Eat

O ver the years, about as many myths about seafood safety have circulated as legends of the high seas. "Oysters are only safe to eat in months containing the letter 'r,'" one saying goes. "If you eat the greenish 'dead men' in blue crabs you may die," says another. Or "drinking milk or eating ice cream with fish will make you sick."

While such myths about seafood safety exist, fish and shellfish remain safe to eat.

In the past few years, concerns about food safety have increased with media scrutiny — seafood included. Some reports proved true, but others were sensational, such as two urging consumers never to eat fresh tuna or any fish found near reefs, such as snapper.

HOW SAFE IS SEAFOOD?

Seafood in the United States is now safer than ever, in part due to a federally mandated inspection program that began in 1997. HACCP, or Hazard Analysis and Critical Control Point, is a science-based, food safety monitoring program used by the food industry to control the risks associated with certain food products. HACCP is designed to protect the food supply against biological, chemical and physical hazards. The regulation is enforced by the U.S. Department of Agriculture and the Food and Drug Administration (FDA).

Though retail markets remain exempt from the regulations, they are encouraged by the FDA to apply the same principles. As a result, you can likely see improvements such as increased use of ice and cleaner facilities in your local market.

The FDA is the federal agency responsible for administration of the National Shellfish Sanitation Program, a voluntary program in which state shellfish control agencies, the shellfish industry, FDA and other federal agencies participate. The program has been in place since 1925. It addresses the sanitary control of fresh and frozen molluscan shellfish — oysters, clams, mussels and scallops — sold in interstate commerce.

Seafood in the United States is now safer than ever, in part due to a federally mandated inspection program that began in 1997. HACCP, or Hazard Analysis and Critical Control Point, is a science-based, food safety monitoring program used by the food industry to control the risks associated with certain food products.

More than half of the reported

acute fish and shellfish

problems result from improper

handling and preparation in

the home or food service

establishment, according to the

National Academy of Sciences.

Just a few simple precautions

will ensure the safety of the

food you prepare.

Based on filed seafood illness and epidemiological studies, the U.S. Centers for Disease Control found the risk of becoming ill from eating seafood to be one in 250,000. If raw and partially cooked molluscan shellfish (oysters, clams, scallops and mussels) are excluded from this number, the risk of eating seafood drops to one in a million. This compares favorably to the rate of eating poultry, which is one in 25,000.

Also, remember that most seafood products usually smell and look unacceptable before they are likely to cause illness. Exceptions include canned and pasteurized products, as well as vacuum-packed seafood.

When you follow the proper precautions, you can be sure that fish and shellfish are safe for you and your family to eat.

SEAFOOD SAFETY AND YOU

Even though seafood inspection programs exist, consumers also play a role in seafood safety. Choose your retail market carefully, and handle and serve food with care in your home.

At the Market

• Buy only from reputable sources. Be wary of roadside vendors.

• Buy only fresh seafood that is properly iced or refrigerated. Fish should be displayed on a thick bed of ice, preferably in a case or under a cover. They should be arranged with the belly down so that melting ice drains away from the fish.

• Don't buy cooked seafood, such as shrimp, crabs or smoked fish if it is in the same case as raw seafood. Cross-contamination may have occurred.

• Don't buy frozen seafood if the packages are damaged or are stacked above the load line of the freezer. If the package is transparent, look for freezer burn or ice crystals. The package may have been stored too long or may have been thawed and refrozen.

• Get seafood home and on ice or into the refrigerator or freezer quickly. If possible, have it iced when you buy it.

• Anglers should follow state and local government advisories about fishing areas and eating fish from certain areas.

At Home

More than half of the reported acute fish and shellfish problems result from improper handling and preparation in the home or food service establishment, according to the National Academy of Sciences. Just a few simple precautions will ensure the safety of the food you prepare.

Storing

The shelf life of fresh seafood depends primarily on three factors: the species, where and when it was landed, and how well it was handled before you bought it. If you live near the coast and buy from a local seafood market, you obviously should be getting fresher fish and shellfish than someone who lives inland and buys from a major distribution center.

The storage times mentioned below are for fish and shellfish that are at their freshest — just when they come from the water.

• Store fresh fish to be used within two days in the refrigerator. Place the fish on a bed of crushed ice and keep it as close to 32 F as possible. If you're going to hold it longer, freeze and use within three to six months.

• Store live oysters in a dry, cool place. Use within seven days. Discard any that die (open).

• Store live clams and mussels in the refrigerator. Place in a shallow container and cover with a damp cloth or paper towel, allowing for adequate ventilation. Use within two to three days. Discard any that die.

• Cook live crabs and lobsters the day you buy them. Discard any that die.

• Shrimp, scallops, and freshly shucked oysters and scallops will keep about seven days in the refrigerator or on ice.

• Cooked, picked crabmeat should be used within seven to 10 days. Pasteurized crabmeat must be refrigerated and can be stored, unopened, for six months. Once it is opened, it should be used within three days.

Preparation

• Before handling seafood, or any other food, wash your hands for at least 20 seconds with hot soapy water. Also wash your hands after going to the bathroom, sneezing or coughing, touching skin or hair, before working with new food or utensils, after finishing food preparation and before serving food.

• Never let raw seafood come in contact with cooked seafood or any other food — raw or cooked. And never place cooked seafood in the same container that held raw seafood unless it has been thoroughly cleaned. Cross-contamination poses the most common source of food-related problems at home.

• Marinate seafood in the refrigerator, not at room temperature. If you are going to use the marinade as a basting sauce or dip, reserve some before adding raw seafood. Dispose of marinade after use because harmful bacteria may build up in the raw seafood juices.

The shelf life of fresh seafood depends primarily on three factors: the species, where and when it was landed, and how well it was handled before you bought it. If you live near the coast and buy from a local seafood market, you obviously should be getting fresher fish and shellfish than someone who lives inland and buys from a major distribution center.

Cook fish for 10 minutes per

inch of thickness. Measure at

the thickest point. If baking,

cook at 450 F. Fry at 375 F.

If you use the one-inch method,

test the fish with a fork or

the tip of a sharp knife

a minute or two earlier,

as variables may occur due to

oven temperatures and exact

distance from the heat source.

• Use a clean cloth after working with raw seafood in the kitchen. Bacteria linger in cloths, towels and sponges. It's really easier and safer to use paper towels and to dispose of them after each use.

• Cut raw seafood on an acrylic cutting board, never a wooden one. Wash the board with detergent and hot water and sanitize it thoroughly after each use. Cleaning products containing chlorine bleach or other antibacterial agents also work well. Or you can use a homemade cleaner made with one tablespoon of Clorox mixed with one gallon of water.

• Wash counters and all utensils with detergent and hot water after each use. If counters have been in contact with raw seafood or juices, sanitize them.

• Scrub live oysters, clams and mussels with a stiff brush under cold, running water before shucking or cooking.

• Always wash fresh vegetables and fruit before cutting. Contaminants on the outside can be transferred to the inside.

• Do not use the same plate that held raw seafood to serve cooked fish or shellfish.

Cooking Seafood

• To help remove bacteria, first rinse seafood under cold, running water.

• Marinate seafood in the refrigerator, never at room temperature.

• Cook seafood thoroughly with a continuous heat source. Avoid interrupted cooking, which can cause bacterial growth. Keep hot foods hot (140 F or higher) and cold foods cold (41 F or lower).

• Never leave cooked seafood out of refrigeration for more than 30 minutes.

• Cook fish for 10 minutes per inch of thickness. Measure at the thickest point. If baking, cook at 450 F. Fry at 375 F. If you use this method, test the fish with a fork or the tip of a sharp knife a minute or two earlier, as variables may occur due to oven temperatures and exact distance from the heat source. Add five minutes to total cooking time if the fish is cooked in a sauce or is wrapped in foil or parchment. The FDA recommends that fish reach an internal temperature of 145 F for 15 seconds.

• The FDA recommends that oysters (in shell) be steamed four to nine minutes or boiled three to five minutes after gaping. Shucked oysters should be fried three minutes at 375 F; broiled, three minutes three inches from heat source; baked, 10 minutes at 450 F; or boiled, three minutes.

• The FDA recommends that clams and mussels be steamed four to nine minutes.

Thawing Frozen Seafood
  • Thaw seafood overnight in the refrigerator. A one-pound package will defrost in about 24 hours.
  • For quicker thawing, place seafood under cold running water. Whole shellfish, such as shrimp and clams, can be placed in a colander with cold water running over them. Place dressed seafood, such as fillets or shucked shellfish, in a tightly closed plastic bag, then immerse it in a deep pan of cold water and allow additional cold water to run over it. A one-pound package will defrost in about an hour.
  • Never thaw seafood at room temperature or with warm or hot water.
  • When using your microwave to thaw fish, defrost at 10 to 30 percent power. Follow the manufacturer's instructions to determine defrosting time for the power of your microwave. A pound of fillets should defrost in about five to six minutes. Be careful to arrange the fish so that the thin edges do not cook while thicker parts are not fully thawed. Fish defrosted in the microwave should be cooked immediately after thawing.

IS IT OK TO EAT RAW SHELLFISH?

Eating raw or partially cooked oysters, clams, mussels and scallops poses significant health risks for some people. Eating these raw or undercooked shellfish accounts for 85 percent of all seafood-borne illnesses. Shellfish need to reach an internal temperature of 145 F to be done. Just-opened shellfish are not fully cooked. A crinkled appearance to the meat typically indicates doneness.

The reason for the high incidence of illness from this handful of popular bivalves is simple. We eat them whole — digestive tract and all — and whatever microorganisms or toxins have accumulated in their guts reaches ours. As filter feeders, bivalve mollusks sit in one place and eat whatever the water brings them. If the water is contaminated by natural toxins, sewage or industrial pollution, so is the oyster, clam, mussel or scallop.

A naturally occurring bacterium, *Vibrio vulnificus*, poses a threat for people with certain medical conditions (see p. 36). Most infections occur from eating raw or partially cooked oysters. The bacterium can also enter the body through an open wound, cut, sore, puncture or burn on skin exposed to sea water or raw shellfish containing the bacteria. *Vibrio vulnificus* can be found in warm water along the coast, especially during the summer months. It does not pose any danger to most healthy people and can be killed by thorough cooking. Freezing does not destroy it. Nor does drinking alcohol or eating with hot pepper sauce.

Eating raw or partially cooked oysters, clams, mussels and scallops poses significant health risks for some people. Eating these raw or undercooked shellfish accounts for 85 percent of all seafood-borne illnesses. Shellfish need to reach a temperature of 145 F to be done. Just-opened shellfish are not fully cooked. A crinkled appearance to the meat typically indicates doneness.

The best way to reduce the risk

of illness is to keep within

the seafood safety net.

Never purchase shellfish from

unknown or uncontrolled

sources. They're no bargain.

Buy only from reputable dealers

who buy from shellfish harvest-

ers licensed under the National

Shellfish Sanitation Program.

Gastroenteritis usually occurs within 16 hours of ingesting the organism. Symptoms include chills, fever, nausea, vomiting, blood poisoning and even death within two days for people with weakened immune systems. More than 50 percent of infections from *Vibrio vulnificus* prove fatal for people with the health conditions listed here.

No major outbreaks of illness have been attributed to *Vibrio vulnificus*, but sporadic cases occur frequently.

WHO IS AT RISK?

People with any of the following medical problems are at risk and should not eat raw or partially cooked shellfish:

• liver disease — from excessive alcohol intake, viral hepatitis, cirrhosis or other causes. This category accounts for most seafood-related illnesses and increases the risk of death more than 200 times.

• gastrointestinal problems, including previous gastric surgery, low stomach acid, or low stomach acid from regular use of antacids

• transplanted organs
• chronic alcohol use
• diabetes
• immune disorders, including HIV infection
• long-term steroid use, as for asthma and arthritis treatment
• hemochromatosis and other iron disorders
• inflammatory bowel disease
• chronic kidney disease
• cancer
• heart disease and blood disorders

Older adults tend to be at increased risk because they suffer from these health conditions more often. Also, pregnant women, infants and very young children should eat fully cooked shellfish.

The best way to reduce the risk of illness is to keep within the seafood safety net. Never purchase shellfish from unknown or uncontrolled sources. They're no bargain. Buy only from reputable dealers who buy from shellfish harvesters licensed under the National Shellfish Sanitation Program. If in doubt, ask to see the shipper's tag that accompanies in-the-shell products. Also, ask to see the shipper's number on shucked oyster containers. Such information tells who shipped the product and where it came from originally.

Other Bacterial Pathogens

Vibrio parahaemolyticus is a bacterium that lives in brackish saltwater and causes gastrointestinal illness in humans. It naturally inhabits coastal waters in the United States.

Most people become infected by eating raw or undercooked shellfish, especially oysters. *Vibrio parahaemolyticus* causes watery diarrhea that is often accompanied by abdominal cramping, nausea, vomiting, fever and chills. The symptoms occur within 24 hours of ingestion and the illness is self-limiting and lasts about three days. Severe disease occurs rarely and usually only in persons with weakened immune systems.

The bacterium can also cause skin infections when an open wound is exposed to warm sea water, but this is less common.

Listeria monocytogenes is a bacterium not commonly associated with seafood, but it may occur in some cooked, ready-to-eat fishery products. It is caused by improper handling practices. The FDA enforces zero tolerance for the presence of listeria in all cooked, ready-to-eat food products. Consumers should be aware that it is harmful when consumed, especially for women of child-bearing age, young children and older adults who may not be able to ward off food-borne infections.

Recall notices are posted when public health agencies find food products tainted with listeria bacteria. Thorough cooking will eliminate this potential bacterial hazard.

IS IT SAFE TO EAT RAW FINFISH?

For most people, sushi, sashimi and other raw fish dishes are safe if made with fresh, commercially frozen fish.

Fish, like all other living things, can contain parasites. However, freezing and cooking kills the parasites.

Most home freezers are not cold enough to kill parasites. If you freeze fish for raw dishes, be sure that your freezer can reach -4 F or lower. The fish must then be kept at this temperature for 168 hours (seven days).

Though freezing kills parasites, it does not kill bacteria. Thus people at risk should not eat raw finfish.

For most people, sushi, sashimi and other raw fish dishes are safe if made with fresh, commercially frozen fish. Fish, like all other living things, can contain parasites. However, freezing and cooking kills the parasites.

Histamine in fish cannot be

destroyed by freezing or

cooking. Although scombroid

poisoning can be a problem in

the commercial seafood

industry, it can also pose a

significant problem for

recreational fishers who do

not handle their catch

properly. Illnesses due to

these natural toxins do pose

serious safety concerns,

but seem to be improving as

people, especially anglers,

ice seafood more and properly.

Norwalk and Similar Viruses

Norwalk viral infection is caused by the Norwalk virus. It and similar viruses are recognized as leading causes of food-borne illness in the United States. They have been linked to intestinal illness in communities, camps, schools, institutions and families. Contaminated water is the most common source of outbreaks. Shellfish and salad ingredients are the foods most often implicated. Eating raw or partially cooked clams and oysters poses a high risk for infection.

The symptoms of infection by the Norwalk virus appear one to two days after eating contaminated food. They include nausea, vomiting, diarrhea and stomach cramps. The illness lasts two to three days. Severe illness is uncommon.

Some viruses are heat-resistant and are not destroyed by cooking.

Natural Toxins

Other seafood safety concerns include scombroid poisoning and ciguatera poisoning, the two most common diseases caused by marine toxins.

Scombroid poisoning, also known as histamine fish poisoning, is caused by consuming scombroid and mackerel-like marine fish that have not been kept at low enough temperatures after being caught. Fish most commonly involved include tunas, mackerels, bluefish, dolphin (mahi-mahi) and amberjacks. When these fish are not quickly and properly iced after capture, bacteria on the surface begin to convert the amino acid histidine to histamine. Large amounts of histamine can cause an allergic response such as rash, diarrhea, facial flushing, sweating, headache and vomiting. There may also be burning or swelling of the mouth, abdominal pain or a metallic taste. The symptoms appear within a few minutes to two hours after eating the fish. Symptoms usually last four to six hours and rarely exceed two days.

Histamine in fish cannot be destroyed by freezing or cooking. Although scombroid poisoning can be a problem in the commercial seafood industry, it can also pose a significant problem for recreational fishers who do not handle their catch properly. Illnesses due to these natural toxins do pose serious safety concerns, but seem to be improving as people, especially anglers, ice seafood more and properly.

Ciguatera occurs most often from eating reef fish that harbor the toxin ciguatera. Ciguatoxic fish are not inherently toxic. The poisonous substance originates in microscopic sea plants. Small fish feeding on these organisms become toxic. They in turn get eaten by larger fish, and in time, the larger fish become toxic, too. Thus the toxin moves up the food chain into the large predatory fish often favored by consumers. While barracuda are commonly associated with ciguatera, some other fish, including grouper, snapper and sea bass that live in tropical reef waters, can be toxic.

Toxic fish cannot be detected by appearance, taste or smell, and cooking does not inactivate the toxin. Vacationers and inexperienced recreational fishers should use care in waters where ciguatera thrives.

Symptoms of ciguatera begin from 30 minutes to six hours after eating contaminated fish. They include nausea, diarrhea, vomiting, headache and muscle aches. These symptoms can be followed by neurological discomforts such as headache, flushing, a tingling or numb sensation on the lips, tongue and mouth, nightmares or hallucinations. In more severe cases, the most definitive symptom is a cold-to-hot sensory reversal so that cold objects feel hot and hot objects feel cold. Symptoms usually last from one to four weeks.

Mercury in Fish

While seafood makes part of a healthy diet, some fish contain high levels of a form of mercury, methylmercury, that can harm an unborn child's developing nervous system if eaten regularly. Nearly all fish contain trace amounts of methylmercury that are not harmful to humans. But large, long-lived fish that feed on other fish accumulate the highest levels and pose the greatest threat to people who eat them regularly.

The FDA advises pregnant women, and women who may become pregnant, not to eat four fish: shark, swordfish, king mackerel and tilefish. It also recommends that nursing mothers and young children not eat these fish.

In 2001, the FDA advised these women to select a variety of other seafood, including shellfish, canned fish, smaller ocean fish and farm-raised fish. The FDA states that they can safely eat 12 ounces of cooked fish per week.

Current FDA advisories on seafood safety can be found online at www.fda.gov.

While seafood makes part of a healthy diet, some fish contain high levels of a form of mercury, methylmercury, that can harm an unborn child's developing nervous system if eaten regularly. Nearly all fish contain trace amounts of methylmercury that are not harmful to humans.

How to
SELECT, HANDLE, CLEAN & STORE SEAFOOD

Keeping seafood fresh after a successful fishing trip at the coast depends

on proper handling and transporting. Adequate storage or freezing

helps ensure continued fresh taste, too. Here, expert tips and more than

60 illustrations assist in bringing home the catch.

How to
SELECT, HANDLE, CLEAN & STORE SEAFOOD

HOOKED ON FRESH FISH AND SHELLFISH

Fish and shellfish are highly perishable and must be properly handled from catch to cook. Mishandling results in poor quality and loss of flavor and nutrients. Be sure that the seafood you buy is fresh. It's a good idea to go to the market to buy fresh seafood, not just a particular species. If your recipe calls for flounder, but the snapper is fresher, buy the snapper. The following indicators will help you determine freshness and quality.

A fresh fish has...
- eyes that are bright, clear, full and protruding. As a fish deteriorates, the eyes become cloudy, discolored and sunken.
- gills that are bright red or pink, free from slime. Avoid fish with gills that are dull pink, gray, brown or green.
- flesh that is firm and elastic and springs back when pressed gently with the finger. It should not separate from the bone. As fish age, the flesh becomes soft and slimy and slips away from the bone. The flesh of fillets and steaks should be firm and elastic and have a fresh-cut appearance with no drying or browning around the edges.
- skin that is shiny and not faded. Characteristic colors and markings fade as a fresh fish gets older.
- scales that adhere tightly. As fish deteriorate, the scales become dull and dry and begin to separate.
- an intestinal cavity (if gutted) that is pink with a bright red blood streak, not a dark or brown one.
- an odor that is ocean-fresh and mild. Fish fresh from the water do not have a "fishy" smell.

Be sure that the seafood you buy is fresh. It's a good idea to go to the market to buy fresh seafood, not just a particular species. If your recipe calls for flounder, but the snapper is fresher, buy the snapper.

Fresh shrimp have...

- a mild odor and firm meat. They are not slippery and retain their natural color. Beware of shrimp that are bright pink or red, both signs of not being properly iced. Avoid shrimp that suffer from black spot, a sign of age or poor handling.

Cooked shrimp have...

- red shells and meat with a red tint and no disagreeable odor.

Live crabs and lobsters...

- show movement of the legs. The tail of a lobster should curl under the body and not hang down when the lobster is picked up.

Cooked crabs and lobsters...

- should have a bright red color and no disagreeable odor.

Clams and oysters in the shell...

- should be alive. Shells should be tightly closed or should close tightly when tapped.

Shucked oysters...

- should be plump with a natural creamy color and clear or slightly opalescent liquid. They should have a mild odor and not contain more than 10 percent liquid.

Fresh scallops...

- should have a sweet odor and be free of excess liquid. The meat of bay and calico scallops is typically creamy white but may be light tan or slightly pink. Sea scallop meat is typically creamy white but may be slightly orange or pink.

Frozen seafood...

- should be solidly frozen with no discoloration or drying (freezer burn) on the flesh, and no disagreeable odor. It should be wrapped with moisture-proof and vapor-proof material that fits closely and is undamaged. Seafood should be stored below the load line of the display case. It should contain clean, uniform pieces that are not frozen together. Breading or coating should be intact.

BRINGING THE CATCH HOME

After a successful fishing trip at the coast, how can you keep your seafood fresh until you get home? If handled properly, fish and shellfish can be transported safely for long distances and can remain fresh for several days.

Handling

You may want to dress fish completely — scale, head and eviscerate, or fillet — so that they are ready to use or freeze when you arrive home. Most seafood markets will dress fish for a nominal fee.

If you do not want to dress fish before traveling, at least head or degill, eviscerate and rinse them well to maintain freshness.

Large fish such as tuna should be bled and gutted immediately upon capture. Pack the body cavity with ice and pack the fish in ice. Cut very large fish into pieces that will fit into your cooler.

The most important thing to remember is that seafood must be kept cold. The colder the temperature, the slower the rate of spoilage.

Superchilling Fish

While packing fish in ice keeps it fresh, a method called "superchilling" is even better. For this, you will need an insulated cooler. Coolers vary from thin-walled foam to heavier-walled plastic ones. The better the insulation, the longer the ice will last and the colder the fish will stay. It's best to use a cooler with a drain.

Local seafood markets usually will sell you flaked or crushed ice. Avoid ice that is rough or jagged as it will bruise the fish.

Before packing the fish, make a salt-ice mixture in a separate container, using about one-half pound of salt for every five pounds of ice. If your cooler does not have a drain, first place a rack in the bottom to keep the seafood out of any water that may accumulate from melting ice.

Line the cooler with 3 to 4 inches of flaked or crushed ice. Layer the fish in the cooler, covering each layer with the salt-ice mixture. Eviscerated fish should be unwrapped and the body cavities filled with ice. Dressed fish and shucked shellfish should be wrapped in heavy, clear plastic film. Shrimp should be headed, left in the shells and wrapped in heavy, clear plastic film or plastic bags.

When the cooler is filled, top the contents with a generous layer of ice and tightly close the lid. Also close the drain plug.

Place the cooler in a cool, shady section of your car, if possible. If you can't do this, use the trunk of the car, making sure that the fish is well-iced. Check your ice and fish at the end of each day. Drain off melted water at night and add more ice. On longer trips, you may need to add more salt.

After you've tried superchilling, you will be able to do it without mixing the ice and salt. To each layer of seafood, just add ice and then lightly sprinkle with salt.

You can also superchill your fish at home. If I have a few fillets or some shrimp, I often place them in a deep pan or tub, cover with ice and sprinkle on some salt, then place in the refrigerator. It's simple and easy, and will keep seafood even fresher than ice alone.

TRANSPORTING LIVE SHELLFISH

Live shellfish can be successfully transported, but great care must be taken to ensure food safety.

A cooler makes the most practical container for holding shellfish during travel.

Crabs

Place 3 to 4 inches of ice in the bottom of the cooler. Cover the ice with waxed cardboard or plastic foam in which holes have been punched. This allows the cold to escape, but keeps the crabs out of contact with ice or water. Place the crabs on the cardboard or foam and cover them with damp burlap or several layers of damp cheesecloth. Leave the cooler lid slightly ajar for air circulation.

Maintain a temperature of 40 F to 50 F. The crabs will be inactive, but they will revive when removed from the cold temperature. Limit holding time to one day. Do not use any crabs that die. Live crabs show movement of the legs.

Oysters

Live oysters need to be kept moist and can be transported in the same way as live crabs. Live oysters will be closed or will close tightly when tapped.

Clams

Clams need a drier environment and greater air circulation than oysters, but they, too, can be successfully carried in this manner or can be placed on top of ice. Maintain a temperature of 35 F to 40 F for oysters and clams. Limit holding time to two to three days. Discard any that are not alive when you reach your destination. The shells of live clams will be tightly closed or will close when you tap them.

GLAZING AND FREEZING FINFISH

When you reach your destination, unpack fish and rinse them under cold running water. If you are not planning to cook them right away, package and freeze them for future use.

Many people freeze fillets, steaks and dressed fish by placing them in plastic or milk containers, then filling them with water. While this works fairly well, there are some disadvantages. The water leaches some of the nutrients from the fish. It takes much longer to freeze, and we know that the faster food is frozen, the higher the quality. Also, it requires a much longer thawing time. And the big containers take up valuable freezer space.

Some seafood specialists recommend wrapping the fish with a high-quality plastic wrap, excluding as much air as possible, then overwrapping with foil or freezer paper.

Others suggest glazing the fish with ice. To do this, dip the fish in cold water, place on a baking sheet and freeze for two hours, then wrap tightly. Some specialists think that the process should be repeated at least four times before wrapping.

Lemon-Gelatin Glaze

Some years ago, our Seafood Lab developed a lemon-gelatin glazing process that we still recommend to protect fish from oxidation and freezer burn.

Measure 1/4 cup of bottled lemon juice into a pint container and fill the rest of the container with water. Dissolve one packet of unflavored gelatin in 1/2 cup of this mixture.

Heat the remaining liquid to boiling, then stir the dissolved gelatin mixture into the boiling liquid. Cool to room temperature.

Dip the fillet or steak in the liquid. Lift it out and allow to drain for a few seconds.

Wrap the fish tightly in a heavy, protective plastic film. We recommend Saran Wrap. Freeze as quickly as possible.

FREEZING SHELLFISH

Shrimp...
- should be headed and frozen in their shells in freezer containers. After filling the carton, cover the shrimp with ice water, leaving enough head space for the water to expand when frozen. Use small or medium containers so that the shrimp will freeze more quickly.

Scallops...
- should be shucked and frozen in airtight containers.

Clams and oysters...
- are best frozen in their shells, which makes them easy to shuck with no loss of juice. This is not always practical and they can be shucked and frozen in airtight containers.

Blue crabs...
- should be cleaned and cooked before freezing. Freeze the cores and claws and thaw them before picking the meat out. The quality of the crabmeat will be superior to that of frozen, picked meat that undergoes significant textural changes.

STORAGE TIMES

Ideally, all frozen seafood should be used within two months for maximum quality. When properly frozen, lean fish such as flounder and catfish should maintain quality up to six months. Fatty fish such as bluefish, mackerel and mullet should be used within three months.

Shrimp, scallops, clams, oysters and crabs can be stored up to three months.

The sooner fish and shellfish are frozen after harvest, the longer the shelf life will be. *(See also page 33.)*

HANDLING HINTS —
FIRST STEPS IN PREPARING SEAFOOD

Market Forms of Fresh Fish

• (1) **Whole or round fish** are sold just as they come from the water. They must be scaled and eviscerated — or gutted — before cooking. If the head is left on, the fish must be degilled. The edible yield is about 45 percent.

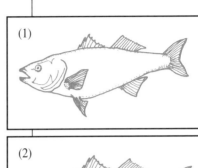

• (2) **Drawn fish** have been eviscerated. They must be scaled and, if the head is left on, must be degilled. The edible portion is about 48 percent.

• (3) **Dressed fish** are ready to cook, usually with head, tail and fins removed. The edible portion is about 67 percent.

• (4) **Fillets** are the sides of the fish cut away from the backbone and are ready to cook. They are usually boneless, with no waste.

• (5) **Steaks** are ready-to-cook, cross-sectional slices of large fish. The edible yield is about 86 percent.

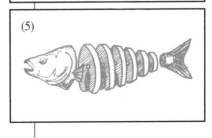

Dressing a Round Fish

• (6) Place fish on a flat surface. With a fish scaler or dull side of a knife, scrape off scales, moving from head to tail.

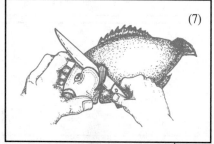

• (7) Remove the head and pectoral fins by cutting through the fish at a 45-degree angle just behind the head.

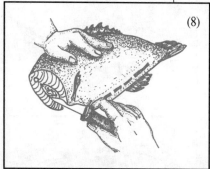

• (8) Cut the entire length of the belly from head to tail.

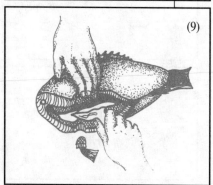

• (9) Remove viscera and all black membranes and blood, particularly the blood streak running along the backbone. Cut around pelvic fins and remove them. Rinse fish well — with attention to cavity — under cold, running water.

Filleting a Round-Bodied Fish

• (10) Scale the fish. At the pectoral fin, just behind the head, cut into flesh at a 45-degree angle toward the head until your knife reaches the backbone.

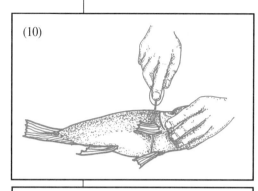

• (11) Turn the knife and follow backbone to the tail, keeping the knife against the backbone. Or, if you prefer, reverse this and cut from the tail to the head. Turn fish over and repeat on the other side.

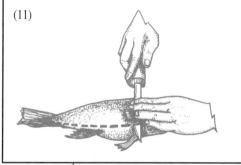

• (12) Rinse the fillet well under cold, running water.

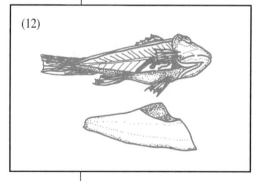

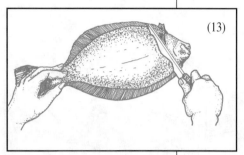

(13)

Filleting a Flat-Bodied Fish

• (13) Scale the fish. Cut down to the backbone at a 45-degree angle just behind the head.

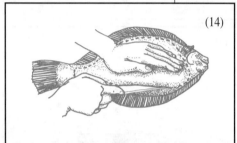

(14)

• (14) Make a cut from nape to tail along each side of the backbone. Slide knife along the backbone to loosen the fillet. Turn fish over and repeat on the other side.

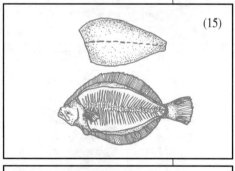

(15)

• (15) You may leave fish as two fillets or cut each in half lengthwise to make four fillets. Rinse well under cold, running water.

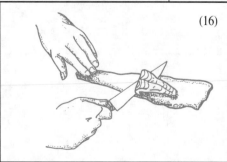

(16)

Skinning a Fillet

• (16) With skin side down, hold tail of fillet. Slide knife between skin and flesh. With the blade almost horizontal, pull the skin taut as you draw the blade toward the large end of the fillet.

Dressing Live Crabs

• (17) Pick up crab by one or both back flippers so that claws cannot pinch you.

• (18) Turn crab over and stab straight down at the point of apron. Make two cuts from this point to form a V-pattern that will remove the face of the crab (eyes and mouth).

• (19) Do not remove knife after removing the face. Firmly press crab shell on cutting surface without breaking the shell. With other hand, grasp crab by legs and claws on the side where you are holding the knife. Pull up. This should pull the crab body free from the shell.

• (20) Remove gray, feathery gills, often called "dead men," which are attached just above the legs. Cut and scrape upward to remove them.

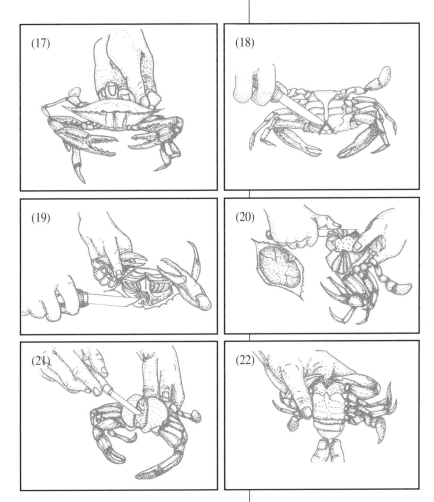

• (21) Remove all loose material — viscera and eggs — from the cavity.

• (22) If apron did not come loose with the shell, remove it. Rinse dressed crab thoroughly under cold, running water. The dressed crab can be used whole or halved.

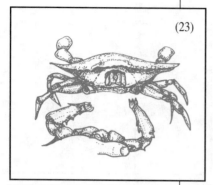

(23)

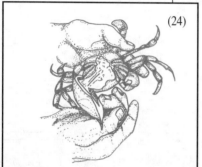

(24)

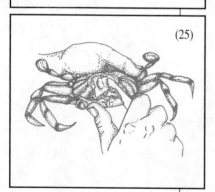

(25)

Dressing and Picking Cooked Crabs

• (23) Holding crab in one hand, grip two large claws and pull down, breaking them off. Save them.

• (24) Lift up one point of top shell and pull off the shell.

• (25) Cut across body just behind eyes to remove the face. Remove gray, feathery gills and internal organs by scraping them out with a knife.

• (26) Cut off legs where they join the body. Do not cut in too far or you will cut the meat.

• (27) This is the most important cut. On one side of crab, make a straight cut from back to front of crab, just above the leg joints, baring top and bottom chambers. Repeat on other side.

• (28) With knife, remove large chunk of white muscle — the lump meat — from each side.

• (29) Remove remaining meat from body by sliding knife under each piece and lifting it out.

• (30) Remove meat from top two chambers.

• (31) Just behind pincer of one claw, crack shell all the way around with knife. Pull meat out or remove it with knife.

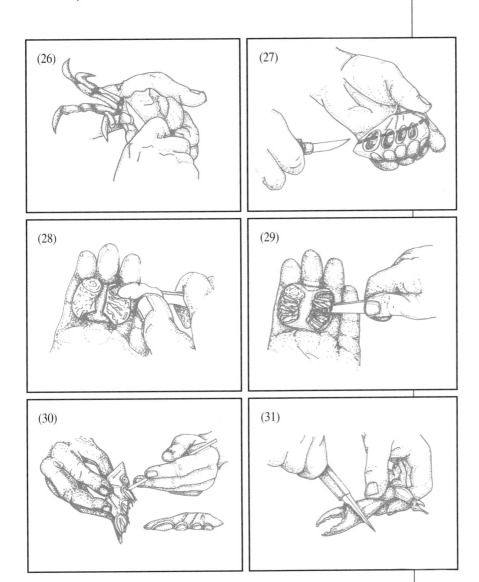

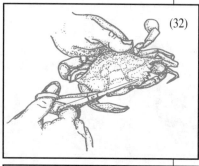

Cleaning Soft-Shell Crabs

• (32) With scissors, cut across body just behind eyes to remove face.

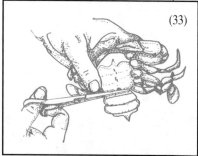

• (33) Turn crab on its back. Lift and remove apron and vein attached to it.

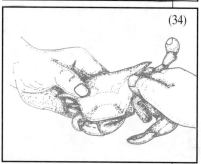

• (34) Turn crab over and lift one side of top shell.

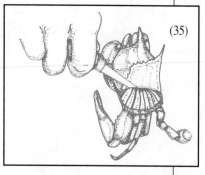

• (35) With small knife, scrape off grayish-white gills. Repeat on other side. Rinse crab gently under cold, running water, then pat dry.

Heading, Peeling and Deveining Shrimp

• (36) Hold a shrimp in one hand. With your thumb behind its head, push the head off. Be sure to push just the head so that you do not lose any meat.

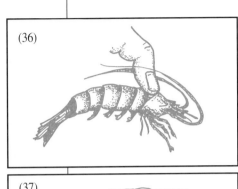

• (37) If using a deveiner, insert it at the head end just above the vein.

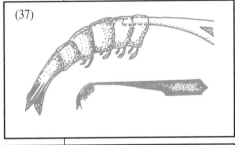

• (38) Push through to the tail and remove the shell. This removes the vein at the same time. Rinse shrimp well under cold running water.

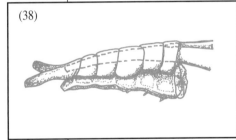

• (39) If you prefer to use a paring knife, shell shrimp with your fingers or knife. To remove the vein, use the knife. Rinse well under cold, running water.

Note: When cooking shrimp in their shells, first head them. After cooking, peel and devein them. To maintain flavor, do not rinse shrimp after cooking.

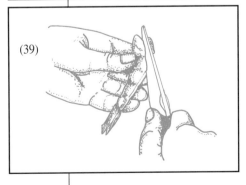

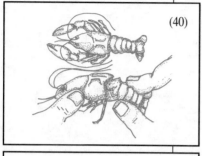

(40)

Peeling Cooked Crawfish

• (40) Separate the tail from the head by twisting and firmly pulling the tail away.

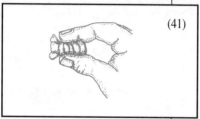

(41)

• (41) Hold the tail between your forefinger and thumb. Squeeze until the shell cracks.

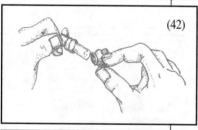

(42)

• (42) Grasp the first three segments from the side and loosen by lifting up and pulling around the meat. This piece can easily be pulled off and discarded.

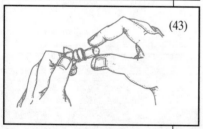

(43)

• (43) Grasp the last segment and tailfin between your thumb and forefinger of one hand. Hold the meat with the other. Gently pull.

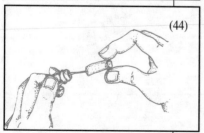

(44)

• (44) The meat should slide out of the shell and the vein should pull free from the meat. If not, remove the vein with a small knife.

Opening Oysters

Oyster shells are especially
sharp. Be sure to wear gloves.

Method 1

• (45) Chip off thin lip of
oyster until there is a small
opening.

• (46) Insert oyster knife and
cut muscle from top and
bottom shells. Twist knife and
pop oyster open.

Method 2

• (47) Work oyster knife into
front of oyster, opposite the
hinge.

• (48) Insert knife and cut
muscle from top and bottom
shell. Twist knife and pop
oyster open.

Method 3

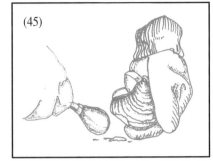

(45)

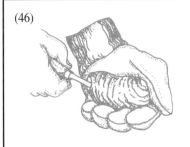

(46)

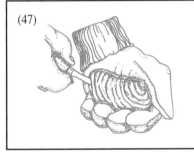

(47)

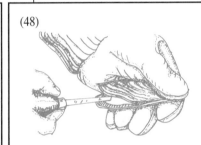

(48)

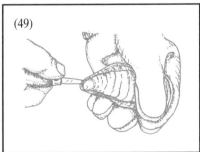

(49)

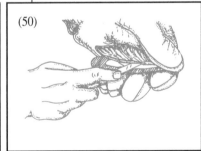

(50)

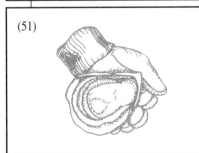

(51)

• (49) Insert oyster knife at hinge and twist to pop open.

• (50) Insert knife at front and cut muscle from top and bottom shell.

Serving

• (51) In all three methods, the oyster is ready to cook or serve on the
half-shell. Before eating or serving raw shellfish, see the safety discussion
on p. 35.

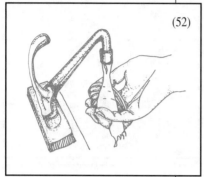

(52)

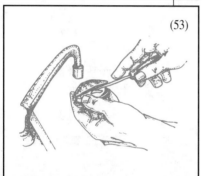

(53)

Opening Clams

Method 1

• (52) The easiest way to open clams is to freeze them, then hold under cold, running water for about 45 seconds.

• (53) You can then easily insert the knife. Cut inside muscles and scrape meat free from top and bottom. This method also saves the clam liquid, which is still frozen around the clam.

Method 2

• (54) In back of clam near the hinge, find a black ligament. Follow to the front, where the ligament ends in a weak spot. Insert knife at this spot.

• (55) Inside are two muscles. Run knife around the shell to sever these.

• (56) Insert knife in front of shell and scrape meat free from top and bottom.

Method 3

• (57) Scrape edge of shell on a cement block or other rough surface to break away some shell and provide an opening for the knife.

• (58) Insert knife and cut muscles. Then go in front and cut meat free.

Serving

• (59) In all three methods, the clam is ready to cook or serve on the half-shell. Before eating or serving raw shellfish, see the safety discussion on p. 35.

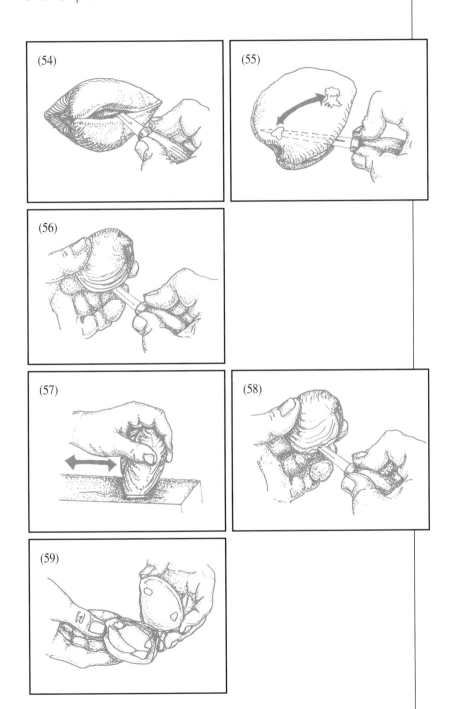

(54)

(55)

(56)

(57)

(58)

(59)

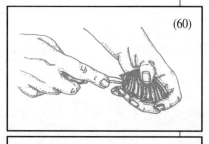

(60)

Opening Scallops

Scallops are marketed shucked, but you can open the ones that you harvest from approved waters.

• (60) Insert knife blade between shells to part them.

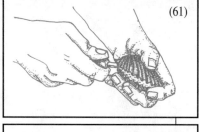

(61)

• (61) Run blade inside one shell to cut muscle.

(62)

• (62) Break hinge open and discard top shell.

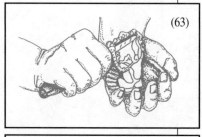

(63)

• (63) Insert knife under viscera and, by pinching viscera between knife and your thumb, push up so that viscera peels away from the white flesh. Discard viscera.

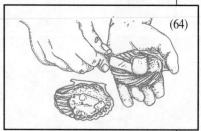

(64)

• (64) Run knife under muscle to free it from remaining shell. Rinse shucked scallops well under cold, running water.

TIPS FROM
the Kitchen

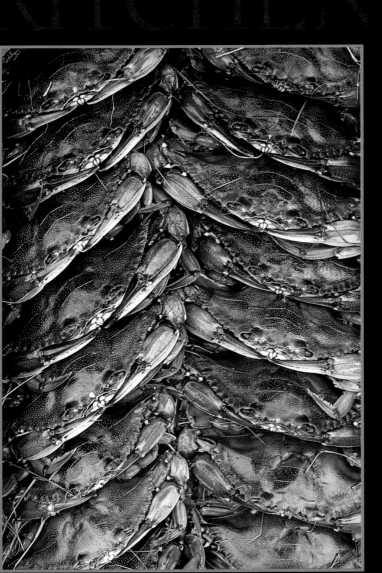

Cooking fish and shellfish is not mysterious. It is easy and usually simple. Many people do not cook seafood because they feel uncomfortable with it. We hope that this book will change that. If you're not a seafood cook, you can become one. If you are already a seafood cook, we hope that you will gain some additional ideas.

TIPS FROM
the Kitchen

This book is about seafood, not just about cooking. By the time you are reading this chapter, you have found answers to many of your questions. In this section and the ones on nutrition, seafood safety, buying and handling fish and shellfish, we provide information on the questions we are asked most often by consumers.

Cooking fish and shellfish is not mysterious. It is easy and usually simple. Many people do not cook seafood because they feel uncomfortable with it. We hope that this book will change that. If you're not a seafood cook, you can become one. If you are already a seafood cook, we hope that you will gain some additional ideas.

The recipes in this book were developed, tested and evaluated on the coast by a dedicated group over a period of 30 years. The first chapter introduced you to these folks. You probably wish that you could have been here with them.

These same Nutrition Leaders also evaluated the foods we prepared. And they were tough! We had some recipe failures. You won't find any of them in this book. Our evaluation system was simple. We used "smiley faces" with a scale of 1 to 5. A 5 is excellent, 4 is very good, 3 is average, 2 is poor, 1 is unacceptable. Actually, we considered anything that received a rating below 4.5 as unacceptable. All the recipes included here received 4.5 or higher. We're very proud of this.

5   4   3   2   1

Most of our preparations are fairly simple. And you won't find any long, stuffy names — no *Marinated Grilled Salmon Fillets on Snow Peas and Cabbage with Watercress Mayonnaise and Ginger Horseradish Butter, Capers, Red Peppers and Corn Relish*. A few of our preparations may sound

The recipes in this book were developed, tested and evaluated on the coast by a dedicated group over a period of 30 years. The first chapter introduced you to these folks. You probably wish that you could have been here with them.

Remember that the first

secret to good seafood cooking

is always to use fresh fish and

shellfish. Always go to the

market to buy fresh fish,

not a particular species.

If the recipe calls for

snapper but the flounder is

fresher, choose the flounder.

a bit complicated at first. If they do, take time to try them. They're worth it.

You will notice that our recipes call for fillets or steaks, not whole fish. Over the years we have found that most cooks prefer the convenience and ease of cooking pieces that do not contain bones. Whole fish are also more difficult to serve because you have to cut through the backbone and this often causes the fish to fall apart, resulting into unattractive portions. Most people have access to pieces of fish such as fillets and steaks, but not many markets sell whole fish unless they're on the coast.

There are advantages, though, to cooking whole fish. Bones add flavor to all meat, including fish. Also, the price per pound is less than that of fillets and steaks. And whole fish add interest to a meal. A small, whole pan-fried flounder on your plate presents a picture that can't be matched by a piece of fish.

You can adapt many recipes to whole fish. The principles are the same. If you want to be adventurous, try some whole, dressed fish.

Remember that the first secret to good seafood cooking is always to use fresh fish and shellfish. Always go to the market to buy fresh fish, not a particular species. If the recipe calls for snapper but the flounder is fresher, choose the flounder.

Following are a few miscellaneous suggestions that will help you create delicious seafood dishes.

Amount to Buy and to Serve

Our fish recipes generally call for a number of fillets or steaks rather than weight. The reason for this is simple. I've watched countless people in the seafood market look at fish and ask for a certain number of pieces. They are deciding the size that will be served to each person.

If I'm going to cook fish for six people, I might buy six small fillets, three medium fillets or two large ones that can be cut into six serving-size pieces. In the 20-plus years that our newsletter reached several thousand people, we found that consumers preferred this. Most people can look at fillets and visualize how many will be needed to feed a certain number of people, but they can't visualize the size of one-fourth or one-third of a pound.

Recipes usually state the number of servings. One hundred grams (about 3.5 ounces) is considered a serving. But in reality, we know that people usually eat more than this. In these recipes we have allowed one-fourth to one-third pound per person. Make them smaller or larger so that they meet your needs.

The following suggestions are based on approximately 3.5 ounces per serving:

- Whole or Round Fish — 3/4 pound
- Dressed Fish — 1/2 pound
- Fillets and Steaks — 1/3 pound
- Oysters and Clams, in the shell — 6
- Oysters and Clams, shucked — 1/6 pint
- Scallops — 1/4 pound
- Crab, cooked meat — 1/4 pound
- Crabs, live — 1 to 2 pounds
- Shrimp, headed — 1/2 pound
- Shrimp, cooked and peeled — 1/4 pound

Judging Doneness

The two biggest problems in seafood cooking are lack of freshness and overcooking.

Fish and shellfish cook quickly, and it's easy to overcook them.

Fish is perfectly cooked just at the point when it turns opaque. Insert a fork or the tip of a sharp knife at its thickest point and gently push the flesh aside, or flake it.

Some fish, such as tuna and shark, do not flake. Cut into the center of these to check for doneness.

Recipes give you a cooking time, such as "about 8 to 10 minutes." You should always check before this suggested time. If it isn't done, you can cook it further, but if you check it at eight minutes and it's overcooked you can't remedy the problem.

Another method of judging doneness is to cook fish for about 10 minutes per inch of thickness, measured at the thickest point of the fish. Again, you should check before the time is up.

Fish should reach an internal temperature of 145 F. It usually isn't practical to use a thermometer, but if it is cooked until opaque and flakes easily it is done.

If you're cooking fish in a sauce or wrapped in foil, add five minutes to the total cooking time. Double the cooking time when cooking frozen fish.

Shrimp, scallops, crabs and lobsters turn opaque when done. Cut into the center to test.

Cook live clams, oysters and mussels until the shells are opened and the flesh is fully cooked. Before you eat them raw or partially cooked, be sure to read the chapter on seafood safety.

The two biggest problems in seafood cooking are lack of freshness and overcooking. Fish and shellfish cook quickly, and it's easy to overcook them. Fish is perfectly cooked just at the point when it turns opaque.

Does it take more time to use

fresh products? Yes, a little more.

But try making a few recipes

with fresh ingredients. Once you

do, you'll see what we mean.

And your family will appreciate

the difference. Besides, we're

dealing with seafood and it

deserves the best ingredients.

Fresh Ingredients

Fresh ingredients *do* make a difference. Unlike many other cooks, we always specify such items as freshly ground black pepper. If you ever grind your own black or white pepper, you'll never buy another box of ground pepper. If you don't have a good pepper mill, indulge yourself. It's a must in food preparation.

There is no substitute for fresh garlic. And dehydrated onion does not impart the sweet flavor of fresh onion.

You will find a world of difference in a dish made with fresh lemon, lime or orange juice rather then processed juice.

In addition, we make our own sauces. While you can sometimes substitute a commercial product, you won't get the same flavor.

You may not believe it, but crumbs made from fresh crackers will be so much tastier than prepared ones. Use unsalted or salted saltines.

In recipes calling for bread, we use Italian bread. It is a simple, basic bread containing only flour, yeast, water and salt. It takes just a second to make fresh bread crumbs in the food processor. For dry bread crumbs, first toast the bread, then process the crumbs.

And cheeses! Once you use freshly grated cheese, you will always grate your own, whether cheddar, Parmesan or any other variety.

Always use real wine, not cooking wine, in your foods. It doesn't need to be expensive. Buy a bottle of dry white wine such as *chenin blanc,* not a fruity or sweet one. Most cooking wines contain preservatives and salt. And you have to wonder how long they were aged — maybe 10 minutes?

Does it take more time to use fresh products? Yes, a little more. But try making a few recipes with fresh ingredients. Once you do, you'll see what we mean. And your family will appreciate the difference. Besides, we're dealing with seafood and it deserves the best ingredients.

Seasonings

Fresh herbs, spices and some vegetables can enhance and add variety to your cooking — not just seafood, but almost all of your cooking.

Herbs are the leaves of plants such as basil and rosemary. Most supermarkets carry a selection of fresh herbs. Many cooks like to grow their own in a garden, window box or in small pots. Herbs are easy to grow and give you fresh ingredients just for the picking.

The oils in herbs are volatile and are what you smell and taste. Chop herbs just before you add them to the food. Add fresh herbs about the last 15 or 20 minutes of cook time.

You won't get the same results if you use dried herbs, but if they are not old and stale you can still create some great dishes. Dried herbs and spices should be stored in airtight containers away from heat and light. One of the best places to store them is in the freezer. They will remain stable up to a year. Always smell them before use. If they do not have their initial fresh scent, replace them.

Generally, use two to three times as much fresh herbs as dried since dried ones are more potent. The exception to this is rosemary; use equal amounts of it. Add dried herbs early in the cooking.

Spices are the bark, root, fruit, berry or seeds of plants. Like herbs, spices such as pepper and ginger are very compatible with seafood.

Black peppercorns are picked and dried when the berries of the pepper plant are not quite ripe. Slightly hot, they have the most intense flavor.

The mature berries of the pepper plant are pink or red. The hull is removed to make white peppercorns. They are less pungent than black ones. White pepper is often used in foods such as white sauces so that the color won't stand out in the food.

Both black and white peppercorns are quite compatible with fish and shellfish. They need to be freshly ground just before using. You're going to love these two fresh spices. And don't forget about the pepper mill mentioned above.

Green peppercorns are unripened berries and usually come packed in brine. Pink peppercorns are not true peppercorns and come from a different plant. Neither of these two is used much, if at all, in seafood cooking.

Many herbs and spices are compatible with fish and shellfish, including the following:

• basil	• fennel	• rosemary
• bay leaves	• ginger	• saffron
• black pepper	• marjoram	• sage
• cayenne pepper	• mustard	• savory
• celery seed	• nutmeg	• tarragon
• chives	• oregano	• white pepper
• curry	• paprika	
• dill	• parsley	

Some root vegetables, such as garlic and onions, make great seasonings for seafood. Both belong to the lily family, along with leeks, shallots and chives, which are also compatible with seafood.

Fresh herbs, spices and some vegetables can enhance and add variety to your cooking — not just seafood, but almost all of your cooking.

Since the odor of raw

garlic is so pungent,

people often ask if it isn't

too strong to use with seafood.

It isn't — once garlic

is cooked, it becomes mild,

mellow and sweet.

Garlic is inexpensive and available year-round. Buy firm, heavy, plump bulbs with dry skin. Store in a cool, dry place. Don't store it in the refrigerator because it will sprout. If you cut into a clove that has started to sprout, remove the sprout to keep it from affecting the flavor of the garlic.

The whole bulb you buy is the head. The individual pieces that make up the head are cloves. Each clove is covered with a paperlike skin.

Before you peel garlic, first cut the stem off the end of the cloves. Some cooks use a small paring knife and their fingers to peel it. Others tap the cloves with the side of a chef's knife or the weight of one hand. You can also buy a garlic peeler at kitchen supply stores. It is an inexpensive tubular piece of plastic about five inches long and a little more than an inch in diameter. You simply place the garlic clove in it and roll it with your hand on the counter top until you hear the paper skin crackle. It takes just a few seconds and the clove is perfectly peeled. To us, this is the easiest way to peel garlic.

If a recipe calls for minced or chopped garlic, you can almost always press it instead. The exception is if you need large chopped pieces or slices. Buy yourself a good garlic press. You'll soon find it indispensable.

Since the odor of raw garlic is so pungent, people often ask if it isn't too strong to use with seafood. It isn't — once garlic is cooked, it becomes mild, mellow and sweet.

Garlic enhances many foods, not just seafood. There is no firm evidence yet, but many studies have indicated that garlic may aid medical treatment for illnesses such as cancer, high cholesterol and blood pressure, as well as other health problems.

Garnishes

Suggestions include the following fruits, herbs and vegetables:
- avocado slices
- asparagus tips, steamed
- broccoli florets
- capers
- carrot curls or sticks
- celery sticks
- cauliflower florets
- corn, baby
- cucumber rounds or sticks
- egg (hard-cooked slices)
- fruit (lemon, lime, orange, tangerine wedges or slices)

- mushrooms (baby, whole or sliced)
- olives (stuffed or black)
- onions (pearl); green (whole or strips); red (rings); spring (whole or strips)
- pepper (red, green or yellow, rings)
- pimento strips
- sprigs (dill, oregano, parsley, sage, tarragon, thyme, watercress)
- tomatoes (cherry or slices)

Also sprinkle with toasted almond slivers, paprika, chopped pimento, freshly ground Parmesan cheese, freshly chopped basil, chives, dill, thyme, diced fresh tomatoes or the zest of lemon, lime or orange.

Side Dishes

We've come a long way in preparing foods to complement fish and shellfish. Not too long ago, seafood usually came served with french fries and coleslaw. Try your favorite dishes. Here are a few ideas:

- corn, creamed or on-the-cob
- small, whole boiled or roasted potatoes
- oven-baked french fries
- baked potatoes
- green beans amandine
- broiled or baked tomato halves
- wild rice
- steamed broccoli, cauliflower, green beans, snow peas, sugar snap peas, cabbage, carrots, Brussels sprouts, mushrooms, spinach, asparagus
- fresh citrus salad

Fats and Oils

The fats that we eat, from animal fats, vegetable shortening and cooking oils, are three types of fatty acids — saturated, polyunsaturated and monounsaturated.

Saturated fats are found mainly in meats and dairy products such as butter and cheese, and in coconut and palm oils. Saturated fats are solid at room temperature.

Polyunsaturated fats are found in oils such as sunflower and soybean oil. They are liquid at room temperature.

Monounsaturated fats are found in such oils as olive and canola. They are liquid at room temperature. Research shows that monounsaturated oils are the most heart-healthy.

The *American Heart Association Cookbook* recommends canola, corn, olive, safflower, sesame, sunflower and vegetable oils. Vegetable oil is a blend of

Research indicates that trans fat lowers the "good" cholesterol and may raise the "bad" cholesterol. Trans fatty acids also raise the total serum cholesterol level. Studies of the health effects of trans fat indicate that it may affect birth weight, insulin levels, immune responses and other medical conditions.

When unsaturated liquid fats are hydrogenated to form solid products such as margarine or vegetable shortening, trans fat results. The more solid the food, the more trans fatty acids. Tub and soft margarines are better for you than stick margarine. Trans fatty acids are also found in crackers, pastries, chips, non-dairy creamers, whipped toppings and many other foods.

oils made from plant sources such as soybeans. The AHA does not recommend peanut oil because it contains 17 percent saturated fat.

While some oils are more heart-healthy than others, remember that all cooking oils contain the same number of calories — nine per gram. The label "light" on oils refers only to the flavor, not the number of calories.

Trans fatty acids, or *trans fat*, found in many foods raise additional concerns among nutritionists. Research indicates that trans fat lowers the "good" cholesterol and may raise the "bad" cholesterol. Trans fatty acids also raise the total serum cholesterol level. Studies of the health effects of trans fat indicate that it may affect birth weight, insulin levels, immune responses and other medical conditions.

When unsaturated liquid fats are hydrogenated to form solid products such as margarine or vegetable shortening, trans fat results. The more solid the food, the more trans fatty acids. Tub and soft margarines are better for you than stick margarine. Trans fatty acids are also found in crackers, pastries, chips, non-dairy creamers, whipped toppings and many other foods.

While nutrition labels list total fat and saturated fat contents, they have not listed trans fatty acids. In 2003, the Food and Drug Administration announced a rule to require the listing of trans fatty acids.

The National Academy of Sciences Institute of Medicine says that trans fatty acids provide no known health benefit and that no safe level of them exists.

As the result of the studies of trans fatty acids, some fast-food chains and makers of snack foods such as chips are beginning to reduce the level of trans fat in their products.

You will notice that we specify "margarine or butter" in our recipes. This doesn't indicate that they are equal in health benefits. While margarine contains more trans fat, butter contains more saturated fat. We list butter as an option only because over the years we have found that it is so compatible with seafood. Our *Steamed Clams in Wine Broth* wouldn't be quite the same if we used margarine. But you're the boss and you get to make the choice.

Ingredient Substitutions

You will notice that not all of our recipes are low in fat. Although we are quick to emphasize the nutritional and health benefits of seafood, we also know that from time to time cooks want to indulge themselves and their guests. Occasionally, we enjoy some cheese or butter or we want to fry some seafood. Moderation is the key.

Remember that you can often substitute ingredients. You will have flavor and texture differences. Most folks don't object, but some purists will. Not all substitutions will work in all recipes; you may have to experiment.

Ingredient	Substitute
• egg	egg substitute
• mayonnaise	reduced calorie or fat-free mayonnaise, low-fat yogurt
• sour cream	non-fat sour cream, plain low-fat yogurt
• whole milk	low-fat or fat-free milk
• heavy cream	skim evaporated milk
• cheddar cheese	low-fat processed cheese, Parmesan cheese
• margarine, butter	diet margarine

Fish Flavors and Substitutions

Different fish have different flavors. But you can almost always substitute in most recipes. Just exchange one type for a similar one. For example, substitute one lean fish for another lean one, a fatter fish for another with about the same fat content. Most of our palates are not so discriminating that we will notice a big difference.

Lean fish are white or light in color and have a mild flavor. Higher fat fish have a more pronounced flavor and are darker in color. You can substitute among the species in each category. Following are some examples.

White or light color, delicate flavor: Atlantic cod, Alaska pollock, brook trout, catfish, cod, grouper, Gulf flounder, halibut, rainbow trout, Southern flounder, summer flounder, tilefish, white sea bass

White or light color, light to moderate flavor: Atlantic salmon, butterfish, catfish, croaker, drum, mahi-mahi, mullet, pompano, porgy, red snapper, sheepshead, spot, spotted sea trout, striped bass, swordfish, whiting

Light, more pronounced flavor: king mackerel, Spanish mackerel

Darker meat, light to moderate flavor: black sea bass, bluefish, salmon, tuna

Remember that the most essential element in the flavor of fish is freshness. If it isn't fresh, the flavor is distorted.

In addition to flavor differences, fish also differ in texture. Fish such as flounder and butterfish have a delicate texture — the meat separates easily and flakes into small pieces. Species such as mullet and trout are moderate in texture and do not flake as easily. Other fish, such as grouper and catfish have a firmer, meatier texture.

Different fish have different flavors. But you can almost always substitute in most recipes. Just exchange one type for a similar one. For example, substitute one lean fish for another lean one, a fatter fish for another with about the same fat content. Most of our palates are not so discriminating that we will notice a big difference.

Texture doesn't affect our selection of fish as much as taste does. But you may choose a particular type if you want to use a certain cooking method. If you want fish to cook directly on your grill, you might choose a firm fish such as tuna or salmon rather than flounder or butterfish, which would come apart during grilling.

Keep in mind that overcooking changes the texture of fish. Any species will be tough, dry and chewy if you cook it too long.

EASY WAYS TO
Cook Seafood

Sometimes the simplest recipes taste the best. Fresh ingredients plus easy

CHAPTER SIX RECIPES:

- Baked Fillet of Flounder Stuffed with Crab
- Oven-Browned Catfish
- Baked Grouper with Green Onion and Mushrooms
- Individual Crab Casseroles
- Baked Trout with Cheese Topping
- Baked Flounder with Creamy Vegetables
- Oysters Casino
- Baked Tuna with Fresh Basil
- Baked Grouper with Basil-Parmesan Butter
- Herb-Broiled Mackerel Steaks
- Broiled Pompano Amandine
- Broiled Shrimp with Fresh Parsley
- Broiled Oysters
- Broiled Snapper with Hollandaise Sauce
- Golden-Brown Flounder Fillets
- Broiled Flounder with Paprika and Herbs
- Mahi-Mahi with Garlic-Ginger Sauce
- Broiled Tuna Provencal
- Spicy Flounder with Garlic Mayonnaise
- Grilled Tuna with Lemon Mayonnaise
- Grilled Garlic Shrimp
- Spotted Trout with Garlic and Tomatoes
- Marinated Charcoal-Grilled Shrimp
- Grilled Scallop Kabobs
- Grilled Tuna with Lime Butter
- Grilled Marinated Tuna with Herb Butter
- Steamed Snapper Fillets with Fresh Thyme
- Steamed Snapper Fillets with Cilantro and White Wine Sauce
- Steamed Flounder Fillets with Fresh Parsley and White Wine Sauce

- Steamed Clams in Wine Broth
- Steamed Shrimp with Soy-Ginger Sauce
- Steamed Flounder with Ginger
- Steamed Snapper Fillets with Mushroom Sauce
- Poached Flounder Fillets with Green Onion and Garlic Butter
- Milk-Poached Flounder with Mornay Sauce
- Poached Snapper with Dill Butter
- Poached Grouper with Seasoned Mayonnaise
- Poached Flounder Fillets in Cream Sauce
- Poached Grouper with Dill Sauce
- Poached Shrimp with Crab Sauce
- Poached Scallops with Béarnaise Sauce
- Beer Batter Fried Oysters
- Spicy Fried Scallops
- Fried Shrimp
- French-Fried Shrimp
- Deep-Fried Flounder
- Breaded Triggerfish
- Pan-Fried Snapper with Garlic Butter
- Fried Clams
- Crispy Flounder Fillets
- Sautéed Tuna Steaks with Tarragon
- Sautéed Mahi-Mahi with Lemon-Butter Sauce
- Sautéed Flounder Amandine
- Snapper Fillets Sautéed with Mushrooms
- Scallop and Vegetable Stir-Fry
- Grouper and Vegetable Stir-Fry
- Shrimp and Broccoli Stir-Fry
- Salmon and Asparagus Stir-Fry
- Catfish Stir-Fry
- Shrimp Stir-Fry with Green Beans and Corn

EASY WAYS TO
Cook Seafood

STRAIGHT FROM THE OVEN — BAKED FRESH FISH AND SHELLFISH

One of the best and easiest ways to cook fish or shellfish is just to slide it in the oven and bake it. Fillets, steaks, dressed fish and shellfish can all be baked. Combine them with favorite vegetables and seasonings and you always produce fresh, intermingled flavors — and satisfying results.

Baking uses dry heat and may require some basting. Lean fish may need to be basted once or twice. Fatty fish need less, if any, basting. You don't even have to use a recipe. Just brush fillets with melted margarine or butter, or use olive or vegetable oil. Top lightly with your favorite seasonings and bake. For added flavor, place the fish on a vegetable bed such as thinly sliced celery with whole leaves, carrots and onions.

Fish cooked with the head on always taste more flavorful than those that are headed, but some people object to this. As with all cooking, cook to your preferences.

Lean fish are more suitable for baking than oily ones. When you bake a fatty fish, you may want to use a rack to keep it from standing in the oil.

When you cook fish in foil, a brown-in bag or parchment, remember that you are actually steaming it instead of baking. These methods create steam in the packages, cooking with moist heat. If fish is baked in foil, add five minutes to the total cooking time and more for large fish.

Baked fish can be simple or fancy. A golden-browned, baked fish is notable for its simplicity. It can also be dressed up with a topping of sauce or vegetables. Fillets also can be rolled up, stuffed and baked. Or you can put stuffing on the flesh side of a fillet, then place another fillet on top, flesh side down. This creates boneless stuffed fish.

There is no need to turn fish when baking since it is surrounded by heat.

You can marinate seafood before baking. Or you can use rubs made with herbs and spices.

Baked fish can be simple or fancy. A golden-browned, baked fish is notable for its simplicity. It can also be dressed up with a topping of sauce or vegetables. Fillets also can be rolled up, stuffed and baked.

Commercially prepared rubs are available at your local grocery and many seafood markets. You can make your own by mixing together seasonings such as herbs, salt, freshly ground pepper, dry mustard and celery seeds. Use your own favorites. Just be sure that they are compatible. Most are.

It's easy to make a simple "butter" to serve with baked fish. Add pressed garlic, fresh lemon juice or favorite herbs to a stick of softened margarine or butter. Then spread on serving portions for special flavors after baking.

Bake fish at 400 F or higher. Cooking at lower temperatures for a longer time dries seafood. Small, thin pieces should be cooked at higher temperatures, 425 F to 450 F, so that they will not dry out. Larger pieces should be cooked more slowly at a lower temperature so that the exterior will not be done before the inside is cooked.

The Canadian, or 10-minute rule, specifies baking fish at 450 F for 10 minutes per inch of thickness. Add up to five minutes to the total cooking time when fish is cooked in a sauce or wrapped in foil.

The standard test for doneness used by many cooks is to cook until the fish flakes easily at the thickest part with a fork or the tip of a sharp knife.

Whichever method you choose, always check for doneness before the end of the cooking time. And don't rely completely on the cooking time stated in a recipe. It's certainly better to check and then cook another minute or so than to wait until the time is up, only to find the fish overcooked. Always keep in mind that fish cooked just a little bit too long will be dry and tough.

Fish should reach an internal temperature of 145 F for 15 seconds. If you want a more thorough test for doneness than the flaking test or 10-minute rule, you can use a small cooking thermometer to check for doneness. You can buy an inexpensive digital or dial thermometer at any discount store.

Be sure to preheat the oven. Preheating for 15 minutes or longer ensures evenly distributed heat. It's a good idea to check your oven with an oven thermometer every month or so. Variations in temperature have adverse effects not just on seafood but also on other dishes.

Increase the temperature by 25 degrees or increase the cooking time when baking more than one dish.

If possible, partially or completely thaw frozen fish before cooking. If you can't, double the cooking time.

For real convenience, try baking fish in dishes that can be brought directly to the table.

The 10-minute rule does not apply to shellfish. Cooking time varies depending on the species, size and additional ingredients.

Many shellfish can be cooked and served in their shells. Oysters, small clams and mussels require only that you scrub the shells well under cold, running water before cooking. To steady the shells and save the juices, place the shells in a bed of rock salt deep enough to keep them level. Try our *Oysters Casino*. And in the sections on clams, oysters and shrimp, you'll find other delicious baked recipes.

Bake some fish or shellfish tonight. You'll have a great meal.

Baked Fillet of Flounder Stuffed with Crab

- 4 medium skinless flounder fillets
- 1/2 pound backfin crabmeat
- 1 cup fresh bread crumbs
- 1 tablespoon dry sherry
- 3 tablespoons freshly grated medium cheddar cheese
- 1/8 teaspoon salt
- 1 egg, beaten
- 2 tablespoons margarine or butter, melted
- salt
- paprika

Remove any shell or cartilage from crabmeat.

In medium bowl, combine crumbs, sherry, cheese, 1/8 teaspoon salt, crabmeat and egg.

Place the two thicker fillets in greased baking dish, skin side down. Spoon stuffing mix over them. Top with 2 remaining thinner fillets, skin side up.

Brush with margarine, then sprinkle lightly with salt. Bake at 400 F until done, about 25 minutes, sprinkling with paprika after 20 minutes. Cut into serving-size pieces. Serves 6 to 8.

Oven-Browned Catfish

- 1 pound catfish fillets
- 3 tablespoons margarine or butter, melted
- 1/4 cup soft bread crumbs
- 1/4 cup freshly grated Parmesan cheese
- 1/2 teaspoon thyme
- 1 teaspoon paprika
- 1/2 teaspoon salt
- 1/4 teaspoon freshly ground black pepper

Place margarine in shallow dish. In separate shallow dish, combine crumbs, Parmesan, thyme, paprika, salt and pepper. Dip fillets in margarine, then in crumb mixture.

Place in lightly greased shallow baking dish. Bake at 425 F until coating is browned and fish flakes easily with a fork, about 10 to 15 minutes. Serves 3 to 4.

Baked Grouper with Green Onion and Mushrooms

- 1 pound grouper fillets
- 1 tablespoon melted margarine or butter
- salt
- freshly ground black pepper
- 3 tablespoons margarine or butter
- 1 cup thinly sliced green onion
- 1/2 pound small mushrooms, sliced
- 2 tablespoons minced fresh dill (or 1 tablespoon dried)

Place fish in greased baking dish. Brush with melted margarine. Sprinkle with salt and pepper.

In small saucepan, melt 3 tablespoons margarine. Add green onion and mushrooms and sauté lightly. Add dill and mix well. Spoon over fish. Bake at 425 F until done, about 15 to 20 minutes. Serves 3 to 4.

Individual Crab Casseroles

- 1 pound backfin crabmeat
- 2 slices bacon
- 1/2 cup chopped onion
- 1/2 cup chopped celery
- 1/4 cup chopped green pepper
- 1/2 teaspoon pressed garlic
- 3/4 cup fresh cracker crumbs
- 1/4 cup margarine or butter, melted
- 1/4 cup milk
- 1 egg, beaten
- 2 tablespoons chopped fresh parsley
- 1 teaspoon dry mustard
- 1 teaspoon Worcestershire sauce
- 1/2 teaspoon salt
- 1/8 teaspoon cayenne pepper

Remove any shell or cartilage from crabmeat.

In medium skillet, cook bacon until crisp. Remove from pan, crumble and set aside. Cook onion, celery, green pepper and garlic in bacon drippings until tender. Remove from heat.

Stir in crumbs, margarine, milk, egg, parsley, mustard, Worcestershire, salt and cayenne. Mix well. Gently stir in crabmeat. Place in 6 well-greased shells or ramekins. Sprinkle bacon over tops. Bake at 350 F until brown and bubbly, about 20 to 25 minutes. Serves 6.

Baked Trout with Cheese Topping
- 1 to 1 1/2 pounds trout fillets
- 1/2 cup mayonnaise
- 1/2 cup sour cream
- 2 teaspoons flour
- 1 tablespoon minced onion
- 1/4 teaspoon cayenne pepper
- 1/8 teaspoon salt
- 1/4 cup fresh lemon juice
- 1/2 cup freshly grated medium cheddar cheese

In small bowl, mix together mayonnaise, sour cream, flour, onion, cayenne and salt. Place fillets in greased, shallow baking dish. Brush with lemon juice. Spread mayonnaise mixture over fillets.

Bake at 400 F until fish is almost done, about 20 minutes. Sprinkle with cheese and continue baking until cheese is melted, about 3 to 4 minutes. Serves 4 to 6.

Baked Flounder with Creamy Vegetables
- 1 1/2 pounds skinless flounder fillets
- 2 tablespoons fresh lemon juice

Vegetable Topping:
- 1/4 cup cream cheese, softened
- 1/3 cup mayonnaise
- 1/2 cup grated carrots
- 1/2 cup chopped tomato
- 1/3 cup sliced green onion, including tops
- 2 tablespoons minced fresh parsley
- 1/4 teaspoon salt
- 1/4 teaspoon freshly ground black pepper

In small bowl, combine cream cheese, mayonnaise, carrots, tomato, green onion, parsley, salt and pepper. Blend well.

Place fillets in greased baking dish. Brush with lemon juice. Spoon topping over fish, covering completely.

Bake at 400 F until done, about 15 to 20 minutes. Serves 4 to 6.

Oysters Casino

- 24 oysters in shell
- 6 bacon slices
- 6 tablespoons margarine or butter, softened
- 1/2 cup finely chopped green onion
- 2 tablespoons finely chopped sweet red pepper
- 1/3 cup finely chopped fresh parsley
- 2 tablespoons fresh bread crumbs
- 2 tablespoons fresh lemon juice
- 1/4 teaspoon salt
- 1/4 teaspoon freshly ground black pepper
- rock salt

Before shucking, scrub oysters thoroughly with a stiff brush under cold, running water. Open oysters. Leave oysters in deep lower shells. Discard top shells.

Cut each bacon slice into 4 parts. Cook over medium heat until almost done. Drain on paper towels. In small bowl, blend together margarine, green onion, red pepper, parsley, crumbs, lemon juice, salt and black pepper.

Place a deep layer of rock salt in baking dish. Place the oysters in their shells on the rock salt, using it to level and stabilize the shells. Spoon margarine mixture over the oysters and top each with bacon. Bake at 450 F until oysters are done and bacon is brown, about 8 to 10 minutes. Serves 4.

Baked Tuna with Fresh Basil

- 4 tuna steaks, about 1 inch thick
- salt
- freshly ground black pepper
- 8 sprigs fresh basil
- 2/3 can diced tomatoes, drained
- 1/2 pound sliced fresh mushrooms
- 1/4 cup dry white wine
- 1/4 stick margarine or butter, melted

Place steaks in shallow baking pan or dish. Sprinkle with salt and pepper. Place 1 basil sprig over each steak. Spread with tomatoes. Place 4 remaining basil sprigs over each steak. Spread with mushrooms. Drizzle with wine, then with margarine.

Bake at 450 F. Check for doneness after 10 minutes. Continue cooking until done. Serves 4.

Baked Grouper with Basil-Parmesan Butter
- 1 large grouper fillet, about 2 to 2 1/2 pounds
- 4 tablespoons melted margarine or butter
- salt
- freshly ground white pepper

Prepare Basil-Parmesan Butter and set aside.

Brush fillets with melted margarine. Lightly salt and pepper. Bake at 450 F until fish flakes easily with a fork, about 30 minutes. Cut into serving-size pieces. Serve with Basil-Parmesan Butter. Serves 6 to 8.

Basil-Parmesan Butter:
- 1/4 pound margarine or butter, softened
- 1/2 cup chopped fresh basil
- 1 tablespoon chopped fresh parsley
- 1/4 cup freshly grated Parmesan cheese
- 1/4 teaspoon freshly ground white pepper
- 1 tablespoon fresh lemon juice

In small bowl, mix together margarine, basil, parsley, Parmesan, pepper and lemon juice. Spread over warm fish.

BROILED SEAFOOD — AN EASY CATCH

Broiling is a simple, quick way to bring out the true flavor and texture of fresh fish. It's so easy to brush a fillet with melted margarine or butter, sprinkle it lightly with salt and freshly ground pepper, and slide it under the broiler for a few minutes.

Broiling is the ideal way to cook fillets, steaks, some shellfish, kabobs and some ramekin dishes. The intense, dry heat cooks very quickly.

You can serve broiled seafood with a sauce or butter if desired, but the fish itself is what is important.

Before broiling, fillets, steaks, shellfish and kabobs should be lightly oiled with margarine, butter, vegetable or olive oil. Use only a small amount on fatty

Broiling is a simple, quick way to bring out the true flavor and texture of fresh fish.

fish such as salmon or tuna. Use more on lean fish such as flounder or snapper.

Most books say basting is essential when broiling. But when cooking thin pieces, you may find that brushing with oil is enough. Lean fish generally require some basting. Fatty fish require less, if any.

You can create flavor differences by adding ingredients such as wine or soy sauce to the basting oil. Just be sure that other flavors don't overpower the seafood.

Marinades add flavor to broiled seafood. Marinades for fatty fish need little or no oil, while those for lean fish need more. Always broil with the skin side down so that you are basting the flesh side.

Some seafood cooks say not to use paprika when broiling. This is true if you're using it as a substitute for browning. However, when it is used for flavor and color, I like to add it just before the cooking time ends. But if allowed to burn, it will taste bitter.

When broiling or grilling, always use a perforated broiling rack. Fish sticks to a wire rack, breaks apart and falls through.

Fully preheat the broiler unless the oven manufacturer recommends differently. If your broiler has a temperature setting, turn it to 550 F. Leave the oven door open or closed according to the manufacturer's instructions.

Pay attention to the distance of the fish from the broiler, intense heat and timing when broiling. Most recipes specify broiling three to four inches from the heat source. The thicker the fish, the farther it should be from the element. This prevents the top from browning too quickly before the inside is done.

It's generally best to broil fillets and steaks that are three-fourths to one inch thick. Cook about six to eight minutes. Thicker pieces require a bit longer.

It isn't necessary to turn fish when broiling unless the pieces are more than one inch thick. If they are, broil the skin side first for eight to 10 minutes. Turn and broil the other side until done — about five to eight minutes.

Broil whole, dressed fish over one inch thick about 10 minutes per side. Most shellfish will broil in about 10 to 15 minutes (total).

Always check for doneness before the end of the cooking time.

As with all seafood, avoid overcooking. Since you're using intense, dry heat, cooking time is brief. Fish should be moist and golden or lightly browned when done. Remember that the fish continues to cook a bit after removal from the oven. If slightly translucent in the middle, it will finish cooking after you take it out. Test for doneness with the tip of a sharp knife or with a fork. The fish will flake easily when done.

To broil in-shell clams and oysters, scrub the shells with a stiff brush under cold, running water. Open and leave on half of the shell (for oysters use the deep half). Place in deep rock salt on a baking pan. To spice up your shellfish, add salt, pepper and melted margarine or butter. Or sprinkle on other ingredients such as a bit of minced onion, parsley or hot pepper sauce. In just a few minutes, you'll have wonderful shellfish.

Broiling and grilling are basically the same method. Both use dry, intense heat. The only difference is that in broiling the heat is above the food while in grilling it is below it. You can substitute most broiling recipes for grilling and vice versa.

Herb-Broiled Mackerel Steaks
- 4 small Spanish mackerel steaks
- 1/4 cup margarine or butter, softened
- 1 tablespoon chopped fresh parsley
- 1 tablespoon thinly sliced green onion, including tops
- 1/2 teaspoon chopped fresh tarragon (or 1/4 dried)
- 1/2 teaspoon chopped fresh thyme (or 1/4 dried)
- 1 teaspoon salt
- 1/8 teaspoon freshly ground black pepper
- 1/8 teaspoon paprika

Place fillets in greased, broiler-safe pan, without rack, skin side down. In small bowl, blend together margarine, parsley, green onion, tarragon, thyme, salt, pepper and paprika. Spread over fillets. Broil about 4 inches from heat until fish flakes with a fork, about 8 to 10 minutes. Baste once or twice with pan juices during cooking. Serves 4.

Broiled Pompano Amandine
- 2 pounds pompano fillets
- 2 tablespoons margarine or butter, melted
- 2 tablespoons vegetable oil
- 1/4 cup flour
- 1 1/2 teaspoons salt
- 1 teaspoon paprika

Combine margarine and oil. Brush over fillets and on broiler rack. In shallow pan or dish, mix flour, salt and paprika. Roll fillets in flour mixture.

Broil about 6 inches from heat, basting as needed. Cook until surface is crusted, about 10 to 15 minutes, or until fish flakes easily when tested with a fork. Place cooked fish on heated serving dish and pour sauce over it. Serves 6 to 8.

While cooking fish, prepare Amandine Sauce.

Amandine Sauce:
- 3 tablespoons margarine or butter
- 1/2 cup slivered almonds
- 2 tablespoons fresh lime juice
- 4 drops Tabasco sauce

In small saucepan, melt margarine over medium heat. Add almonds and brown lightly. Remove almonds and scatter over cooked fillets. Add lime juice and Tabasco to remaining margarine. Heat and pour over fish.

Broiled Shrimp with Fresh Parsley
- 1 pound medium or large shrimp
- 1/4 cup soy sauce
- 1/4 cup vegetable oil
- 1/4 cup fresh lemon juice
- 1/4 cup snipped fresh parsley
- 1/4 teaspoon salt
- 1/8 teaspoon freshly ground black pepper
- 1/2 teaspoon Tabasco sauce

Peel shrimp, leaving on tail section. In shallow dish, combine soy sauce, oil, lemon juice, parsley, salt, pepper and Tabasco. Place shrimp in mixture and marinate in refrigerator 15 minutes.

Broil about 4 inches from heat until done, about 5 to 6 minutes, turning once. Serves 3 to 4.

Broiled Oysters
- 1 pint oysters, drained
- 2 slices bacon
- 2 tablespoons margarine or butter
- 1 teaspoon fresh lemon juice
- 1/4 teaspoon freshly ground black pepper
- 1/4 cup thinly sliced green onion
- flour

Fry bacon until crisp. Remove bacon from pan, reserving 1 1/2 table-spoons bacon grease. Add margarine to pan and melt. Add lemon juice, pepper and green onion. Cook until onion is tender, about 2 minutes.

Place oysters in lightly greased shells or ramekins. Dust lightly with flour. Spoon margarine mixture over oysters. Broil about 4 inches from heat until done, about 8 to 10 minutes. Sprinkle with crumbled bacon. Serves 4.

Broiled Snapper with Hollandaise Sauce
- 4 medium snapper fillets
- 2 tablespoons margarine or butter, melted
- salt
- freshly ground black pepper

Brush fillets with margarine. Lightly salt and pepper. Broil about 4 inches from heat until fish flakes with a fork, about 10 minutes. Serves 6 to 8.

While fish is cooking, prepare Cooked Hollandaise Sauce.

Cooked Hollandaise Sauce:
- 3 egg yolks
- 1/4 cup water
- 1 tablespoon fresh lemon juice
- 1/2 cup firm cold butter, cut into eighths
- 1/4 teaspoon salt
- 1/8 teaspoon paprika
- 1/16 teaspoon cayenne pepper

In a small saucepan, beat together egg yolks, water and lemon juice. Cook over very low heat, stirring constantly, until yolk mixture bubbles at edges. Stir in butter, one piece at a time, until melted and sauce is thickened. Stir in salt, paprika and cayenne. Remove from heat. Pour over cooked fish. Makes about 3/4 cup.

Golden-Brown Flounder Fillets
- 6 small flounder (or other white) fillets
- 4 tablespoons margarine or butter, melted
- 1 tablespoon grated onion
- 2 tablespoons fresh lemon juice
- 1 teaspoon salt
- 1/4 teaspoon freshly ground black pepper
- paprika
- lemon wedges (optional)

In small bowl, combine margarine, onion, lemon juice, salt, pepper and paprika. Place fillets on greased broiler rack, skin side down. Baste with margarine mixture. Broil about 4 inches from heat until done, about 8 to 10 minutes, basting and sprinkling with paprika after first 5 minutes. Serves 6.

Broiled Flounder with Paprika and Herbs
- 6 small flounder fillets
- salt
- 1 teaspoon paprika
- freshly ground black pepper
- 1/2 cup softened butter or margarine
- 2 tablespoons minced green onion
- 2 tablespoons minced fresh parsley
- 1 tablespoon minced fresh tarragon (or 3/4 teaspoon dried)
- 1 tablespoon fresh lemon juice

Lightly grease broiler rack. Place fillets on the rack. Sprinkle lightly with salt, then with the paprika and pepper.

Spread margarine on top of fillets, sprinkle with onion and broil about 4 inches from heat, spreading more margarine on once or twice. Broil until fish flakes easily, about 8 to 10 minutes. Sprinkle with parsley and lemon juice. Pour sauce from the pan over all. Serves 6.

Mahi-Mahi with Garlic-Ginger Sauce
- 1 1/2 pounds medium mahi-mahi fillets, cut into serving-size pieces
- 1 tablespoon extra virgin olive oil
- 1/2 teaspoon salt
- 1/4 teaspoon freshly ground black pepper
- 1 tablespoon pressed garlic
- 1 tablespoon minced fresh ginger
- 1 teaspoon fresh lime juice
- 2 teaspoons chopped fresh parsley

In small bowl, combine olive oil, salt, pepper, garlic, ginger and lime juice. Brush over fish.

To broil, place fish about 4 inches from heat, depending upon thickness. (Remember: the thicker the piece, the farther from the heat in grilling and broiling.) Cook until one side is done, about 4 to 5 minutes. Turn over and repeat on other side. Serves 6 to 8.

Broiled Tuna Provencal
- 4 tuna steaks, about 1 inch thick
- 1 tablespoon extra virgin olive oil
- 1 tablespoon fresh lemon juice
- salt
- freshly ground black pepper

Prepare Provencal Sauce and keep warm.

Combine olive oil and lemon juice. Place steaks on greased broiler rack and brush them with oil mixture. Lightly salt and pepper.

Place steaks about 6 inches from heat source and broil until top side is tender, about 8 minutes. Turn and repeat until done, about 6 minutes. Serve with Provencal Sauce.

Provencal Sauce:
- 2 tablespoons extra virgin olive oil
- 1 teaspoon pressed garlic
- 6 canned chopped tomatoes, drained
- 1 teaspoon chopped fresh basil
- 1 tablespoon chopped fresh parsley
- 1/2 teaspoon salt
- 1/4 teaspoon freshly ground black pepper

In small saucepan, heat oil. Add garlic and sauté until tender. Add tomatoes and basil. Cover and simmer 10 to 15 minutes. Add parsley. Spoon over hot fish.

WHERE THERE'S SMOKE, THERE'S GRILLED SEAFOOD

In ancient times, men and women cooked over an open fire as an alternative to eating raw food. Today, with all our advances and conveniences, we still love to cook outdoors over a flame. And it's not just burgers and steaks anymore. A meal of fresh seafood, prepared simply outdoors and eaten in the company of friends, is one of life's real pleasures. Most of our Nutrition Leaders hold fond memories of family and neighbors gathering for oyster roasts by the shore, or fish fresh from the boat and hot off the grill.

Once considered a summertime activity, grilling is now enjoyed year-round for those of us in mild climates. On a recent Christmas Eve, a friend and I enjoyed a fish and shrimp cookout.

In addition to great flavor, grilled seafood is easy, quick and convenient. And it doesn't heat up the kitchen. It's also healthful, requiring little, if any, added fat. As in baking or broiling, you may need to use a little oil and baste lean fish for grilling, but not with oilier fish. In general no elaborate seasonings, sauces or marinades are needed.

In ancient times, men and women cooked over an open fire as an alternative to eating raw food. Today, with all our advances and conveniences, we still love to cook outdoors over a flame. And it's not just burgers and steaks anymore.

Selecting seafood to grill

Fish in any market form — drawn, dressed, steaks or fillets — may be cooked over coals. You can grill any fish that you can broil. Shellfish, depending on the recipe, may be grilled in the shell or shucked. Use the freshest fish and shellfish you can find. Lack of quality means lack of good flavor.

Firm fish such as shark or tuna can be cooked directly on the grill. With careful handling, medium-firm fish such as salmon or grouper can be cooked the same way. Steaks and skin-on fillets should be about one inch thick if they are to be cooked directly on the grill. When cooking skin-on fillets, begin grilling with the skin side down.

Small foods such as shucked shellfish, pieces of fish and vegetables grill easily on skewers. Create your own kabobs by alternating a variety of foods such as different seafoods, vegetables and fruit. Try using pineapple and bell pepper chunks on a skewer with sea scallops, for example, or onion wedges and button mushrooms with shrimp.

Choosing grilling accessories

You can use metal or bamboo skewers. Just remember to soak bamboo skewers in water for 30 minutes before using to prevent burning.

You will find that using a hinged metal grill or fish basket will make almost all seafood grilling easier. Long handles make these utensils easy to use, and they adjust to the fish's thickness. When it's time to turn the food, simply flip the hinged grill or basket.

You can find inexpensive hinged grills and baskets at discount or hardware stores, or sometimes in supermarkets. Always oil the grill before placing food in it.

Delicate fish such as flounder or trout, thin fillets and shucked shellfish always should be cooked in a hinged grill. This maintains their shape and prevents them from falling into the fire.

While thin fillets do not have to be turned, they will maintain more grilled flavor if they are.

Grilling tips

Do not overcook. Fish should always be moist and tender, never dry and chewy. Cook only until meat flakes easily when tested with a fork or tip of a sharp knife. Crustaceans are low in fat and will dry out quickly. Watch shrimp and crabs carefully and remove from the heat quickly.

You don't need a recipe for grilling oysters and clams in the shell. Just scrub the shells under cold, running water, then place them on the grill. Place oysters with the deep shell on the bottom. Grill until the shells open and the meat is done, about 7 to 12 minutes for oysters, 5 to 8 minutes for clams.

Always use a clean rack. Preheat it, then brush with vegetable oil or spray. Cook seafood about four inches above moderately hot coals. Depending upon size, fillets will cook in 6 to 12 minutes per inch of thickness. Turn once. And always check for doneness before the cooking time is up.

When cooking drawn or dressed fish, score each side. Make three cuts diagonally along each side to ensure even cooking.

Use a covered grill if you can. It provides faster cooking and keeps the seafood moist and tender. If you use an open grill, your cooking time will vary due to wind and air temperature.

Seafood tastes great when cooked on a grill, whether charcoal or gas. Gas is more convenient, and the fire will always be about the same temperature as the setting. But gas grills don't sear or brown as well as charcoal. Charcoal has the advantage of adding smoke and wood flavor, too, even though you have to light the fire and keep it going.

For additional smoked flavor, add hardwood chips such as hickory or oak to coals. A smoky flavor enhances fatty fish such as mackerel, but may overwhelm leaner fish such as flounder. Be careful when using mesquite, it may overpower the flavor of the food. When using chips, follow the package directions, then adjust to your preferences.

Me — I'm a purist. I love the delicate flavor that charcoal imparts to food. No chips, no gas grill. You, too, should follow your personal tastes.

You can baste seafood with oil or melted butter or margarine when grilling. Some people use a favorite salad dressing or mayonnaise. Remember that oily fish such as salmon and mackerel retain moisture and need little or no basting.

Spicing it up with marinades, rubs and herbs

Many cooks like to marinate seafood before grilling. Always make marinades in a nonreactive container such as glass or stainless steel, never in aluminum or any other metal that can cause chemical action or add an off-flavor to the food. To prevent grill flare-ups, limit the amount of oil used. If a flare-up occurs, cover the grill or use water from a spray bottle to put out the flame. Be careful to avoid scattering ashes onto the food.

Marinating seafood 15 to 30 minutes usually proves sufficient. Marinating for longer periods in high-acid mixtures (wine, vinegar, citrus juices) causes fish and shellfish to turn opaque and firm with a cooked appearance. This will make them dry and tough.

If you plan to use the marinade for basting, reserve some before placing the seafood in it. Never baste cooked fish or shellfish with marinade that has been used on raw seafood. The food can become contaminated with harmful bacteria.

Tasty rubs provide another alternative for spicing up grilled seafoood. A rub is a concentrated blend of herbs and spices. You can create your own flavors, such as Mexican, Creole or herb. Commercial marinades, rubs and sauces are easy to use and are often sold at seafood markets or your grocery store. Simply rub or sprinkle the mixture over the surface of the seafood before cooking.

No time for a recipe? Then keep it simple and quick. Try brushing a fillet with melted margarine, butter or oil, sprinkle with salt and pepper, and place it on the grill for a few minutes. Or spread mayonnaise or a garlic or herb butter over the fish. In a flash, it's ready and tastes wonderful.

For subtle flavors, try tossing herbs such as bay, basil, thyme, tarragon or rosemary on the hot coals. The herbs should be soaked for 30 minutes before using.

To complement your meal, try grilling your vegetables, too. Corn-in-the-husk, garlic, mushrooms, tomatoes, squash, eggplant, potatoes and other vegetables cook up great on the grill.

Spicy Flounder with Garlic Mayonnaise

- 1 1/2 pounds flounder fillets
- 1/2 tablespoon freshly ground black pepper
- 1/2 tablespoon freshly ground white pepper
- 3/4 teaspoon cayenne pepper
- 1 tablespoon dried thyme
- 1 tablespoon dried oregano
- 1 tablespoon garlic powder
- 1 tablespoon onion powder
- 1 tablespoon chili powder
- 3/4 teaspoon ground cumin

Prepare Garlic Mayonnaise and refrigerate.

Combine black pepper, white pepper, cayenne, thyme, oregano, garlic powder, onion powder, chili powder and cumin. Pour onto plate. Dredge fillets in mixture. Place in greased, hinged wire grill.

Grill, skin side down, about 4 inches from coals until one side is done, about 5 to 6 minutes. Turn and repeat on other side until fish flakes easily, about 5 to 6 minutes. Spread with Garlic Mayonnaise. Cut into serving-size pieces. Serves 4 to 6.

Garlic Mayonnaise:
- 1 1/2 cups mayonnaise
- 1/2 teaspoon pressed garlic
- 1/2 tablespoon fresh lemon juice
- 1/2 tablespoon Dijon mustard
- 1/4 teaspoon dried tarragon

In small bowl, combine mayonnaise, garlic, lemon juice, mustard and tarragon. Refrigerate until ready to use. Spread over cooked fillets.

Grilled Tuna with Lemon Mayonnaise
- 4 tuna steaks, about 1 inch thick
- 1/4 cup vegetable oil
- salt
- freshly ground black pepper

Prepare Lemon Mayonnaise and set aside.

Brush steaks with oil and sprinkle with salt and pepper. Grill about 4 inches from coals until done on one side, about 6 to 7 minutes. Turn and repeat on other side. Spread with Lemon Mayonnaise. Serves 4.

Lemon Mayonnaise:
- 1 cup mayonnaise
- 3 tablespoons fresh lemon juice
- 1/8 teaspoon cayenne pepper
- 1/8 teaspoon salt
- 3 tablespoons lime zest

In small bowl, combine mayonnaise, juice, cayenne, salt, cayenne and zest. Set aside for flavors to blend. Serve over cooked steaks.

Grilled Garlic Shrimp
- 1 pound medium or large shrimp, peeled
- 3/4 cup margarine or butter
- 10 cloves garlic, minced
- 2 tablespoons fresh lemon juice
- 1/4 teaspoon cayenne pepper
- 1/2 teaspoon dried dill
- 1/4 teaspoon sugar

Melt margarine in heavy saucepan over medium heat. Add garlic, lemon juice, cayenne, dill and sugar. Bring to a boil and simmer one minute. Remove from heat and cool. Place shrimp in sauce and marinate in refrigerator 20 to 30 minutes.

Thread shrimp on skewers. Grill about 4 inches from coals until cooked on one side, 3 to 4 minutes. Turn and repeat on other side. Serves 3 to 4.

Spotted Trout with Garlic and Tomatoes
- 4 small trout fillets
- 3/4 cup canned chopped tomatoes, drained
- 1/2 teaspoon dried oregano
- 1/2 teaspoon salt
- 1/8 teaspoon freshly ground black pepper
- 1/2 teaspoon pressed garlic
- 2 tablespoons melted margarine or butter
- 1/2 teaspoon crumbled dried rosemary
- vegetable oil

In small bowl, combine tomatoes, oregano, salt, pepper and garlic. Bring to a boil and heat thoroughly. Keep warm.

Brush fillets with melted margarine. Sprinkle with rosemary. Place in greased, hinged wire grill and cook, skin side down, about 4 inches from coals 5 to 6 minutes. Turn and repeat on other side until fish flakes easily with a fork, about 5 to 6 minutes. Place fillets on platter. Pour tomato mixture over fillets. Serves 4.

Marinated Charcoal-Grilled Shrimp
- 2 pounds medium or large shrimp, peeled
- 2 tablespoons fresh lime juice
- 1 tablespoon olive oil
- 3/4 teaspoon freshly ground black pepper
- 1/2 teaspoon salt
- 1/8 teaspoon dill
- 1/8 teaspoon sugar
- 1/2 teaspoon cumin
- 1/2 teaspoon basil
- 1 1/2 teaspoons finely chopped fresh garlic
- 2 teaspoons minced green onion
- melted margarine or butter (optional)

In large shallow dish, combine lime juice, oil, pepper, salt, dill, sugar, cumin, basil, garlic and onion. Place shrimp in mixture and marinate in refrigerator for 20 to 30 minutes, turning if necessary. Remove shrimp from marinade and thread on skewers. Discard marinade.

Grill about 4 inches from coals until done on one side, about 3 to 4 minutes. Turn and repeat on other side. Serve with melted margarine, if desired. Serves 6 to 8.

Grilled Scallop Kabobs
- 1 1/2 pounds bay scallops (or sea scallops, halved)
- 1 can (13 1/2 ounces) pineapple chunks, drained
- 1/2 pound button mushrooms
- 1 sweet red pepper, cut into 1/2-inch squares
- 1/4 cup vegetable oil
- 1/4 cup fresh lemon juice
- 1/4 cup chopped fresh parsley
- 1/4 cup soy sauce
- 1/4 teaspoon salt
- 1/8 teaspoon freshly ground black pepper

Place scallops, pineapple, mushrooms and red pepper in medium bowl.

In separate small bowl, combine oil, lemon juice, parsley, soy sauce, salt and pepper. Reserve 1/3 cup. Pour remainder over scallop mixture and marinate in refrigerator 30 minutes, stirring occasionally.

Alternate scallops, pineapple, mushrooms and red pepper on skewers. Grill about 4 inches from moderately hot coals until one side is golden, about 4 to 5 minutes. Baste with reserved sauce. Turn and cook until other side is golden and scallops are tender. Serves 6 to 8.

Grilled Tuna with Lime Butter
- 4 tuna steaks, about 1 inch thick
- 1/4 cup vegetable oil
- salt
- freshly ground black pepper

Prepare Lime Butter and set aside.

Brush steaks with oil on both sides. Sprinkle with salt and pepper. Grill about 4 inches from coals until done on one side, about 6 to 7 minutes. Turn and repeat on other side. Spread with Lime Butter. Serves 4.

Lime Butter:
- 3/4 cup margarine or butter, softened
- 3 tablespoons fresh lime juice
- 3 teaspoons lime zest

In small bowl, combine margarine, juice and lime zest. Set aside for flavors to blend. Serve over cooked steaks.

Grilled Marinated Tuna with Herb Butter

- 8 tuna steaks
- 1/2 cup vegetable oil
- 1/3 cup soy sauce
- 1/4 cup fresh lemon juice
- 1 teaspoon lemon zest
- 1 garlic clove, minced

Prepare Herb Butter and set aside.

In small bowl, combine oil, soy sauce, lemon juice, zest and garlic. Blend well.

Place steaks in single layer in shallow baking dish. Pour marinade over them, reserving 1/3 cup. Marinate in refrigerator about 45 minutes, turning occasionally.

Drain fish. Discard used marinade. Place steaks in well-greased hinged grill. Cook about 4 inches from heat until done on one side, about 6 to 8 minutes. Baste with reserved marinade and turn. Cook on other side until done, about 6 to 8 minutes. Spread with Herb Butter. Serves 8.

Herb Butter:
- 3/4 cup margarine or butter, softened
- 2 tablespoons minced green onion
- 2 tablespoons minced fresh parsley
- 1 tablespoon minced fresh tarragon
- 1 teaspoon Dijon mustard

In small bowl, combine margarine, green onion, parsley, tarragon and mustard. Set aside for flavors to blend. Serve over tuna steaks.

STEAMING PLATTERS OF SEAFOOD

Steaming offers one of the best preparation methods for accenting the natural tastes of seafood. The delicate textures and pure flavors are enhanced because the seafood cooks in its own liquid.

Steaming fish and shellfish is easy. In steaming, food cooks over liquid. And any seafood can be steamed — fillets, steaks, dressed fish and shellfish in the shell or shucked.

Fish and shellfish can be cooked over water or other liquid enhanced with flavorings such as wine and fresh herbs, which impart a subtle taste. Seasoning the seafood itself produces a more distinct flavor. Steamed seafood needs little or no fat for cooking.

Shellfish in the shell can be steamed to preserve juices that blend with the cooking liquid to form a broth. Try our *Steamed Clams in Wine Sauce* for a simple and tasteful meal.

Clams can be steamed over water, wine or fish stock with added herbs, butter, garlic or other ingredients. When the clams are done, serve the liquid as a dipping sauce. You've just created your own recipe. Do not, however, try this with oysters. The shells cannot be cleaned well enough to yield a potable broth.

Lean fish such as flounder, grouper and snapper usually steam better than oily fish, which have a stronger flavor. Meaty fish such as tuna are less suited for steaming.

A variety of steamers is available, ranging from electric to stove-top to bamboo. Steamers for clams, oysters and crabs can be small enough to make a meal for your family or large enough to feed a crowd outdoors.

If you don't have a steamer, you can improvise. Use a vegetable steamer, roasting trivet or roasting pan with rack. Always oil the rack or steamer except when steaming unshucked shellfish. Be sure to use a pot large enough for steam to circulate freely. And use a tight-fitting lid.

A great way to steam seafood is to arrange it in a shallow dish above the liquid. Seafood steamed this way collects juices and the flavors become more pronounced. Use leftover juice in place of sauce or as the base for one. Use a low, flare-sided, heat-proof platter. If you don't have a rack, support the dish with a trivet or canning jar rings.

For a basic steamed fish dish, arrange four fillets or steaks on a platter. Pour a couple tablespoons of dry white wine over them. Sprinkle with salt, freshly ground black pepper, minced green onion and minced fresh parsley. Set the platter over steam, cover and cook until the fish flakes easily with a fork, about eight to 10 minutes. This makes an easy dinner for four.

Another popular method of steaming is with a Yunnan pot — an unglazed clay or glazed ceramic bowl with a lid and a central chimney. Place the food in the trough surrounding the chimney, then set the pot over a saucepan of steaming water. Steam rises up the chimney, condenses on the lid and falls over the food in a light mist.

Steaming fish and shellfish is easy. In steaming, food cooks over liquid. And any seafood can be steamed — fillets, steaks, dressed fish and shellfish in the shell or shucked.

Seafood can also be steamed in a brown-in bag, parchment or packets of aluminum foil. But do not use foil if the recipe contains any acidic ingredients such as lemon juice or wine.

Did you ever wonder who orders those bamboo steamers you see advertised on TV? They make great seafood steamers. Large ones have more than one rack and can accommodate more seafood or other foods such as vegetables.

Cooking time determines the amount of liquid needed for steaming. For most seafood, about an inch of liquid is adequate. With a bamboo steamer you need more. Pour the liquid to within an inch or two of the steamer base. Use a wok or large pot over which the steamer fits securely.

Start the cooking time when the liquid begins to boil, steam is visible, and food is placed over it and covered. The liquid should bubble but not boil vigorously. Remember that fish will continue to cook in a covered pot after the heat is off. Remove the seafood immediately when done.

Steamed Snapper Fillets with Fresh Thyme

- 4 medium snapper fillets
- 1 tablespoon margarine or butter
- 1 cup thinly sliced green onion, including some tops
- 1/3 cup dry white wine
- 1 cup heavy cream
- 1/8 teaspoon salt
- 1/8 teaspoon freshly ground white pepper
- 2 tablespoons chopped fresh thyme
- 1 teaspoon cornstarch

In small saucepan, melt margarine over medium heat. Add onion and sauté until tender. Add wine and cook, stirring until most of the liquid has evaporated. Blend in cream, salt and pepper. Bring to boil and simmer for 3 to 4 minutes, stirring constantly. Remove a small amount into a bowl and mix with cornstarch. Return to sauce. Add thyme and simmer, stirring constantly, until sauce is desired consistency. Keep warm.

Place about 1 inch of water in bottom of steamer. Bring to boil. Lightly salt and pepper fillets. Place on oiled steamer rack. Lay a sprig of thyme over each. Cover and steam until fish flakes easily with a fork, about 10 minutes.

Transfer fish to warm serving plates. Spoon sauce over fillets. Cut into serving-size pieces. Serves 6 to 8.

Steamed Snapper Fillets with Cilantro and White Wine Sauce
• 6 medium snapper fillets
• salt
• freshly ground white pepper
• 1 cup chopped fresh cilantro
    Prepare White Wine Sauce and keep warm.
    Cut fillets into halves. Sprinkle with salt, pepper and cilantro. Place in one layer on oiled steamer rack above boiling water. Steam for about 10 minutes, or until fish flakes easily with a fork. Serve with White Wine Sauce. Serves 12.

White Wine Sauce:
• 1 2/3 cups dry white wine
• 1 tablespoon chopped green onion
• 1 tablespoon chopped fresh parsley
• 2 tablespoons margarine or butter
• 3 tablespoons flour
• 2/3 cup chicken broth
• 1/2 cup heavy cream
• 1/2 teaspoon salt
• 1/4 teaspoon freshly ground white pepper
    Heat 2/3 cup wine in small saucepan over medium heat. Add onion and parsley and simmer until reduced by half.
    Meanwhile, melt margarine in small saucepan over medium heat. Add flour and stir until smooth. Slowly add broth and remaining 1 cup wine, stirring to blend. Cook over low heat, stirring until sauce is smooth and thick.
    Strain onion and parsley mix. Add liquid to sauce and mix well. Add cream gradually, stirring constantly. Add salt and pepper. Simmer, continuing to stir, until sauce is desired consistency. Spoon over steamed fillets.

Steamed Flounder Fillets with Fresh Parsley and White Wine Sauce
• 6 medium flounder fillets
• 1 cup chopped fresh parsley
• salt
• freshly ground black pepper
    Prepare White Wine Sauce, p. 94, and set aside.
    Sprinkle fillets with parsley, salt and pepper. Place in single layer on oiled steamer rack above boiling water. Steam until fish flakes easily with a fork, about 10 minutes. Serves 12.

White Wine Sauce:
- 6 tablespoons margarine or butter
- 1 1/2 cups sliced mushrooms
- 1/2 cup thinly sliced green onion
- 1 cup dry white wine
- 2 1/2 cups fish or chicken broth
- 1/2 teaspoon salt
- 1/4 teaspoon freshly ground white pepper
- 1/4 cup flour
- 2 cups heavy cream
- 1 tablespoon fresh lemon juice

Melt 1 tablespoon margarine in medium saucepan over medium heat. Add mushrooms and green onion and cook, stirring, for 1 minute. Add wine, 1/2 cup broth, salt and pepper. Simmer until liquid is reduced by half.

Melt 3 tablespoons margarine in small saucepan over medium heat. Add flour and stir until well mixed. Stir in remaining broth. Blend well, bring to boil and simmer for 10 minutes. Add to mushroom mixture, stir and simmer for 10 minutes.

Add cream gradually, stirring constantly. Add remaining 2 tablespoons margarine and lemon juice. Simmer, stirring constantly, until desired consistency, stirring occasionally, about 15 minutes. Serve over steamed fish.

Steamed Clams in Wine Broth
- 4 pounds cherrystone or littleneck clams
- 6 tablespoons margarine or butter, melted
- 3/4 cup dry white wine
- 3/4 cup water
- 1 1/2 tablespoons chopped fresh parsley
- 1/4 teaspoon Tabasco sauce

Discard any clams that are open or do not open when tapped. Under cold, running water, scrub clams thoroughly with a stiff brush.

Bring margarine, wine, water, parsley and Tabasco to boil in bottom of steamer. Arrange clams on rack and place in steamer. Cover. Steam until clams open, about 8 to 10 minutes. Discard any that do not open.

Divide clams into 3 or 4 serving bowls. Ladle broth over them. Serves 4.

Steamed Shrimp with Soy-Ginger Sauce
- 1 pound medium or large shrimp, peeled
- 1/2 teaspoon dried tarragon
- 1/2 teaspoon salt
- 1/2 teaspoon celery seed
- 1/8 teaspoon cayenne pepper
- 1 can beer, room temperature

Prepare Soy-Ginger Sauce and set aside for flavors to mingle.

Mix tarragon, salt, celery seed and cayenne in small bowl. Place shrimp in single layer on oiled steamer rack. Sprinkle with the seasoning mix. Place in refrigerator for 30 minutes. Bring beer to boil in bottom of steamer. Place rack in steamer and cover. Steam until shrimp are done, about 5 minutes. Serve with sauce for dipping. Serves 3 to 4.

Soy-Ginger Sauce:
- 1/4 cup vegetable oil
- 4 tablespoons soy sauce
- 1/2 cup finely chopped green onion, including tops
- 1 tablespoon finely shredded ginger root

In small bowl, combine oil, soy sauce, green onion and ginger. Mix well. Place in individual serving containers. Use as dipping sauce.

Steamed Flounder with Ginger
- 1 1/2 pounds flounder fillets
- 1/4 cup dry sherry
- 3 tablespoons vegetable oil
- 9 tablespoons thinly sliced green onion, including tops
- 1 1/2 tablespoons finely chopped fresh ginger
- 3 tablespoons soy sauce
- 1/4 teaspoon freshly ground white pepper

Cut fillets into serving-size pieces. Place on rack, drizzle with sherry and salt lightly. Place on rack over boiling water. Cover and steam until done, about 8 to 10 minutes. Remove fish to warm platter. Serves 4 to 6.

While fish is cooking, heat oil in small skillet. Add onion and ginger and stir-fry until tender, about 2 minutes. Add soy sauce and pepper. Mix well. Remove from heat. Pour over hot fish.

Steamed Snapper Fillets with Mushroom Sauce
- 4 medium snapper fillets
- 3 tablespoons melted margarine or butter
- salt
- freshly ground white pepper

Prepare Mushroom Sauce and keep warm.

Cut fillets into serving-size pieces. Brush fillets with margarine and lightly salt and pepper. Place in single layer on oiled steamer rack over boiling water and cook until done, about 8 to 10 minutes. Remove from rack. Pour Mushroom Sauce over fillets. Serves 6 to 8.

Mushroom Sauce:
- 1/2 pound button mushrooms
- 2 tablespoons margarine or butter
- 1/4 cup minced green onion, including tops
- 1/4 teaspoon salt
- 1 tablespoon flour
- 1/4 teaspoon freshly ground white pepper
- 1/4 cup dry white wine
- 1/2 cup heavy cream

Clean mushrooms and cut into thin slices. In small saucepan, melt margarine over medium heat. Sauté mushrooms and green onion until tender. Add salt and pepper. Blend in flour.

Add wine. Add cream slowly, stirring constantly, and cook until slightly thickened, about 5 minutes. Serve over hot fish.

POACHED FISH — AN EASY DISH

Many people think that poaching is a mysterious and difficult way to cook fish. In reality, poaching is one of the easiest cooking methods. And it certainly produces some of the most delicious fish you'll ever eat.

Simply defined, poaching is cooking in an aromatic broth.

Fish are usually poached in a court bouillon — a simmered mixture of vegetables, seasonings, water and wine or vinegar. But you can also use milk, fish or chicken stock or lightly seasoned water.

One of the simplest ways I know to cook fish requires no special ingredients and no measuring. Melt about one-third of a stick of margarine or butter in a long, shallow pan or electric skillet. Sprinkle with garlic powder, salt

Many people think that poaching is a mysterious and difficult way to cook fish. In reality, poaching is one of the easiest cooking methods.

and freshly ground black pepper. Add enough water to cover your fish. Pour in about one cup of dry white wine and add a bay leaf. Bring to a boil.

Place your fillets in the broth and lower the heat. Cook until the fish flakes easily when tested with a fork. This will take about eight to 10 minutes or more for thicker fillets. You will have delicious, delicately flavored fish, with no masking of the true flavor. I cook whole, dressed fish this way to make flaked fish. (See section on flaking fish, p. 172.)

Court bouillon most often consists of water, dry white wine, onions, celery, carrots and parsley, with some thyme and a bay leaf. You can add your favorite ingredients and seasonings. Chopping or slicing vegetables thinly causes them to release more flavor. Allow the court bouillon to simmer 20 to 30 minutes or more before adding the fish.

To poach seafood, completely submerge it in a single layer in the cooking liquid. Have enough liquid in the pan so that the fish will be covered when you put it in. If you're not sure you have enough liquid, test the amount by quickly submerging the raw fish in the cold liquid and removing it. Or measure the fish at its thickest point, then use liquid twice that deep.

When poaching, the surface of the water should quiver or shimmer, but not bubble. You may see tiny bubbles on the bottom of the pan, but they should not be rising. Because fish is delicate it should never be boiled. Boiling breaks apart the flesh and cooks it unevenly.

Almost any fish can be poached, but those that flake into small pieces, such as snapper and trout, work best. And lean fish such as flounder and grouper cook better this way than fatty fish such as mackerel, which have a stronger flavor.

Dressed fish, steaks and fillets can be poached. Use pieces that are at least one-half inch thick. Always place in a single layer to poach.

Our recipes call for fillets. Many people do not like to serve whole fish because it can be difficult to cut through the bone, and bones show up in the servings. Using fillets eliminates these problems.

Likewise, some people do not like the skin of fish. So when poaching fish, I often use skinless fillets. They also tend not to curl when cooking. If you like the skin, it's fine to leave it on. One exception is steaks, which should be poached with the skin on to keep them from coming apart. Remove the skin after poaching.

As with all cooking methods, poaching time is determined by the thickness of the fish. Remove fish immediately when done to prevent further cooking.

Overcooking is the most common problem in seafood preparation. People sometimes ask, "How can fish be dry if it is cooked in water?" At some time we've all left chicken or another meat in the cooking liquid for too long and found the meat dry and tough. It's true for fish, too. Actually, fish may become even drier than other meats.

For ease in poaching large fish or fillets, place them in a layer of cheese-cloth before cooking. Double the cloth for very large fish. Allow several inches of extra cloth on each end. Twist the ends and make knots to use as handles when lifting the fish.

Once you've tried poaching fish, you may want to buy a fish poacher. They work wonderfully. Since they are deep enough to hold a whole fish and equipped with a rack for lowering and lifting the fish, they make poaching a snap. For years when I was doing my "road show" on how to cook fish, I had only a long skillet. When I finally got a poacher, I realized how much easier life could be!

If you don't have a poacher, use a long shallow pan that will fit over two burners of the stove, an oblong electric skillet or a roaster with a bottom rack. Always use a nonreactive pan since most poaching recipes call for wine or lemon juice, which are acidic.

Remember that seafood forms and species can be substituted in recipes. For example, you can use fillets instead of steaks or steaks instead of whole fish. Simply adjust the cooking time. To substitute species — say snapper for flounder — use one lean fish in place of another, a mild-flavored fish for another with mild flavor, or a delicately textured fish for another. Always go to the market to buy fresh fish, not a particular species.

You'll notice that many of our ingredients for the poaching liquids in our recipes are similar. But feel free to add or take away ingredients that you choose, keeping in mind that you are creating flavor differences. For example, some poaching recipes call for leeks, which are expensive. You can substitute shallots, green onion or possibly even a mild onion. The resulting flavor will vary, but very few of us have such discriminating tastes that we will notice a big difference.

Poached fish may be served hot, warm or cold. Such dishes are usually served with a sauce, flavored butter or other topping. But they can also be served just as they come from the liquid with their delicate flavors.

If you've never tried poaching fish in milk, you're in for a real treat. The subtle flavors are delightful. Try our *Milk-Poached Flounder with Mornay Sauce*.

After you've poached fish, you can strain the broth as a base for other sauces or freeze it for use later.

Poached Flounder Fillets with Green Onion and Garlic Butter

- 6 small flounder fillets
- 6 cups water
- 1 1/2 cups dry white wine
- 1/2 cup thinly sliced onion
- 1/4 cup thinly sliced carrots
- 1/4 cup coarsely chopped celery
- 1/4 teaspoon whole black peppercorns
- 1 teaspoon salt
- 1/4 teaspoon dried thyme
- 1 bay leaf
- 1 clove garlic, peeled
- 2 sprigs fresh parsley

Prepare Green Onion and Garlic Butter and set aside.

Combine ingredients for poaching liquid in fish poacher or large, shallow pan. Bring to boil. Partially cover, reduce heat and simmer 20 to 30 minutes.

Place fish in liquid, submerging it entirely. Poach until fish flakes easily when tested with a fork, about 10 minutes. Gently remove to serving platter. Spread with butter. Serves 6.

Green Onion and Garlic Butter:

- 1/2 cup margarine or butter, softened
- 2 tablespoons minced green onion
- 2 cloves garlic, pressed
- 1/4 teaspoon freshly ground white pepper
- 1 teaspoon fresh lemon juice
- 3 tablespoons minced, fresh parsley

Place margarine in small bowl. Add onion, garlic, pepper and lemon juice and blend well. Add parsley and blend gently. Spread on hot fish.

Milk-Poached Flounder with Mornay Sauce

- 4 small flounder fillets
- 3 cups milk
- 1 1/2 cups water
- 1 large onion, sliced
- 1 carrot, chopped
- 1 bay leaf
- 1/2 teaspoon whole black peppercorns

Prepare Mornay Sauce and set aside.

Place ingredients for poaching in fish poacher or large, shallow pan. Bring to boil, partially cover, then simmer about 10 minutes.

Place fish in liquid, submerging it completely. Poach until fish flakes easily when tested with a fork, about 10 minutes. Serves 4.

Mornay Sauce:
- 1 tablespoon margarine or butter
- 1 tablespoon flour
- 1/2 cup fish or chicken broth
- 1/8 teaspoon freshly ground white pepper
- 1/2 cup heavy cream
- 1 egg, beaten
- 1/2 cup freshly grated Swiss cheese
- 1/16 teaspoon cayenne pepper
- 1/8 teaspoon salt

Melt margarine in medium saucepan over medium heat. Blend in flour, stirring with a whisk. Add broth gradually, stirring constantly. Cook, stirring constantly, until thickened. Add white pepper.

Blend cream and egg together. Gradually add to thickened sauce. Cook over low heat, stirring constantly, until thickened. Do not allow to boil.

Add cheese to sauce. Cook over low heat until cheese is melted. Add cayenne pepper and salt. Serve over poached fish.

Poached Snapper with Dill Butter
- 6 small snapper fillets
- 6 cups water
- 2 cups dry white wine
- 1 large onion, sliced
- 2 carrots, sliced
- 4 celery stalks, with leaves, sliced
- 3 sprigs fresh parsley
- 1 bay leaf
- 3 sprigs fresh thyme
- 1 teaspoon salt
- 1 teaspoon black peppercorns, crushed

Prepare Dill Butter and set aside.

Combine poaching ingredients in fish poacher or large, shallow pan. Bring to boil. Partially cover, reduce heat and simmer for 20 to 30 minutes.

Gently place fish in poaching liquid. Cook, uncovered, until fish flakes easily when tested with a fork, about 10 minutes. Carefully remove to serving platter. Serves 6.

Dill Butter:
- 1 stick butter or margarine, softened
- 1 clove garlic, minced
- 1/4 teaspoon salt
- 1/4 teaspoon freshly ground white pepper
- 1 teaspoon fresh lemon juice
- 4 tablespoons minced, fresh dill

Place margarine in small bowl. Add garlic, salt, pepper and lemon juice and blend well. Gently stir in dill. Spread on hot fish.

Poached Grouper with Seasoned Mayonnaise
- 2 large skinless grouper fillets
- 8 cups water
- 1 cup dry white wine
- 3 tablespoons margarine or butter
- 2 lemon slices
- 1 large onion, sliced
- 2 carrots, chopped
- 2 stalks celery, including leaves, sliced
- 3 sprigs fresh parsley
- 1 bay leaf
- 1 teaspoon salt
- 1/4 teaspoon whole black peppercorns

Bring poaching ingredients to boil in fish poacher or large, shallow pan. Partially cover, reduce heat and simmer 20 to 30 minutes. While liquid is simmering, prepare Seasoned Mayonnaise.

Gently place fillets in poaching liquid. Cook until fish flakes easily when tested with a fork, about 20 minutes. Serves 8 to 10.

Seasoned Mayonnaise:
- 2/3 cup mayonnaise
- 1 tablespoon Dijon mustard
- 1 tablespoon white wine vinegar
- 1/4 teaspoon freshly ground white pepper
- 1 teaspoon pressed garlic
- 1/4 teaspoon Tabasco sauce

Place mayonnaise in top of double boiler over heated water. Add mustard, wine vinegar, pepper, garlic and Tabasco, blending thoroughly. Continue to stir gently until mayonnaise is warm. Keep warm until ready to use. Spoon over poached fish.

Poached Flounder Fillets in Cream Sauce
- 6 small flounder fillets
- 2 1/2 cups milk
- 1 teaspoon salt
- 1/4 teaspoon whole black peppercorns
- 1 large onion, sliced
- 3 sprigs fresh thyme
- 1 bay leaf
- 2 whole cloves
- 4 sprigs fresh parsley
- 1/4 teaspoon Tabasco sauce

Place poaching ingredients in fish poacher or large, shallow pan. Bring to boil. Reduce heat, partially cover and simmer 20 to 30 minutes.

Place fish in liquid, submerging it completely. Cook until fish flakes easily with a fork, about 10 minutes. Remove to serving platter and keep warm. Reserve poaching liquid to use in sauce. Serves 6.

Cream Sauce:
- 2 tablespoons margarine or butter
- 3 tablespoons cornstarch
- 2 cups poaching liquid
- 1/2 cup heavy cream
- 1/4 teaspoon freshly grated nutmeg

Melt margarine in medium saucepan over moderate heat. Add cornstarch, stirring with a wire whisk. Gradually add poaching liquid, stirring constantly. Continue to stir until thickened and smooth. Gradually stir in cream. Add nutmeg. Cook over very low heat for 5 minutes. Spoon sauce over warm fish.

Poached Grouper with Dill Sauce
- 3 small grouper fillets
- 6 cups water
- 1 teaspoon salt
- 1/2 cup thinly sliced carrots
- 1 large onion, chopped
- 1/2 cup green onion, thinly sliced
- 1/2 teaspoon dried thyme
- 1/2 teaspoon dried tarragon
- 2 small bay leaves
- 4 springs fresh parsley
- 1/2 teaspoon black peppercorns
- 1 lemon, sliced

Combine ingredients for poaching liquid in fish poacher or large, shallow pan. Bring to boil. Reduce heat, partially cover and simmer for 30 minutes. While liquid is simmering, prepare Dill Sauce.

Place fillets in liquid, submerging entirely. Poach until fish flakes easily when tested with a fork, about 15 minutes. Gently remove to serving platter. Spread Dill Sauce over fish. Serves 6.

Dill Sauce:
- 1 cup sour cream
- 1/2 cup mayonnaise
- 3 tablespoons minced, fresh dill
- 1/2 teaspoon minced garlic
- 1 teaspoon fresh lemon juice
- 1/2 teaspoon freshly ground white pepper

In small bowl, combine sour cream and mayonnaise. Add dill, garlic, lemon juice and pepper and blend will. Spread on hot fish.

Poached Shrimp with Crab Sauce
- 2 pounds peeled shrimp
- 8 cups water
- 2 teaspoons salt
- 1/8 teaspoon freshly ground white pepper
- 1/16 teaspoon cayenne pepper
- 1/2 teaspoon fresh lemon juice
- 1/2 small bay leaf
- 1/4 teaspoon dried thyme leaves

Prepare poaching liquid and simmer about 15 minutes. Meanwhile, prepare Crab Sauce.

Place shrimp in liquid and poach (remember not to boil or even simmer) until done, about 2 to 3 minutes. Remove to warm platter with slotted spoon. Pour Crab Sauce over shrimp. Serves 6 to 8.

Crab Sauce:
- 1 cup backfin crabmeat
- 1 tablespoon margarine or butter
- 1 tablespoon flour
- 1/2 cup fish or chicken broth
- 1/4 teaspoon salt
- 1/8 teaspoon freshly ground white pepper
- 1/2 cup heavy cream
- 2 egg yolks
- 1/8 teaspoon nutmeg

Remove all shell or cartilage from crabmeat.

Melt margarine and blend in flour, stirring with a whisk. Add broth gradually, stirring constantly, until thick. Add salt and pepper.

Beat cream and egg yolks together and gradually add to sauce. Cook, stirring, over low heat until somewhat thickened. Do not boil. Blend in crabmeat gently. If sauce is too thick, add more broth. Continue to cook over low heat until heated thoroughly, about 3 to 5 minutes. Do not boil. Add nutmeg. Serve over poached shrimp.

Poached Scallops with Béarnaise Sauce
- 2 pounds sea scallops
- 6 cups water
- 3/4 teaspoon salt
- 1/2 teaspoon freshly ground white pepper
- 1/2 cup thinly sliced carrots
- 3/4 cup coarsely chopped onion
- 3/4 cup coarsely chopped celery
- 1 cup dry white wine

Prepare poaching liquid and simmer about 15 minutes. Meanwhile, prepare Béarnaise Sauce.

Place scallops in liquid and poach (remember not to boil or even simmer) until done, about 4 or 5 minutes. Remove to warm platter with slotted spoon. Pour Béarnaise Sauce over scallops. Serves 6 to 8.

Béarnaise Sauce:

- 3 tablespoons dry white wine
- 2 teaspoons minced onion
- 2 teaspoons chopped fresh tarragon (or 1 teaspoon dried)
- 1 tablespoon chopped fresh parsley
- 1/4 teaspoon freshly ground white pepper
- 3 egg yolks
- 1/4 cup water
- 2 tablespoons fresh lemon juice
- 1/2 cup margarine or butter, cut into eighths
- 1/8 teaspoon salt
- 1/8 teaspoon paprika
- 1/8 teaspoon cayenne pepper

In small saucepan, combine wine, onion, tarragon, parsley and white pepper and bring to boil. Simmer until almost all liquid has evaporated. Keep hot.

In small saucepan, whisk together egg yolks, water and lemon juice. Cook over very low heat (or use a double boiler), stirring constantly, until mixture boils at edges. Stir in butter, one piece at a time, until melted and sauce is thick. Add salt, paprika and cayenne. Remove from heat and blend in wine sauce. Serve over hot fillets.

SOMETIMES IT'S OK TO FRY SEAFOOD

"Frying" has almost become a dirty word in seafood circles in recent years, and much of the criticism is deserved. We know that grease-laden foods add fat and calories we do not need. But remember that our bodies need some fat. The problem is that we eat too much of it.

Obviously, frying adds some fat and calories. But many of the calories and much of the fat added to fried seafood result from improper cooking. Cooked quickly and with very little oil, fried fish and shellfish can be surprisingly light and tasteful.

The keys to good frying are proper temperature and fast cooking. The ideal temperature for frying fish is 375 F. With cooler oil, the food absorbs too much fat and the fish becomes soggy. If the oil is too hot, the fish may brown too quickly and burn. Also, most oils begin to smoke when they reach 400 F.

Oil, a combination of oil and butter, or clarified butter can be used for frying. Most vegetable oils work fine. Because they are tasteless (except olive oil) they do not mask the flavor of the food.

The keys to good frying are proper temperature and fast cooking. The ideal temperature for frying fish is 375 F. With cooler oil, the food absorbs too much fat and the fish becomes soggy.

We generally use canola oil because it has the lowest level of saturated fat of any vegetable oil. It also contains a relatively high level of monounsaturated fatty acids. Safflower oil ranks second to canola in low levels of saturated fat.

Butter burns at 248 F. Since 375 F is needed for frying, the water and milk solids in butter must first be removed. The fat, or clarified butter, that remains is used for frying. Clarified butter can be used for pan-frying but is best suited for sautéing.

Clarifying Butter

Cut butter into one-inch chunks and melt over low heat. Remove from heat and cool for a few minutes, then skim the foam off the top.

Set butter aside until the solids have settled to the bottom, about 20 minutes. Gently pour the transparent (clarified) fat into another container, leaving the solids behind.

Clarified butter loses about one-fourth to one-third of the original volume, so melt more than the recipe calls for. Two sticks of butter will yield about three-fourths cup of clarified butter. Any unused butter may be covered and kept in the refrigerator for several weeks.

Frying Tips

Oil should reach 375 F before adding fish. If using a deep-fryer, check the thermostat for accuracy with a cooking thermometer. Or drop a one-inch cube of bread into the oil. It should brown in 30 to 45 seconds.

Fry only a small amount of fish at a time so that the temperature remains constant. If it drops, allow it to return to 375 F before adding the next batch.

The high temperature will quickly form a crust that will seal in the juices and prevent the food from soaking up oil.

Check recipes for exact temperatures, as the cooking method determines what is needed. For example, sautéed shrimp cook at a lower temperature than frying.

Seafood is done when it is golden brown. Remove from the oil immediately and drain the fish or shellfish on paper towels. Be careful not to overcook or the food will dry out. A minute can make a difference. It's like that steak on the grill — give it just a few more seconds and it's overdone.

Lean, firm fish such as flounder are more suitable for frying than fatty ones. Oily fish such as salmon are too rich in flavor to fry. Thin fillets and dressed fish no more than about three-fourths of an inch thick fry better than large or thick pieces. While most shellfish can be fried, shrimp and oysters are the most popular.

The term "frying" in this chapter includes deep-frying, pan-frying, sautéing and stir-frying. We define and discuss each term, then recipes follow.

Almost all seafood can be fried. If you enjoy fried seafood — and most of us do — it can be part of a healthy diet. By regularly limiting the amount of fat and calories in our diet, we can occasionally select and enjoy fried fish and shellfish. As with many other things in life, moderation is the key.

Deep-Frying

No cooking method except deep-frying results in such a contrast of a crispy outside and tender inside. Just see how much seafood is fried, not only at home, but also in restaurants. Many an eatery has built a lasting reputation on the basis of "Calabash" cooking — the fried seafood named after the Carolina location.

To deep fry, choose a deep-fryer, Dutch oven, wok or deep, heavy pan. Add only enough oil to fill one-third of the container. This provides room for the bubbling that occurs when the fish is dropped in and for the space taken up by the food. The seafood should be immersed in the oil. Vegetable oil makes the best medium for deep-frying.

Fish and shellfish need to be coated with a batter, dipped in beaten egg and coated with cornmeal, or coated with flour, cornmeal or crumbs before deep-frying.

Most batters contain flour, seasonings and a liquid — most often milk, water or beer. Be sure that the batter is thick enough to coat the food evenly. Beaten egg whites make a light batter, while baking soda causes the batter to puff up. Use a wire strainer, slotted spoon or tongs to drop the seafood into the oil and another utensil to remove it. Coat your seafood just before placing it in the fryer so that the coating will not absorb moisture, causing it to be thick and heavy.

As always, be sure not to overcook.

Beer Batter Fried Oysters

- 1 pint oysters
- 1/2 cup flour
- 6 tablespoons beer, room temperature
- 1 tablespoon vegetable oil
- 1/4 teaspoon salt
- 1/4 teaspoon freshly ground black pepper
- 3 egg whites, stiffly beaten
- oil for frying

In small bowl, combine flour, beer, oil, salt and pepper. Fold in egg whites. Roll oysters in batter. Fry in deep fat at 375 F until golden brown, about 10 minutes. Serves 3 to 4.

Spicy Fried Scallops

- 1 pound sea scallops
- 2 large eggs
- 1/4 teaspoon cayenne pepper (more to taste)
- 1 1/2 tablespoons chopped fresh thyme
- 3/4 teaspoon salt
- 1 cup flour
- 2 cups oil
- lemon wedges (optional)

Place eggs in shallow bowl. Add cayenne, thyme and salt and beat well.

Place flour in another bowl. Dredge scallops in flour and shake to remove excess. Dip into egg mixture.

Deep-fry at 350 F until golden brown, about 2 to 3 minutes. Drain on paper towels. Serve with lemon wedges. Serves 3 to 4.

Fried Shrimp

- 1 pound medium or large shrimp
- 2/3 cup flour
- 1/2 teaspoon salt
- 1/4 teaspoon freshly ground black pepper
- 1 egg, beaten
- 2/3 cup fresh cracker crumbs
- oil for frying

In shallow dish, combine flour, salt and pepper. Beat the egg in a small bowl. Place crumbs in another shallow dish. Dredge shrimp in flour mixture, then in egg, then in crumbs. Fry in deep fat at 3750 F until golden brown, about 4 to 5 minutes. Serves 3 to 4.

French-Fried Shrimp
- 1 pound medium shrimp
- 2 eggs, beaten
- 1 teaspoon salt
- 1/4 teaspoon freshly ground black pepper
- 1/4 teaspoon paprika
- 1/4 teaspoon Tabasco sauce
- 1/2 cup flour
- 1/2 cup dry bread crumbs
- oil for frying

Peel shrimp, leaving last section of shell on tail. Combine egg, salt, pepper, paprika and Tabasco in medium bowl.

Combine flour and crumbs in medium shallow dish. Dip each shrimp in egg mixture, then in flour mixture. Fry in deep fat, 350 F, until golden brown, about 6 to 8 minutes. Drain on paper towels. Serves 3 to 4.

Deep-Fried Flounder
- 1 pound flounder fillets, cut into 2-inch pieces
- 1 egg, beaten
- 1 tablespoon milk
- 1/2 teaspoon salt
- 1/4 teaspoon freshly ground black pepper
- 1/2 cup cornmeal
- oil for frying

In small bowl, combine egg, milk, salt and pepper. Place cornmeal in shallow dish. Dip fish in egg mixture, then roll in cornmeal. Fry in deep fat at 375 F until golden brown, about 8 to 10 minutes. Drain on paper towels. Serves 3 to 4. (Smaller, thinner pieces near the tail will require about 2 minutes less cooking time.)

Pan-Frying

Vegetable oil, a mixture of oil and butter, or clarified butter create the best medium for pan-frying. Occasionally a recipe calls for bacon fat, usually in an old "handed-down" recipe. Some coastal cooks insist on its use in special dishes. It isn't necessary. You decide.

Pan-frying uses much less oil than deep-frying. Food is not immersed in the oil, but is cooked in a shallow layer of oil about one-fourth inch deep.

The principle of pan-frying is the same as deep-frying. An exterior crust forms quickly and seals in juices. Again, you must maintain the 375 F temperature for fish. Otherwise, the food turns greasy or even soggy, adding calories and fat.

Small fillets, pan-dressed fish and steaks can be pan-fried. Fillets should be about one-half inch thick. Pan-dressed fish need to be no more than about three-fourths inch thick. Otherwise, when the crust is browned the fish will not be done inside.

Many shellfish — shrimp, oysters, soft crabs, scallops and clams — are often pan-fried.

Seafood can be dusted with flour, cornmeal or crumbs, or a combination before pan-frying. Sometimes it is dipped in liquid — water or milk — then in the dry ingredient. Our *Breaded Triggerfish* is a delicious example of this. Thick, firm fish do not require a coating but it can be added.

To pan-fry, place the seafood in the hot oil and cook until brown on one side, then turn and repeat on the other side. Drain the food on paper towels.

Breaded Triggerfish

- 2 pounds triggerfish, cut into 1-inch chunks
- 2 eggs
- 3 tablespoons water
- 1 teaspoon salt
- 1/2 teaspoon freshly ground white pepper
- 1 cup flour
- 1 1/2 cups fresh bread crumbs
- 1/2 cup vegetable oil
- 1/2 cup margarine or butter

Beat eggs with water, salt and pepper. Dredge fish thoroughly in flour. Dip into egg mixture and let excess drain off. Coat with bread crumbs.

Heat oil in large skillet. Add butter and heat to 375 F. Cook fish until golden brown on one side, about 5 to 6 minutes. Turn and repeat on other side. Drain on paper towels. Serves 6 to 8.

Pan-Fried Snapper with Garlic Butter
- 1 1/2 pounds snapper fillets
- 1/4 cup milk
- salt
- freshly ground black pepper
- flour
- 3 tablespoons vegetable oil
- 6 tablespoons margarine or butter
- 4 teaspoons pressed garlic
- 1 tablespoon fresh lemon juice

Place milk in shallow bowl. Dip fillets in milk and drain off excess. Lightly salt and pepper, then dredge lightly in flour.

Heat oil over medium-high heat. Add 3 tablespoons butter and heat to 375 F. Cook fillets until golden on one side, about 3 to 4 minutes. Turn and repeat on other side. Remove to warm platter.

Wipe pan clean with paper towel. Melt remaining 3 tablespoons margarine, shaking pan until margarine foams and turns slightly brown. Add garlic and sauté lightly; do not allow it to brown. Sprinkle fillets with lemon juice and drizzle garlic butter over them. Serves 4 to 6.

Fried Clams
- 1 pint clams
- 1 egg, beaten
- 1 tablespoon milk
- 1/2 teaspoon salt (see *Note* below)
- 1/4 teaspoon freshly ground black pepper
- 1/4 teaspoon paprika
- 1 cup dry bread crumbs
- oil for frying

Drain clams. In medium bowl, combine egg, milk, salt, pepper and paprika. Put crumbs in shallow dish. Dip clams in egg mixture, then roll in crumbs.

Heat oil in medium skillet. Fry clams at 375 F until brown on one side, about 3 minutes. Turn and repeat on other side. Drain on paper towels. Serves 4 to 5.

Note: Before adding the salt, taste the heated clam liquor. Some clams are very salty. The first time we cooked this, we added the salt. The result was a dish that was too salty to eat. To taste the liquor, first heat a few spoonfuls on the stove top or in the microwave. Be sure that the temperature reaches 145 F for several minutes. Remember not to taste the raw liquid if you are at risk for Vibrio vulnificus. *See the chapter on seafood safety, pp. 35-36.*

Crispy Flounder Fillets
- 2 pounds flounder fillets
- 2 tablespoons dry vermouth
- 1 bay leaf
- 9 tablespoons vegetable oil
- salt
- freshly ground black pepper
- 1 cup flour
- 2 eggs, beaten
- 2 1/2 cups dry breadcrumbs
- 6 tablespoons margarine or butter
- 1 teaspoon pressed garlic
- 2 tablespoons chopped fresh parsley
- 1/2 teaspoon dried thyme leaves
- 2 tablespoons fresh lemon juice

Combine vermouth, bay leaf, and 6 tablespoons oil. Marinate fillets 20 to 30 minutes, depending on size.

Remove fish from marinade and discard marinade. Salt and pepper fillets, then dredge in flour. Brush with eggs. Dip into breadcrumbs, pressing crumbs on firmly but gently.

In medium skillet, heat remaining 3 tablespoons of vegetable oil over medium-high heat. Add 3 tablespoons margarine and heat. Cook fish until golden on one side, about 3 to 4 minutes. Turn and repeat on other side. Remove to warm platter.

Wipe skillet with paper towel. Add remaining 3 tablespoons butter and cook until foamy and brown. Add garlic and cook lightly but do not brown. Add parsley, thyme and lemon juice. Drizzle over fish. Serves 6 to 8.

Sautéing

The term "sauté" is often used interchangeably with "pan-fry." There is a distinction, though. Sautéing is much quicker. The term comes from the French word meaning "to jump." To sauté indicates cooking quickly — into the pan, fast cook, out of the pan.

Sautéing uses just enough oil to cover the bottom of the pan, and it almost always calls for butter. You can use clarified butter, oil and butter, or oil. If you use both oil and butter, heat the oil, then add the butter. If you want the best possible flavor from sautéing, use clarified butter. You'll be glad you did.

Always have the oil or butter heated before you cook seafood. If you don't, the food will become soggy when you place it in the cooking liquid. Sauté fish, clams, soft-shell crabs and oysters at 375 F. Sauté shrimp and scallops at 350 F.

Even though frying seafood in unclarified butter is not usually recommended because of the high temperature needed, I sometimes sauté a small, thin fillet in melted butter. Because it is thin, you can get it in and out of the pan so quickly that it's done and golden brown before the butter burns.

The only coating you should use for sautéing is a thin layer of flour. Dust the fish lightly and shake or pat gently to remove the excess.

Many fillets can be sautéed without a coating. Pat lightly with paper towels to remove excess moisture. Our *Sautéed Tuna Steaks with Tarragon* are great with a minimum of added ingredients.

As in pan-frying, cook until golden brown on one side, then turn and repeat on the other side.

Sautéed Tuna Steaks with Tarragon
- 4 tuna steaks, about 1 inch thick
- 2/3 cup dry white wine
- 1 tablespoon finely chopped fresh tarragon or 1 teaspoon dried
- salt
- freshly ground black pepper
- 1/4 cup margarine or butter

In small bowl, mix wine and tarragon. Lightly salt and pepper fish. Melt margarine in large skillet and heat. Add steaks and cook until brown and done on one side, about 5 to 6 minutes. Spoon tarragon wine over steaks as they cook. Turn and repeat on other side. Place fish on serving platter and pour remaining wine mix over them. Serves 4.

Sautéed Mahi-Mahi with Lemon-Butter Sauce
- 2 pounds mahi-mahi fillets, cut into serving-size pieces
- 1/2 cup flour
- 1 teaspoon salt
- 1/4 teaspoon freshly ground white pepper
- 1 cup milk
- 3 tablespoons vegetable oil
- 3 tablespoons margarine or butter

Trim all dark meat from fish. Rinse fish thoroughly and gently pat dry with paper towels.

Mix flour, salt and pepper in large shallow dish. Pour milk into another. Dip fillets in milk, drain, then dip in flour mixture.

In large skillet, heat oil. Add 3 tablespoons butter and heat. Sauté fillets until golden on one side, about 6 to 8 minutes, longer if pieces are thicker. Turn and repeat on other side. Drain on paper towels. Serves 6 to 8.

Lemon-Butter Sauce:
- 2 tablespoons margarine or butter
- 1/4 teaspoon freshly ground white pepper
- 2 tablespoons fresh lemon juice

Melt margarine in small pan. Add pepper and lemon juice and heat. Pour over fillets.

Sautéed Flounder Amandine
- 4 small flounder fillets
- 1/2 cup flour
- 3/4 teaspoon salt
- 1/4 teaspoon freshly ground black pepper
- 1/16 teaspoon cayenne pepper
- 3 tablespoons vegetable oil
- 4 tablespoons margarine or butter
- 1/3 cup sliced almonds
- 1 tablespoon fresh lemon juice

Dry fillets thoroughly by patting gently with paper towels.

In shallow bowl, combine flour, salt, pepper and cayenne. Dredge fillets in mixture.

Heat oil in large skillet. Add 3 tablespoons margarine. Melt margarine and heat. Sauté fillets until golden brown on one side, about 4 to 5 minutes. Turn and repeat on other side. Remove fish to warm platter.

Wipe pan clean. Melt remaining tablespoon margarine. When it begins to brown, add almonds. Cook until browned, about 2 to 3 minutes. Mix thoroughly and return to heat for 1 minute. Spread over warm fillets. Serves 4.

Snapper Fillets Sautéed with Mushrooms
- 6 small snapper fillets
- salt
- freshly ground black pepper
- 2/3 cup flour
- 3 tablespoons vegetable oil
- 4 tablespoons margarine or butter
- 1 cup thinly sliced small mushrooms
- 2 tablespoons fresh lime juice
- 3 tablespoons finely chopped freshly parsley

Lightly salt and pepper fish. Dredge lightly in flour.

Heat oil in large skillet. Add 3 tablespoons margarine and heat. Sauté fish until golden brown on one side, about 5 to 6 minutes. Turn and repeat on other side. Transfer to warm platter.

In same pan, melt 1 tablespoon margarine over high heat. Add mushrooms and sauté until liquid is gone and mushrooms are browned. Arrange over fillets and sprinkle with lime juice and parsley. Serves 6.

Stir-Frying

An Asian technique, stir-frying has become a common cooking method in our culture. It is associated with healthful food because of little added fat, less meat than traditional and more fresh vegetables cooked just until tender but still crunchy.

Stir-frying calls for high heat, hot oil and very fast cooking. Most stir-fry meals cook in less than 10 minutes. Preparing the ingredients takes more time than the cooking.

When stir-frying first became popular, everyone thought that it was necessary to have a wok. In China, woks were placed on cylindrical pits containing fire that heated the sides as well as the bottom. Since the stove top does not provide the heat needed for the sides of a wok, most cooks prefer a large, heavy skillet, one with sloping sides if possible. Be sure that it is wide enough and deep enough for tossing the food. You frequently see food being cooked in a wok in a restaurant; it usually fits in a gas burner that provides heat to the sides.

Seafood is ideal for stir-frying. Use firm seafood that will hold together. Shrimp and scallops are just the right size. Cut fish into small chunks or bite-size pieces. Catfish, tuna, salmon and other firm fish cook quickly and remain tender.

Don't crowd the food when stir-frying. You don't have to put all the ingredients in the pan at one time. Cook in batches, then assemble when everything is done. Too much volume cools the pan and steams the food, making it soft.

Some recipes call for cooking the meat first, then removing it and cooking the vegetables. Others reverse the order. Since seafood cooks so quickly, you can often cook the vegetables until almost done, then add the fish or shellfish, cook slightly, then add the sauce. Choose the method that seems most comfortable for you. The steps are the same.

Vegetable oil is commonly used for stir-frying. Since olive oil burns at the temperature suggested for stir-frying, it is not generally recommended. I stir-fry regularly and use extra-virgin olive oil exclusively, however. I just cook at a slightly lower temperature. If you have concerns about polyunsaturated oils, you might want to try olive oil. (See section on oils, pp. 67-68.)

Have all the ingredients ready before you begin to cook. Since stir-frying is fast, you won't have time to chop vegetables or make a sauce once you start.

While stir-frying is just what it says — stirring and frying — you will often see recipes that begin in an open pan, then use steam with a lid on near the end. I sometimes use this method to speed up the tenderizing of the vegetables. Either way works.

Most of the sauces included here are fairly basic and delicious. Sherry, soy sauce and sesame oil are stir-fry standards. Try our *Shrimp and Broccoli Stir-Fry*.

You can buy prepared sauces for stir-frying, but you may have to try several before finding one you like. Or try packets of seasoned dry mixes to which you add ingredients such as oil and soy sauce. You may like some of them.

So many vegetables complement seafood that only rice is needed to complete the meal.

Try stir-frying — it's good for you.

Scallop and Vegetable Stir-Fry
- 1 pound bay scallops (or sea scallops, halved)
- 6 tablespoons soy sauce
- 2 teaspoons cornstarch
- 1/3 cup vegetable oil
- 2 cups red bell pepper, thinly sliced
- 1/2 cup green onion, including tops, sliced
- 1 1/2 cups sliced onion
- 4 cups zucchini, split lengthwise and thinly sliced
- 1/2 pound sliced mushrooms
- 1 tablespoon minced garlic
- 1 tablespoon minced fresh ginger
- cooked rice (optional)

In small bowl, mix soy sauce and cornstarch. Heat oil in large skillet over high heat. Add bell pepper, green onion, sliced onion, zucchini and mushrooms and stir. Add garlic and ginger. Stir-fry until vegetables are crisp-tender, about 4 or 5 minutes. Add scallops and stir-fry until almost done. Stir soy mixture and add to pan. Stir until thickened and scallops are opaque, about 2 to 3 minutes. Serve over rice, if desired. Serves 4 to 6.

Grouper and Vegetable Stir-Fry

- 1 pound grouper, cut into 1-inch chunks
- 6 tablespoons vegetable oil
- salt
- freshly ground black pepper
- 1 medium head cauliflower, cut into bite-size pieces
- 1 medium green or red bell pepper, cut into strips
- 2 teaspoons minced fresh ginger
- 2 teaspoons minced garlic
- 1/2 teaspoon dried hot red pepper flakes
- 4 tablespoons water
- 6 tablespoons soy sauce
- cooked rice (optional)

Heat 2 tablespoons oil in large skillet over high heat. Lightly salt and pepper fish and and cook until golden and almost done, about 3 to 4 minutes. Remove with slotted spoon. Heat remaining oil. Add cauliflower to skillet. Stir in ginger, garlic and pepper flakes. Add water and cook, stirring occasionally, until vegetables are crisp-tender, about 3 to 4 minutes. Stir in soy sauce and mix well. Add fish and cook until done, about 2 to 3 minutes. Serve over rice, if desired. Serves 6.

Shrimp and Broccoli Stir-Fry

- 1 1/2 pounds medium shrimp, peeled (deveined, if desired)
- 4 tablespoons sherry
- 2 tablespoons soy sauce
- 2 tablespoons sesame oil
- 4 tablespoons vegetable oil
- 1 cup sliced onion
- salt
- 1 head broccoli, cut into bite-size pieces
- freshly ground black pepper
- cooked rice

In small bowl, combine sherry, soy sauce and sesame oil. Set aside.

Heat 2 tablespoons oil in large skillet over high heat. Add onion and broccoli and stir-fry until crisp tender, about 4 or 5 minutes. Remove vegetables. Heat remaining oil in skillet. Lightly salt and pepper shrimp and add to pan. Stir-fry until cooked through and pink, about 4 to 5 minutes. Stir in sauce, return vegetables to skillet and stir-fry just to heat through, about 1 minute. Serve over rice, if desired. Serves 6 to 8.

Salmon and Asparagus Stir-Fry

- 1 pound salmon, cut into 1-inch chunks
- 1 pound asparagus
- 3 tablespoons oyster sauce
- 1 1/2 tablespoons dry sherry
- 3 teaspoons sesame oil
- 1/4 teaspoon freshly ground black pepper
- 4 tablespoons vegetable oil
- salt
- freshly ground black pepper
- 8 ounces mushrooms, sliced
- cooked rice (optional)

Wash asparagus, snap off tough ends and snap into bite-size pieces.

In small container, combine oyster sauce, sherry, sesame oil and pepper.

Heat 2 tablespoons vegetable oil in large skillet. Lightly salt and pepper salmon and add to pan. Cook until almost done, stirring occasionally, about 4 minutes. Remove salmon with slotted spoon.

Add remaining 2 tablespoons oil and heat. Lightly salt the asparagus and add to the skillet. Cook until crisp tender, about 2 to 3 minutes. Add mushrooms and cook about 2 minutes. Stir in sauce mixture and toss to coat well. Return salmon to pan and stir until done, about 2 to 3 minutes. Serve over rice, if desired. Serves 6 to 8.

Catfish Stir-Fry

- 4 medium catfish fillets, cut into 1-inch chunks
- 3 tablespoons soy sauce
- 1 tablespoon dry sherry
- 1 teaspoon minced fresh ginger
- 1/4 cup minced green onion, including tops
- 2 teaspoons cornstarch
- 4 tablespoons vegetable oil
- salt
- freshly ground black pepper
- 1 cup thickly sliced celery
- 3/4 pound snow peas
- 1 cup sliced fresh mushrooms
- cooked rice (optional)

Combine soy sauce, sherry, ginger, onion and cornstarch. Set aside.

Heat 2 tablespoons vegetable oil in large skillet. Lightly salt and pepper fish. Add to pan and stir-fry until almost done, about 2 to 3 minutes. Remove fish with slotted spoon.

Add remaining 2 tablespoons oil and heat. Add celery and snow peas and cook 2 to 3 minutes. Add mushrooms and cook until tender, about 2 minutes.

Stir in sauce mixture and cook until thickened, about 2 to 3 minutes. Add fish to pan and cook until done, about 2 minutes. Serve over rice, if desired. Serves 8 to 10.

Shrimp Stir-Fry with Green Beans and Corn

- 1 1/2 pounds medium shrimp, peeled (deveined, if desired)
- 2 tablespoons soy sauce
- 2 tablespoons dry sherry
- 2 tablespoons sesame oil
- 2 tablespoons oyster sauce
- 4 tablespoons vegetable oil
- salt
- freshly ground black pepper
- 1 tablespoon minced fresh ginger
- 1 cup sliced green onion, including tops
- 2 cloves garlic, finely chopped
- 1 pound green beans, ends trimmed, snapped into bite-size pieces
- 1 can baby corn, drained
- cooked rice (optional)

In small bowl, combine soy sauce, sherry, sesame oil and oyster sauce. Set aside.

Heat 1 tablespoon vegetable oil in large skillet. Lightly salt and pepper shrimp and add to skillet. Stir-fry until shrimp turn pink, about 2 to 3 minutes. Remove shrimp. Add remaining oil to skillet and heat. Add ginger, onion and garlic and stir-fry about 1 minute. Lightly salt green beans and corn and add to skillet. Cook 2 to 3 minutes. Stir in sauce, cover and steam until crisp tender, about 2 minutes. Return shrimp to pan and stir-fry until heated through, about 1 minute. Serve over rice, if desired. Serves 6 to 8.

Specialty
SEAFOOD

From family get-togethers to special-occasion dinners, seafood adds something extra to a meal. A variety of flavors, fresh taste and elegant to fun presentations makes serving fresh fish and shellfish real crowd-pleasers. Over the years, the Nutrition Leaders have created some of the best-tasting speciality seafoods around for appetizers, salads, soups, pasta, dressings and more.

CHAPTER SEVEN RECIPES:

- Shrimp Dip
- Tangy Crab Dip
- Creamy Crab Dip
- Crab-Stuffed Cherry Tomatoes
- Clam Dip
- Smoked Fish Spread
- Hot Crab Dip
- Shrimp Christmas Tree
- Baked Oysters with Bacon
- Crab-Stuffed Mushrooms
- Buttery Shrimp
- Crab Salad Deluxe
- Shrimp Salad
- Crab and Shrimp Salad
- Shrimp Salad with Dill
- Seafood-Stuffed Avocados
- Flaked Fish Salad
- Crab Soup Deluxe
- Fisherman's Stew
- Scallop Bisque
- Down East Clam Chowder
- Italian Fish Stew
- Oyster Soup
- Manhattan-Style Clam Chowder
- Shrimp Bisque
- Cream of Shrimp Soup
- French-Toasted Shrimp Sandwich
- Hot Crab and Cheese Sandwich
- Open-Face Oyster Sandwich
- Happy Clamburger
- Hot Seafood Sandwich
  with Mushroom Sauce
- Hot Soft-Crab Sandwich
- Fisherman's Burger
- Flaked Fish Casserole au Gratin
- Shrimp Casserole
- Crab Imperial
- Deluxe Deviled Crab
- Heavenly Seafood Casserole
- Baked Scallops

- Scalloped Clams
- Scalloped Oysters
- Shrimp-Crab Casserole
- Fettucini with Trout-Cheese Sauce
- Crab-Noodle Casserole
- Linguine with Clam Sauce
- Vermicelli with Shrimp
  and Tomatoes
- Pasta with Clam-Vegetable Sauce
- Stir-Fried Noodles with Shrimp
- Linguine with Shrimp Sauce
- Carolina Baked Flounder
- Deviled Clams
- Southern-Fried Oysters
- Fish Chowder
- Spicy Seafood Gumbo
- Crab Savannah
- Creole Bouillabaisse
- Creole Sautéed Mahi-Mahi
- Carolina Fish Stew
- Shrimp and Oyster Jambalaya
- Cooked Mayonnaise
- Cold Poached Bluefish with
  Dill Mayonnaise
- Steamed Flounder with
  Shrimp Sauce
- Sautéed Spanish Mackerel
  with Provencal Sauce
- Flounder Fillets with
  Black Butter Sauce
- Baked Grouper with
  Lemon-Chive Butter
- Broiled Mahi-Mahi with
  Green Onion Butter
- Baked Spotted Trout with
  Parsley Butter
- Broiled Flounder with
  Garlic-Basil Butter
- Poached Flounder with
  Herb Butter

- Baked Fish with
  Herb-Butter Sauce
- Broiled Fillets with Dill Sauce
- Basil-Parmesan Marinated
  Flounder
- Citrus-Marinated Fillets
- Italian-Marinated Catfish
- Orange-Marinated Snapper
- Marinated Grilled Shrimp
- Deviled Crab with Fish
- Fish Flake and Macaroni Salad
- Fish and Shrimp Casserole
- Seafood-Vegetable Casserole
- Fancy Fish Spread
- Choice Fish Cakes
- Seafood Pizza
- Red Snapper with
  Bacon-Mushroom Stuffing
- Vegetable-Stuffed Flounder Fillets
- Flounder Fillets with Crab Stuffing
- Stuffed Mahi-Mahi with
  Egg Sauce
- Baked Grouper with
  Orange-Rice Stuffing
- Red Snapper Fillets with
  Shrimp Stuffing
- Flounder Fillets with
  Parmesan Stuffing
- Flounder with Fresh Mushrooms
  in Parchment
- Parmesan Snapper in Parchment
- Savory Shrimp in Parchment
- Fillets with Herb Butter
  in Parchment
- Flounder with Fine Herbs
  in Parchment
- Parmesan Flounder in Parchment
- Orange-Nutmeg Flounder
  in Parchment
- Herbed Shrimp in Parchment

Specialty
SEAFOOD

SEAFOOD APPETIZERS

When hosting a big party, a small dinner or a casual or formal gathering, let seafood be part of your menu.

You can serve a diverse selection of appetizers when you use seafood. And since many seafood preparations are light, your guests can enjoy them and still look forward to the main course. Or you can serve a selection of seafood appetizers with other foods such as raw vegetables, crackers and fruit for lunch or a light evening meal. Our appetizers easily convert to full meals. *Baked Oysters with Bacon*, for example, makes a great main course. Just allow for larger portions.

For large groups, plan to have mostly cold appetizers, with only a couple hot ones. Then you can enjoy your guests and spend minimal time in the kitchen.

Many popular publications contain recipes for seafood appetizers. But I find that many of the recipes are complex and not well tested. Plus, some are time-consuming to prepare, and when complete, often do not taste as good as the descriptions make them sound.

We've found that some of the simplest appetizers taste best. Simplicity also shortens preparation time. And many of the recipes, such as cold spreads and dips, can be prepared ahead of time. In fact, they often taste better when made a day before serving.

Canapes, or toast or bread topped with spreads, make popular appetizers. Use fish or shellfish and vary the base. Our *Basic Fish Flake Salad* can be used as a spread on thin toast, crackers, wafers or toasted or plain bread. Most of our dips and spreads can be used this way, too. Assorted breads such as white, rye, whole wheat and oatmeal add extra flavor and interest.

Fish and shellfish appetizers add elegance and variety for holiday get-togethers, too. Our *Shrimp Christmas Tree*, for example, is easy to make and offers a light, tasty alternative to the heavy foods and calorie-ridden sweets that abound during the holiday season. And seafood dishes such as *Citrus-Marinated Fillets* also make simple and elegant main courses for holiday dinners.

You can serve a diverse selection of appetizers when you use seafood. And since many seafood preparations are light, your guests can enjoy them and still look forward to the main course. Or you can serve a selection of seafood appetizers with other foods such as raw vegetables, crackers and fruit for lunch or a light evening meal.

Shrimp Dip

- 1 1/2 pounds small or medium shrimp
- 3 ounces cream cheese, softened
- 1/2 cup mayonnaise
- 3 tablespoons finely chopped onion
- 1 1/2 teaspoons prepared mustard
- 2 tablespoons fresh lemon juice
- 1/2 teaspoon Worcestershire sauce
- 1/4 teaspoon Tabasco sauce
- 1 cup light cream

Cook shrimp in salted or seasoned water. Drain, peel and devein. Chop finely.

Combine cream cheese and mayonnaise. Add onion, mustard, lemon juice, Worcestershire and Tabasco. Blend in cream and mix until smooth. Gently stir in shrimp. Chill. Serve with assorted vegetables. May also be used as a spread with assorted crackers. Makes about 3 cups.

Tangy Crab Dip

- 1 pound backfin crabmeat
- 8 ounces cream cheese, softened
- 1/2 cup sour cream
- 1/2 cup mayonnaise
- 1 tablespoon fresh lemon juice
- 1/2 teaspoon Tabasco sauce
- 4 tablespoons minced green onion, including tops
- 1/2 teaspoon pressed garlic
- 2 teaspoons horseradish

Remove any shell or cartilage from crabmeat. Combine cream cheese, sour cream and mayonnaise in medium bowl. Add lemon juice, Tabasco, onion, garlic and horseradish. Gently fold in crabmeat. Chill thoroughly. Serve with chips or assorted crackers. Makes about 2 1/2 cups.

Creamy Crab Dip

- 1 pound backfin crabmeat
- 12 ounces cream cheese, softened
- 1/2 cup light cream
- 4 teaspoons fresh lime juice
- 3 tablespoons Worcestershire sauce
- 1 teaspoon pressed garlic
- 1/4 teaspoon Tabasco sauce
- 4 teaspoons finely chopped fresh parsley
- 1/2 teaspoon freshly ground white pepper
- paprika

Remove any shell or cartilage from crabmeat. In medium bowl, blend cream and cream cheese together. Add lime juice, Worcestershire, garlic, Tabasco, parsley and white pepper. Mix thoroughly. Gently fold in crabmeat. Chill thoroughly. Place in serving bowl and sprinkle with paprika. Serve with assorted vegetables. Makes about 3 cups.

Crab-Stuffed Cherry Tomatoes

- 1 cup backfin crabmeat
- 1 pound cherry tomatoes
- 1/4 cup mayonnaise
- 2 tablespoons finely chopped green onion, including tops
- 1 teaspoon fresh lemon juice
- 1/4 teaspoon salt
- 1/4 teaspoon freshly ground white pepper
- 1/2 teaspoon Tabasco sauce
- fresh parsley sprigs

Remove any shell or cartilage from crabmeat.

Wash, dry and hollow tomatoes. Invert and drain on paper towels. In medium bowl, mix mayonnaise, onion and lemon juice. Add salt, pepper and Tabasco and stir. Gently fold in crabmeat. Stuff tomatoes. Chill thoroughly. Garnish serving dish with parsley sprigs. Makes 25 to 30 appetizers.

Note: You can substitute chopped cooked shrimp for the crab meat.

Clam Dip

* 1 cup cooked clams, minced, liquid reserved
* 6 ounces cream cheese, softened
* 2 teaspoons fresh lemon juice
* 2 teaspoons grated onion
* 1 teaspoon Worcestershire sauce
* 1/8 teaspoon Tabasco sauce
* 1/4 teaspoon salt
* 1 teaspoon minced fresh parsley

Blend together cream cheese, lemon juice, onion, Worcestershire, Tabasco, salt and parsley. Add clams and mix well. Add reserved liquid until desired consistency is reached. Chill thoroughly. Serve with assorted crackers and chips. Makes about 2 cups.

Smoked Fish Spread

* 1 pound smoked fish
* 1 pound cream cheese, softened
* 2 tablespoons fresh lemon juice
* 2 tablespoons finely chopped onion
* 1/4 cup chopped sweet pickles
* 1/2 cup finely chopped celery
* 4 tablespoons horseradish
* 1/2 teaspoon Tabasco sauce
* 1/4 cup chopped fresh parsley
* 3/4 cup light cream

Flake fish. Blend together cream cheese, lemon juice, onion, pickles, celery, horseradish, Tabasco and parsley. Add fish. Blend in cream. Serve with crackers. Makes about 3 cups.

Hot Crab Dip

* 1 pound backfin crabmeat
* 8 ounces cream cheese, softened
* 1 tablespoon milk
* 2 tablespoons grated onion
* 1 tablespoon fresh lemon juice
* 1 teaspoon horseradish
* 1/4 teaspoon freshly ground white pepper
* paprika

Remove any shell or cartilage from crabmeat.

Mix cream cheese, milk, onion, lemon juice, horseradish and pepper in medium bowl. Gently fold in crabmeat. Place in 8-inch pie dish. Sprinkle with paprika. Bake at 350 F for 15 to 20 minutes or until bubbly. Serve with assorted crackers.

Shrimp Christmas Tree
- 2 pounds medium shrimp
- 1 bunch curly endive
- 1 foam cone, about 1 1/2 feet tall
- 1 box small round toothpicks
- cocktail sauce

Prepare Cocktail Sauce ahead of time (even the day before) and chill thoroughly.

Simmer shrimp in salted or seasoned water until pink and tender, about 3 to 5 minutes. Drain and peel. Devein if desired. Chill thoroughly.

Separate, wash and dry endive.

Starting at the base of the cone and working up, cover the cone with overlapping leaves of endive. Fasten endive to the cone with toothpick halves. Cover fully with greens to resemble a Christmas tree. Use toothpicks to attach shrimp to the tree in loose spiral.

For flair, add a red bow to the top of your tree. Provide cocktail sauce for dipping shrimp.

The tree can be assembled several hours in advance. But be sure it is tightly wrapped in plastic to keep the shrimp from drying out. Refrigerate until ready to serve. Serves 15 to 20.

Cocktail Sauce:
- 1 1/2 cups catsup
- 1 tablespoon fresh lemon juice
- 1 tablespoon Worcestershire sauce
- 2 1/2 tablespoons prepared horseradish (more to taste)
- 1/4 teaspoon Tabasco sauce (more to taste)
- 1/8 teaspoon freshly ground black pepper

In small bowl, combine catsup, lemon juice, Worcestershire, horseradish, Tabasco and pepper. Chill thoroughly. Refrigerate until ready to use.

Baked Oysters with Bacon

- 2 dozen large unshucked oysters
- 6 slices bacon
- 1 cup fresh cracker crumbs
- 1/2 cup mayonnaise
- 2 tablespoons thinly sliced green onion, including tops
- 1 teaspoon fresh lemon juice
- 1 teaspoon Tabasco sauce
- 1/2 teaspoon Dijon mustard
- 1/2 cup freshly grated Parmesan cheese
- rock salt

Scrub oysters with stiff brush under cold, running water. Shuck, reserving deep half of shells. Drain oysters.

Cut bacon slices into quarters. Cook until limp, but not brown.

In small bowl, combine crumbs, mayonnaise, onion, lemon juice, Tabasco and mustard.

Place deep layer of rock salt in bottom of large pan or baking dish. Arrange reserved shells in rock salt, being sure that they are level. Place one oyster in each shell. Spread crumb mixture over each. Top with a piece of bacon, then sprinkle with cheese. Bake at 450 F until bacon is crisp and oysters are done, about 8 to 10 minutes. Serves 4 to 6.

Crab-Stuffed Mushrooms

- 1/2 pound backfin crabmeat
- 1 1/2 pounds large fresh mushrooms
- 1/2 cup light cream
- 1 tablespoon margarine or butter
- 1/2 cup fresh cracker crumbs
- 1 teaspoon dry mustard
- 1 tablespoon minced onion
- 1 tablespoon finely chopped fresh parsley
- 1/4 teaspoon salt
- 1/2 teaspoon prepared horseradish
- 1/4 teaspoon freshly ground black pepper
- 2 tablespoons margarine or butter, melted

Remove any shell or cartilage from crabmeat. Remove stems and clean mushrooms with damp paper towel.

Combine milk and 1 tablespoon margarine in small saucepan. Cook over low heat until margarine melts, stirring frequently. Remove from heat. Stir in crumbs, mustard, onion, salt, horseradish and pepper. Gently stir in crabmeat.

Spoon mixture into mushroom caps. Place in lightly greased baking dish. Brush tops with melted margarine. Bake at 350 F for 18 to 20 minutes or until thoroughly heated. Serves about 18.

Note: You can substitute chopped, cooked shrimp for the crabmeat.

Buttery Shrimp
- 1 pound large shrimp
- 1/4 cup margarine or butter
- 1 teaspoon pressed garlic
- 1/4 teaspoon salt
- 1/4 teaspoon freshly ground white pepper
- 1/4 cup finely chopped parsley

Shell and devein shrimp. Melt margarine in large skillet. Add garlic, salt and pepper and mix well. Stir in parsley. Add shrimp to hot mixture and sauté on one side until done, about 2 to 3 minutes. Turn and repeat on other side. Serves about 15.

A SALAD BAR OF FISH AND SHELLFISH

Say "seafood salad" and most people think of tuna salad. But seafood salads offer an almost limitless variety of tastes beyond the traditional lunch of canned tuna, boiled egg, celery and mayonnaise. Made with fish or shellfish, seafood salads can be simple or fancy, light or substantial, but they are always attractive and nutritious. Plus they are easy to prepare and delicious, too.

You'll be surprised how simply seafood salads come together. If you don't believe it, try one of our recipes such as *Crab Salad Deluxe*. Or create your own. Mix some shrimp or crab with vegetables such as celery, onion or green peas, and blend with mayonnaise, salt and a little freshly ground pepper. You can even use leftover cooked fish. Then serve your fresh salad on a bed of greenery with cherry tomatoes. Vary the lettuce bed for variety. Instead of the usual iceberg, try the delicate, buttery flavor of Boston or Bibb lettuce. Or use red leaf lettuce for some added color.

When creating seafood salads, you can use one type of seafood or a combination. We used shrimp, crab, flaked fish or a combination for the six recipes included here. We tried several with scallops and oysters, but none met our taste tests.

Made with fish or shellfish, seafood salads can be simple or fancy, light or substantial, but they are always attractive and nutritious. Plus they are easy to prepare and delicious, too.

We suggest serving these recipes as main dishes as they are hearty and full of flavor. Try them at lunch with fresh fruit and light crackers. Or prepare them for dinner, adding lightly steamed vegetables and hot bread. To save time, many of these salads taste excellent when prepared one day and served the next.

Remember to handle seafood gently. Be careful not to overcook it. And always modify recipes so that they suit your preferences.

Another wonderful recipe, *Fish Flake and Macaroni Salad*, can be found in the section on flaked fish. This salad containing shell macaroni and vegetables almost makes a meal in itself. We've served it to hundreds of people, always with good reviews.

For garnishing ideas, see Chapter 5, pp. 66-67.

Crab Salad Deluxe

- 1 pound lump or backfin crabmeat
- 1 1/2 cups chopped celery
- 1/4 cup chopped red onion
- 2 tablespoons finely chopped green pepper
- 1/3 cup finely chopped fresh parsley
- 1/2 cup mayonnaise
- 4 teaspoons fresh lemon juice
- 1/4 teaspoon salt
- 1/4 teaspoon freshly ground white pepper
- lettuce leaves

Carefully remove any shell or cartilage from crabmeat. In medium bowl, combine celery, onion, green pepper and parsley. Add crabmeat. Combine mayonnaise, lemon juice, salt and pepper. Add to crabmeat mixture. Mix gently but well. Avoid breaking up crabmeat. Chill for several hours. Serve on lettuce leaves. Serves 6 to 8.

Shrimp Salad

- 1 pound cooked small shrimp, peeled, deveined and coarsely chopped
- 1/2 cup mayonnaise
- 2 tablespoons fresh lemon juice
- 1/2 cup chopped celery
- 1/4 teaspoon Tabasco sauce
- 1/4 teaspoon salt
- 1/8 teaspoon freshly ground white pepper
- 2 hard-cooked eggs, diced
- lettuce leaves

In medium bowl, combine mayonnaise, lemon juice, celery, Tabasco, salt and pepper. Gently stir in egg and shrimp. Mix thoroughly. Chill several hours or overnight. Serve on lettuce leaves. Garnish with tomato wedges. Serves 4.

Crab and Shrimp Salad

- 3/4 pound backfin crabmeat
- 1 1/2 pounds cooked small shrimp
- 1/4 cup chopped green pepper
- 1/4 cup grated onion
- 1 cup chopped celery
- 1 cup mayonnaise
- 1 teaspoon Worcestershire sauce
- 1/2 teaspoon salt
- 1/8 teaspoon freshly ground white pepper
- lettuce leaves

Boil shrimp in salted or seasoned water until pink, about 3 to 4 minutes.

Carefully remove any shell or cartilage from crabmeat. Combine green pepper, onion and celery in medium bowl. Add crabmeat and shrimp. Combine mayonnaise, Worcestershire, salt and pepper. Add to crab-shrimp mixture. Mix thoroughly but gently to avoid breaking up crabmeat. Chill for several hours. Serve on lettuce leaves. Serves 8 to 10.

Shrimp Salad with Dill

- 1 1/2 pounds small shrimp
- 1 1/2 cups water
- 1/2 teaspoon chopped garlic
- 1/2 teaspoon celery seeds
- 1/4 teaspoon cayenne pepper
- 1/2 cup chopped celery
- 1/2 cup mayonnaise
- 1/4 teaspoon freshly ground white pepper
- 4 teaspoons chopped fresh dill weed
- lettuce leaves

Bring water, garlic, celery seeds and cayenne to boil in medium saucepan. Reduce heat and simmer for 10 minutes. Bring back to boil and add shrimp. When liquid returns to boil, stir and cook until shrimp are pink, about 3 to 4 minutes. Drain in a colander.

Place shrimp in medium bowl. Add celery, mayonnaise, pepper and dill and mix thoroughly. Chill well. Serve on lettuce leaves. Serves 6.

Seafood-Stuffed Avocados

- 1/2 pound backfin crabmeat
- 1/2 pound cooked small shrimp, peeled and deveined
- 3 tablespoons mayonnaise
- 3 tablespoons sour cream
- 1/4 teaspoon salt
- 1/4 teaspoon freshly ground white pepper
- 3 avocados, chilled
- paprika
- lettuce leaves

Carefully remove any shell or cartilage from crabmeat. In medium bowl, lightly toss crabmeat and shrimp. In small bowl, combine mayonnaise, sour cream, salt and pepper. Add to crab and shrimp. Mix gently but thoroughly. Chill for several hours.

When ready to serve, peel avocados and cut in half lengthwise. Pile centers with salad. Sprinkle with paprika. Place on lettuce leaves. Serves 6.

Flaked Fish Salad

- 2 cups cooked flaked fish
- 1/2 cup mayonnaise
- 1/2 cup finely chopped celery
- 1/4 cup finely chopped onion
- 2 tablespoons finely chopped pimento
- 1 tablespoon fresh lemon juice
- 1/2 teaspoon salt
- 1/4 teaspoon freshly ground white pepper
- lettuce

Place mayonnaise in medium bowl. Add celery, onion, pimento, lemon juice, salt and pepper. Mix thoroughly. Gently blend in flaked fish.

Chill well, overnight if possible. Serve on bed of greenery. Garnished with tomato wedges. Serves 4 to 6.

SEAFOOD SOUPS: A FINE KETTLE OF FISH ... AND SHELLFISH

Chock full of vegetables and seafood, soups and stews make a hearty meal. On a cold day, a hot bowl of scallop bisque or old-fashioned clam chowder needs only a good crusty bread or cornbread to round it out.

Restaurants and gourmets often serve soup as the first course of a large meal. But many of us consider these warm, tasteful bowls of goodness to be a light lunch or the main course at dinner. Seafood soups such as stews, chowders and bisques offer a variety of delicious meals. They can look elegant, too, as many recipes call for ingredients such as clams in the shell, soft or hard crabs or shrimp in the shell. Made ahead, these seafood hits make the perfect solution for entertaining large groups of family or friends. And soups can be especially healthful because all the nutrients are reserved in the liquid.

Lean, white, firm fish cook best in soups. Delicate, fatter fish break apart. Grouper and catfish are ideal. Medium firm fish such as snapper, flounder and spotted sea trout work equally as well. As in all seafood cookery, handle fish carefully. And always avoid overcooking, which causes dryness and toughness. Yes, this happens even though the fish or shellfish is being cooked in water.

Remember that you can always substitute species. Go to the market to buy fresh fish that is in season, not a particular species. And use your favorite seasonings. It's often a good idea to follow a recipe the first time you make a dish, then modify it to your tastes the next time. Use the ingredients that you enjoy.

We've included eight of our all-time best soup recipes here. For tasty gumbo recipes, turn to pp. 155, 233, 259. And our favorite, top-rated *She-Crab Soup* recipe can be found on p. 193.

Crab Soup Deluxe
- 1 pound lump crabmeat
- 3 tablespoons margarine or butter
- 2 1/2 cups chopped onion
- 1/2 teaspoon pressed garlic
- 3 14 1/2-ounce cans chopped tomatoes, undrained
- 1 teaspoon salt
- 1/8 teaspoon freshly ground black pepper
- 1/8 teaspoon Tabasco sauce
- 1/2 teaspoon marjoram
- 1/2 teaspoon ground thyme
- 1/2 teaspoon fresh lemon juice
- zest of 1 lemon
- 1 tablespoon finely chopped fresh parsley

Seafood soups — such as stews, chowders and bisques — offer a variety of delicious meals. They can look elegant, too, as many recipes call for ingredients such as clams in the shell, soft or hard crabs or shrimp in the shell.

Remove any shell or cartilage from crabmeat.

Melt margarine in large saucepan over medium heat. Sauté onion and garlic until tender but not brown. Add tomatoes salt, pepper, Tabasco, marjoram, thyme, lemon juice and lemon zest. Bring to boil. Reduce heat and simmer 30 minutes until flavors are mingled and tomato liquid is reduced. Add parsley and crabmeat. Heat thoroughly, but do not overcook crabmeat. Serve immediately. Serves 8 to 10.

Fisherman's Stew
- 2 pounds firm, skinless fillets, cut in 1-inch cubes
- 2 tablespoons margarine or butter
- 1 cup chopped onion
- 1/2 teaspoon pressed garlic
- 2 14 1/2-ounce cans chopped tomatoes, undrained
- 3 cups water
- 1 teaspoon basil leaves, dried
- 1 teaspoon thyme leaves, dried
- 1/4 teaspoon crushed red pepper
- 1 teaspoon salt
- 4 cups winter squash, cut into 1-inch cubes
- 2 ears corn, cut crosswise into 1-inch pieces

Melt margarine in large saucepan over medium heat. Add onion and garlic and cook until tender. Add tomatoes, water, basil, thyme, pepper, salt, squash and corn. Cover and bring to boil. Reduce heat and simmer until squash and corn are done, about 10 to 15 minutes. Add fish and continue to cook until it flakes easily with a fork, about 10 minutes. Serves 10 to 12.

Scallop Bisque
- 1 pound scallops
- 4 ounces fresh mushrooms, sliced
- 5 tablespoons margarine or butter
- 1/2 teaspoon dry mustard
- 1 teaspoon salt
- 1/4 teaspoon freshly ground white pepper
- 4 tablespoons flour
- 1 quart milk
- paprika

In large saucepan, lightly sauté mushrooms in 1 tablespoon margarine over medium heat. Remove mushrooms. Purée mushrooms and scallops in food processor.

Melt remaining margarine. Add puréed scallops and mushrooms, mustard, salt and pepper. Cook for 5 minutes, stirring occasionally. Blend in flour. Add milk gradually, stirring constantly, and cook until thick. Place in soup bowls and sprinkle with paprika. Serves 6.

Down East Clam Chowder
- 1 quart coarsely chopped chowder clams
- 1/4 pound salt pork, sliced
- 1 quart water
- 1/2 cup chopped onion
- 1 teaspoon salt
- 1/4 teaspoon freshly ground black pepper
- 4 cups diced potatoes
- 1 cup instant potato flakes for thickening (optional)

In large saucepan, fry pork over medium heat until crisp. Remove pork and discard. Add clams, water, onion, salt and pepper to pan. Bring to boil. Reduce heat and cook slowly until clams are tender, about 1 1/2 hours. Add potatoes and onion, and cook until potatoes are done, about 20 minutes. Add mashed potatoes and simmer until thickened, about 5 minutes. Serves 10 to 12.

Italian Fish Stew
- 1 pound each of two species of firm fish, skinless and cut in 2-inch pieces
- 3 dozen littleneck or cherrystone clams, in shells
- 1/4 cup olive oil
- 1 cup thinly sliced onion
- 1/2 teaspoon pressed garlic
- 3/4 cup sliced celery
- 1/2 cup diced carrot
- 2 tablespoons coarsely chopped fresh parsley
- 1 8-ounce can tomato sauce
- 1/4 teaspoon salt
- 1/8 teaspoon freshly ground black pepper
- 1 teaspoon dried basil leaves
- 1/2 cup dry white wine

Heat olive oil in large skillet over medium heat. Add onion, garlic, celery, carrot and parsley and sauté lightly. Add tomato sauce, salt, pepper and basil.

Lightly season fish with salt and pepper, then place on top of vegetables. Cover pan and simmer for 5 minutes. Add clams hinge side down. Cover and simmer 10 minutes. Pour wine over fish and blend with sauce, leaving the fish and clams on top. Turn heat up and cook, basting occasionally, until fish is done and clams are open, about 8 to 10 minutes. (If fish is done and most of the clams are open, place them in serving bowls and return the unopened clams in the pan until they open.) Discard any clams that do not open. Serves 10 to 12.

Oyster Soup

- 2 pints standard oysters, undrained
- hot water
- 6 tablespoons margarine or butter
- 4 tablespoons flour
- 1/2 cup thinly sliced green onion tops
- 3 tablespoons finely chopped fresh parsley
- 1 teaspoon salt
- 1/2 teaspoon freshly ground white pepper

Strain oyster liquor into a measuring cup. Chop oysters coarsely. Heat liquor over medium heat, add chopped oysters and simmer for 5 minutes. Remove oysters and reserve. Add hot water to the reserved liquor to make 5 cups.

Melt margarine in large saucepan over medium heat. Add flour gradually, stirring constantly until smooth. Gradually add the hot liquid, whisking constantly, and cook until smooth. Add onion, parsley, salt and pepper. Simmer for 15 minutes. Add reserved oysters and heat thoroughly. Serve immediately. Serves 8 to 10.

Manhattan-Style Clam Chowder
- 1 quart coarsely chopped chowder clams
- 4 bacon strips
- 2 cups chopped carrots
- 1 1/2 cups chopped celery
- 2 cups chopped onion
- 1/2 cup finely chopped green pepper
- 1 tablespoon minced garlic
- 1 teaspoon salt
- 1/4 teaspoon freshly ground black pepper
- 1/8 teaspoon cayenne pepper
- 1 teaspoon thyme leaves
- 1 bay leaf
- 1 quart water
- 1 14 1/2-ounce can chopped tomatoes, undrained
- 4 cups diced potatoes
- 1 cup finely chopped fresh parsley

    Fry bacon in large pot over medium heat. Remove bacon and reserve. Add carrots, celery, onion, green pepper and garlic and sauté lightly. Add salt, black pepper, cayenne, thyme and bay leaf. Add water, tomatoes and clams. Bring to boil. Reduce heat and cook slowly until clams are tender, about 1 1/2 hours. Add potatoes and cook until done, about 20 minutes. Stir in parsley. Pour in individual serving bowls. Sprinkle with reserved bacon. Serves 8 to 10.

Shrimp Bisque
- 2 pounds shrimp, unshelled
- 1/4 cup chopped onion
- 1/4 cup chopped celery
- 4 tablespoons margarine or butter
- 4 tablespoons flour
- 1 teaspoon salt
- 1/4 teaspoon freshly ground white pepper
- 1/4 teaspoon paprika
- 2 cups milk
- 2 cups light cream
- 1/4 cup finely chopped fresh parsley

Boil shrimp, peel and purée in food processor. In medium saucepan, melt margarine. Add onion and celery and cook until tender. Blend in flour, salt, pepper and paprika. Add milk slowly and cook, stirring constantly, until mixture begins to thicken. Add cream and continue to cook until thick, about 20 minutes. Add shrimp and heat. Garnish with chopped parsley. Serves 8 to 10.

Cream of Shrimp Soup
- 1 1/2 pounds shrimp, in shells
- 1 cup light cream
- 2 tablespoons margarine or butter
- 1/3 cup minced onion
- 1/2 cup minced celery
- 3 tablespoons flour
- 3/4 teaspoon salt
- 1/2 teaspoon paprika
- 1/2 teaspoon freshly ground white pepper
- 1 teaspoon Worcestershire sauce
- 2 cups milk
- 1 cup heavy cream
- 1 tablespoon minced fresh parsley

Cook shrimp in salted water. Peel and devein. Purée with light cream in food processor or mince and combine with cream.

Melt margarine in top of double boiler. Sauté onion and celery until just translucent. Blend in flour, then salt, paprika, pepper and Worcestershire. Add shrimp mixture.

Slowly blend in milk and cream, stirring constantly until slightly thickened. Pour into individual serving bowls and sprinkle with parsley. Serves 6 to 8.

ANY TIME IS SEAFOOD SANDWICH TIME

What comes to mind when someone mentions a seafood sandwich?

Probably a bland, breaded, fried, square piece of fish from the local fast food eatery. Topped, of course, with a slice of processed cheese and a blob of tartar sauce.

Now imagine such goodies as *French-Toasted Shrimp Sandwich, Hot Crab and Cheese Sandwich, Fisherman's Burger* or other delicious seafood sandwiches. Our *Hot Crab and Cheese Sandwich,* for example, melts fresh Monterey Jack and cheddar cheeses over a pound of crabmeat and English muffins.

Over the years, we've developed a variety of seafood sandwiches using fish, shrimp, crab and other seafood. We've varied the breads, too, including cornbread and English muffins.

Many seafood salads, such as shrimp and crab salads, make great sandwich fillings. Dress them up with lettuce and tomato or eat them plain. Not included here, but certainly an option, are the familiar and popular fried shrimp burgers and oyster burgers.

Sandwiches containing fish or shellfish often provide a good way to entice children to eat seafood. For some reason, if it's in a sandwich, children seem to like it better. And you can make a seafood sandwich even more appealing to children by using cookie cutters to turn bread slices into fun seaside shapes such as fish or starfish. Pretend celery slices are seaweed and carrot curls are coral. This is a fun way to get your kids to eat a healthy meal.

Seafood sandwiches can be a nutritious and delicious meal for adults, too. Next time you think of special sandwiches, think of seafood. And feel free to create your own favorites.

A number of these preparations, combined with a fresh vegetable salad or a bowl of soup, make filling and fantastic evening meals.

Over the years, we've developed a variety of seafood sandwiches using fish, shrimp, crab and other seafood. We've varied the breads, too, including cornbread and English muffins.

French-Toasted Shrimp Sandwich

- 2 cups cooked shrimp, coarsely chopped
- 1/2 cup finely chopped celery
- 2 tablespoons finely chopped onion
- 1 teaspoon Worcestershire sauce
- 1/2 teaspoon prepared mustard
- 1/2 cup mayonnaise
- 1/2 teaspoon salt
- 1/4 teaspoon freshly ground black pepper
- 12 slices white sandwich bread
- 2 eggs, beaten
- 1/4 cup milk
- 4 tablespoons margarine or butter

Combine shrimp, celery, onion, Worcestershire, mustard, mayonnaise, 1/4 teaspoon salt and pepper in medium bowl. Spread on 6 bread slices. Top with remaining slices.

In shallow dish, combine eggs, milk and 1/4 teaspoon salt. Melt margarine in large skillet. Dip sandwiches in egg mixture. Fry sandwiches over medium heat until golden brown on one side, about 6 to 8 minutes. Turn and cook on other side until filling is hot and bread is golden brown. Cut in halves. Serves 6.

Hot Crab and Cheese Sandwich

- 1 pound backfin crabmeat
- 1 tablespoon margarine or butter
- 2 tablespoons flour
- 3/4 cup milk
- 3/4 cup chopped celery, including leaves
- 1/2 teaspoon salt
- 1/4 teaspoon freshly ground black pepper
- 1/4 cup finely chopped green pepper
- 1/4 cup finely chopped onion
- 2 cups freshly grated medium cheddar cheese
- 1 cup freshly grated Monterey Jack cheese
- 3 English muffins, split and lightly toasted

Remove any shell or cartilage from crabmeat. In medium saucepan, melt margarine over medium heat. Stir in flour. Add milk gradually, stirring constantly. Add celery, salt and black pepper and cook until thickened, stirring constantly. Add green pepper and onion. Gently stir in crabmeat. Heat thoroughly but do not boil.

Stir in cheeses. Place generous helpings on halves of toasted muffins. Bake at 350 F until cheese is melted and lightly browned, about 15 to 20 minutes. Serves 6.

Open-Face Oyster Sandwich

- 1 pint standard oysters, drained
- 1/2 cup margarine or butter
- 1 teaspoon pressed garlic
- 6 thick slices French bread
- 1 cup freshly grated mozzarella cheese

In small saucepan, melt 1/4 cup margarine over medium heat. Add garlic and cook until soft. Remove from heat. Brush garlic butter on one side of each bread slice. Place, garlic side up, in shallow baking pan. Cook at 350 F until toasted.

While bread is toasting, melt 1/4 cup margarine in large skillet. Add oysters and cook at 375 F until done on one side, about 2 to 3 minutes. Turn and repeat on other side.

Use a slotted spoon to lift oysters out and place on toast. Spread with cheese. Place under broiler until cheese is melted, about 5 minutes. Serves 6.

Happy Clamburger

- 1 cup chopped cherrystone or littleneck clams
- 1 egg, beaten
- 1 tablespoon fresh lemon juice
- 1 tablespoon chopped fresh parsley
- 1 tablespoon grated onion
- 1/4 teaspoon salt
- 1/4 teaspoon freshly ground black pepper
- 1 cup dry bread crumbs
- vegetable oil for frying
- 6 sandwich buns, split and toasted

In medium bowl, combine clams, egg, lemon juice, parsley, onion, salt, pepper and 1/2 cup crumbs. Shape into 6 patties. Roll in remaining crumbs. In large skillet, fry cakes in hot oil, 375 F, until brown on one side, about 5 minutes. Turn and repeat on other side. Serve in toasted buns. Serves 6.

Hot Seafood Sandwich with Mushroom Sauce

- 1 1/2 pounds fish fillets
- salt
- freshly ground black pepper
- cornmeal
- 1 box cornbread mix

Prepare pan of cornbread according to package directions. Keep warm. Prepare Mushroom Sauce and keep warm.

Cut fish into serving-size pieces. Sprinkle with salt and pepper, then roll in cornmeal. Fry in hot oil at 375 F until crisp and brown, about 6 to 8 minutes. Drain on paper towels. Serve on sliced hot cornbread with Mushroom Sauce. Serves 4 to 6.

Mushroom Sauce:

- 4 tablespoons margarine or butter
- 3 tablespoons flour
- 2 cups milk
- 3/4 teaspoon ground thyme
- 1/2 teaspoon salt
- 2 cups sliced fresh mushrooms

In medium saucepan, melt margarine over medium heat. Stir in flour. Add milk gradually, stirring constantly. Add thyme and salt. Cook, stirring constantly, until thickened. Stir in mushrooms. Spoon over fried fish on hot cornbread.

Hot Soft-Crab Sandwich

- 8 soft-shell crabs, cleaned
- salt
- freshly ground black pepper
- flour
- 1/2 cup margarine or butter
- 8 sandwich rolls, warmed
- mayonnaise or tartar sauce (see recipe p. 235)

Sprinkle crabs lightly with salt and pepper. Dust with flour. Heat margarine in large skillet over medium heat until sizzling. Sauté crabs until crisp and brown on one side, about 4 to 5 minutes. Turn and repeat on other side. Drain on paper towels. Serve on warm rolls with mayonnaise or tartar sauce. Serves 8.

Fisherman's Burger
- 2 cups cooked, flaked fish (see p. 172)
- 1 egg, beaten
- 1/3 cup freshly grated Parmesan cheese
- 1 tablespoon chopped fresh parsley
- 1 teaspoon pressed garlic
- 1/2 teaspoon salt
- 1/4 teaspoon freshly grated black pepper
- 1/2 cup dry bread crumbs
- vegetable oil for frying
- 6 sesame seed rolls, toasted
- tartar sauce (see recipe, p. 235)

Combine egg, cheese, parsley, garlic, salt and pepper in medium bowl. Gently fold in flaked fish. Shape into 6 patties. Roll lightly in crumbs. Fry in hot oil, about 375 F, until brown on one side, about 4 to 5 minutes. Turn and repeat on other side. Drain on paper towels. Serve in toasted buns with tartar sauce. Serves 6.

SEAFOOD CASSEROLES — TASTY COMBINATIONS

These days, only a few seafood cookbooks list casseroles as a category. This may be because casseroles have become the "poor child" of food preparations, something to be prepared by those with few talents and little culinary taste. Not so! From basic *Scalloped Oysters* to a *Heavenly Seafood Casserole* of shrimp, scallops, fish and crab, we know seafood casseroles to be an exciting way to prepare seafood. By combining fresh fish or shellfish with cheeses, pungent herbs and fresh vegetables, we find the flavors always to be elegant and the meal — delicious.

While the word "casserole" originally meant the dish itself, we now use the word to mean the food contained in the dish as well. We all go to covered-dish suppers where we enjoy casserole dishes with several ingredients combined into one preparation.

Although many good casserole recipes use pasta or rice as fillers or extenders, our preparations feature fish and shellfish without many additions — just seasonings, a few vegetables or some crumbs. Our casseroles include fish, shrimp, oysters, scallops, clams and crabmeat as the main ingredients. Some feature one species; others combine several. With a vegetable or salad and a loaf of hearty bread, seafood casseroles provide a nutritious and complete meal.

Although many good casserole recipes use pasta or rice as fillers or extenders, our preparations feature fish and shellfish without many additions — just seasonings, a few vegetables or some crumbs. Our casseroles include fish, shrimp, oysters, scallops, clams and crab meat as the main ingredients.

Nine delicious, time-tested recipes follow. For instructions on using finfish in casseroles, see the section on flaked fish, p. 172. For more seafood casseroles, check the index under specific titles such as "Shrimp."

Flaked Fish Casserole au Gratin
- 4 cups cooked flaked fish (see p. 172)
- 1/4 cup margarine or butter
- 1/4 cup flour
- 1/2 teaspoon dry mustard
- 1 teaspoon salt
- 1/4 teaspoon freshly ground black pepper
- 2 cups milk
- 1 cup grated medium cheddar cheese
- 1/2 cup fresh cracker crumbs
- 2 tablespoons margarine or butter, melted

In medium saucepan, melt 1/4 cup margarine. Add flour, mustard, salt and pepper. Stir in milk gradually and cook until thick. Add cheese and stir until melted.

In greased 1 1/2-quart casserole, place a layer of flaked fish, then a layer of sauce. Continue alternating layers, ending with sauce. Combine crumbs with melted margarine and sprinkle over top. Bake at 350 F for 40 minutes or until golden brown and bubbly. Serves 8 to 10.

Shrimp Casserole
- 1 1/2 pounds small shrimp (or medium, cut into pieces)
- 1/4 cup margarine or butter
- 1 clove garlic, pressed
- 1 1/2 tablespoons chopped fresh parsley
- 1/8 teaspoon paprika
- 1/8 teaspoon cayenne pepper
- 2 tablespoons dry sherry
- 1/2 cup soft bread crumbs

Cook shrimp in salted or seasoned water.

Melt margarine in medium saucepan. Add garlic, parsley, paprika, cayenne and sherry and mix well. Cover and simmer about 5 minutes. Add shrimp and crumbs and stir lightly.

Place in lightly greased 1-quart casserole and bake at 325 F for 20 to 30 minutes or until heated and bubbly. Serves 6.

Crab Imperial
- 1 pound backfin crabmeat
- 1 egg, beaten
- 1/4 cup mayonnaise
- 3/4 teaspoon Worcestershire sauce
- 1/4 teaspoon salt
- 1/16 teaspoon thyme
- 1/16 teaspoon oregano
- 1/16 teaspoon dry mustard
- 1/4 teaspoon Tabasco sauce
- 1 teaspoon parsley flakes
- paprika

    Remove any shell or cartilage from crabmeat. In large bowl, mix egg, mayonnaise, Worcestershire, salt, thyme, oregano, mustard and Tabasco. Gently mix in crabmeat. Place in lightly greased 1-quart casserole. Sprinkle with parsley and paprika. Bake at 350 F until mixture is lightly browned and bubbly, about 25 minutes. Serves 4 to 6.

Deluxe Deviled Crab
- 1 pound backfin crabmeat
- 1 cup fresh cracker crumbs
- 1 tablespoon fresh lemon juice
- 1 teaspoon Worcestershire sauce
- 1/2 cup minced onion
- 1/4 teaspoon Tabasco sauce
- 1/4 teaspoon cayenne pepper
- 1 teaspoon dry mustard
- 1/4 cup chopped fresh parsley
- 1/3 cup margarine or butter, melted
- 1/4 cup milk
- 1/4 teaspoon salt
- 1/4 teaspoon freshly ground black pepper
- 1/2 cup fresh cracker crumbs
- 2 tablespoons margarine or butter, melted

Remove any shell or cartilage from crabmeat. In large bowl, mix 1 cup cracker crumbs, lemon juice, Worcestershire, onion, Tabasco, cayenne, mustard, parsley, margarine, milk, salt and pepper. Gently mix in crabmeat. Place in lightly greased 1-quart casserole. Combine crumbs and 2 tablespoons melted margarine. Spread over top of crab mixture. Bake at 375 F for 20 to 25 minutes or until lightly browned and bubbly. Serves 6.

Heavenly Seafood Casserole

- 1/2 pound small shrimp in shell
- 1/2 pound bay scallops (or sea scallops quartered)
- 1/2 pound cooked, flaked flounder (or other white fish)
- 1/2 pound crabmeat
- 6 tablespoons margarine or butter
- 6 tablespoons flour
- 2 cups milk
- 1 tablespoon dry sherry
- 1 1/2 teaspoons Worcestershire sauce
- 4 tablespoons freshly grated Parmesan cheese
- 3/4 teaspoon salt
- 1/8 teaspoon freshly ground white pepper
- 1/2 teaspoon paprika
- 1/4 cup dry bread crumbs

Remove any shell or cartilage from crabmeat. Cook shrimp in salted or seasoned water until pink, about 3 to 4 minutes. Remove shrimp, reserving water. Cook scallops in same water about 2 to 3 minutes, just until tender. Drain well.

Peel shrimp.

Melt margarine in medium saucepan and blend in flour. Add milk gradually and cook over low heat, stirring constantly, until thick. Add sherry, Worcestershire, 1 tablespoon Parmesan, salt, pepper and paprika. Blend well. Add shrimp, scallops, flaked fish and crabmeat. Pour into 1 1/2-quart casserole.

Mix remaining Parmesan with bread crumbs and sprinkle over top. Bake at 375 F about 20 to 25 minutes, or until heated and bubbly. Serves 8 to 10.

Baked Scallops
- 1 pound bay scallops (or sea scallops quartered)
- 1/2 teaspoon salt
- 3 tablespoons margarine or butter
- 1 cup chopped celery
- 1 cup chopped fresh mushrooms
- 1/4 cup finely chopped green pepper
- 4 tablespoons margarine or butter
- 6 tablespoons flour
- 3/4 teaspoon salt
- 1/4 teaspoon freshly ground black pepper
- 2 cups milk
- 1 cup soft bread crumbs mixed with 3 tablespoons melted margarine or butter
- 1/4 cup freshly grated medium cheddar cheese

Rinse scallops and pat dry with paper towels. Sprinkle with 1/2 teaspoon salt. In medium skillet, melt 3 tablespoons margarine. Add celery, mushrooms and green pepper and cook until tender.

In separate medium saucepan, melt 4 tablespoons margarine over low heat. Blend in flour, 3/4 teaspoon salt and black pepper. Add milk gradually and stir until thickened.

Combine scallops, vegetables and sauce. Pour into greased 1 1/2-quart casserole. Combine bread crumbs and cheese and sprinkle over top. Bake at 350 F about 30 minutes or until golden brown and bubbly. Serves 6.

Scalloped Clams
- 2 pints cherrystone clams (about 36 large cherrystones)
- 1 tablespoon fresh lemon juice
- 2 cups unsalted saltine cracker crumbs, in large pieces
- 1/8 teaspoon freshly ground black pepper
- 2 tablespoons chopped fresh parsley
- 2 tablespoons minced onion
- 5 tablespoons margarine or butter, softened
- 1 pint light cream
- 1/2 teaspoon Worcestershire sauce
- 1 tablespoon dry sherry

Shuck clams, reserving liquor. Drain and chop clams. Mix with lemon juice.

In medium bowl, combine crumbs, pepper, parsley, onion and softened margarine. Sprinkle 1/3 of crumb mixture in 1-quart greased casserole. Cover with half of the clams, one-third of the crumbs, then the remaining clams.

See note below before this step. Combine reserved clam liquor with enough cream to make 1 cup. Stir in Worcestershire and sherry. Pour over clams. Top with remaining 1/3 of the crumb mixture. Bake at 375 F until thoroughly cooked and bubbly, about 40 minutes. Let stand 5 minutes before serving. Serves 8 to 10.

Note: Taste cooked clam liquid for salt content. To taste the liquid, boil a small amount for 1 minute before tasting. Do NOT taste the raw liquid. If it is very salty, reduce the amount of clam liquid called for and increase the amount of cream. Or you may need to use cream entirely. We've found this step to be essential; many clams are very salty.

Scalloped Oysters

- 1 pint standard oysters (or selects, cut in half)
- 1/3 cup oyster liquor
- 35 fresh saltine crackers, made into coarse crumbs
- 1/4 cup finely chopped green onion, including tops
- salt
- freshly ground black pepper
- 1/3 cup heavy cream
- 1 tablespoon Worcestershire sauce
- 1/8 teaspoon Tabasco sauce
- 1/4 cup dry white wine
- 3 tablespoons margarine or butter, melted

Drain oysters well, reserving 1/3 cup oyster liquor.

Place 1/4 of the crumbs in lightly greased small casserole dish. Cover with 1/2 of the oysters and 1/2 of the green onion. Lightly salt (remember that the oysters are salty). Sprinkle with black pepper. Repeat, then sprinkle with the remainder of the crumbs. Drizzle with melted margarine.

Combine oyster liquor with cream, Worcestershire, Tabasco and wine and pour over the casserole. Bake at 400 F until brown and bubbly, about 25 minutes. Serves 4 to 6.

Shrimp-Crab Casserole

- 1 pound small shrimp in shell
- 1 pound crabmeat
- 1 1/4 cups thinly sliced celery
- 1/3 cup finely chopped onion
- 1/3 cup mayonnaise
- 1 teaspoon Worcestershire sauce
- 1/2 teaspoon salt
- 1/4 teaspoon freshly ground white pepper
- 3/4 cup fine dry bread crumbs
- 2 tablespoons margarine or butter, melted

Remove any shell or cartilage from crabmeat. Cook shrimp in salted or seasoned water. Peel and cut into halves, lengthwise. Gently combine shrimp and crabmeat in medium bowl. In small bowl combine celery, onion, mayonnaise, Worcestershire, salt and pepper. Blend well. Carefully stir into shrimp/crab mixture.

Place in lightly greased casserole dish. Combine crumbs and margarine and sprinkle over top. Bake at 350 F until lightly browned and bubbly, about 30 minutes. Serves 8 to 10.

SEAFOOD AND PASTA — A PERFECT CATCH

When many of us were growing up, there was no "pasta." Of course we knew about macaroni and cheese and spaghetti and meatballs, but that was the extent of our pasta knowledge. Today, more than 600 different shapes exist on the market, with new ones regularly being designed.

One of the most popular of modern foods, pasta can be served in a variety of ways and combinations. We've created some great combinations of fish and shellfish with pasta such as our *Fettucini with Trout-Cheese Sauce.*

The word "pasta" comes from the Italian word for "paste" and means a combination of flour and water. There are two main types: dry or factory-made with water and paste; and fresh or homemade with flour and eggs. Some fresh pasta is available in the refrigerated section of your supermarket, but it is considerably more expensive than dry pasta. Occasionally some fresh pasta is frozen.

Top-quality pasta is made with refined durum wheat. American-grown durum wheat is considered one of the best in the world, and its pasta ranks among the world's finest. While most pasta is made from durum wheat, others are made from whole wheat, rice, corn or soy flour. Some are colored and

One of the most popular of modern foods, pasta can be served in a variety of ways and combinations. We've created some great combinations of fish and shellfish with pasta such as our Fettucini with Trout-Cheese Sauce.

flavored with spinach, carrot or tomato purée. Included among those we enjoyed were whole wheat spaghetti and spinach fettucini. Experiment with different flavors and colors.

Many types of pasta are interchangeable, but some are more suited to particular sauces than others. For example, delicate noodles are compatible with cream sauces, but spaghetti is usually enhanced by heavier sauces. We made several preparations with large pastas such as manicotti and giant shells, but we did not think they were as compatible with seafood as smaller types.

Pasta should be cooked "al dente" — not soft, yet tender and firm "to the tooth." Cooking times vary for different shapes and sizes. Also, the same type may vary in cooking time among manufacturers. Always follow package directions. Try to coordinate cooking times so that pasta and sauce are done at the same time.

Large pastas such as macaroni and spaghetti must be cooked in plenty of boiling water. Otherwise they become sticky. Miniature pastas such as small shells and small wheels, which do not require as much water, make excellent additions to soups and stews.

Contrary to popular belief, pasta is not fattening. One cup of cooked pasta contains about 200 calories, less than one gram of fat and no cholesterol. The rich sauces and cheeses we pour over pasta make dishes high in calories and fat. Obviously, a tomato-based sauce is less fattening than a cream or cheese sauce.

Remember, too, that the amount of an ingredient used is important. Three ounces of freshly grated Parmesan cheese contain about 390 calories. But if your recipe calls for one-half cup and serves four or six people, you can still have great flavor without many calories. And you can substitute cheeses such as mozzarella that have fewer calories.

You'll enjoy your food more if you grate fresh cheeses instead of buying grated ones. The flavor is fresher and more intense. In addition, you will have fewer calories and additives as well as less salt, fat and cholesterol.

Most of our pasta recipes almost make a meal in themselves. Just add a crisp vegetable salad, and enjoy a little taste of Italy.

Fettucini with Trout-Cheese Sauce

- 4 medium skinless trout fillets
- 1/4 teaspoon salt
- 1/4 cup margarine or butter
- 1/4 cup flour
- 1/2 cup dry white wine
- 1 cup light cream
- 1/2 cup freshly grated Parmesan cheese
- 1/4 cup freshly grated Romano cheese
- 1/4 cup chopped green onion, including tops
- 1/4 teaspoon freshly ground black pepper
- 1 pound spinach fettucini

Cut fillets into 1-inch strips. Sprinkle with salt. In heavy medium skillet, melt margarine over medium heat. Sauté trout 4 or 5 minutes or until done. Remove and set aside.

Stir flour into remaining margarine. Add wine. Slowly blend in cream. Cook over medium heat, stirring constantly, until sauce thickens. Stir in 1/4 cup Parmesan, Romano, onion and pepper. When thoroughly blended, add fish and cook just until fish is heated through.

Meanwhile, cook fettucini according to package directions. Drain. Place on serving plates and top with sauce. Sprinkle with remaining 1/4 cup Parmesan. Serves 8 to 10.

Crab-Noodle Casserole

- 1 pound backfin crabmeat
- 1/4 cup margarine or butter
- 3 tablespoons flour
- 2 cups milk
- 1/2 cup heavy cream
- 1 1/2 teaspoons salt
- 3/4 teaspoon paprika
- 1/4 teaspoon freshly ground white pepper
- 1 tablespoon minced onion
- 1/4 cup dry sherry
- 6 ounces broad egg noodles
- 3 tablespoons margarine or butter, melted
- 1 cup soft bread crumbs

Remove any shell or cartilage from crabmeat. In medium saucepan, melt 1/4 cup margarine over medium heat. Stir in flour. Add milk and cream gradually and cook, stirring constantly, until thickened. Add salt, paprika, pepper and onion. Stir in crab meat. When it is heated, remove from heat. Add sherry.

Meanwhile, cook noodles according to package directions. Drain and stir into crab mixture. Place in 1-quart lightly greased casserole. Mix bread crumbs with 3 tablespoons melted margarine and sprinkle over top. Bake at 375 F for 30 minutes or until thoroughly heated and bubbly. Serves 4 to 6.

Linguine with Clam Sauce

- 1 pint clams, chopped, liquor reserved
- 1/4 cup margarine or butter
- 1/4 cup olive oil
- 1 cup chopped green onion, including tops
- clam liquor plus enough water to equal 1 cup
- 1 14 1/2-ounce can chopped tomatoes, undrained
- 1 1/2 teaspoons garlic, minced
- 1 1/2 teaspoons chopped fresh parsley
- 1/2 teaspoon oregano
- 1/2 teaspoon basil
- 1/4 teaspoon freshly ground black pepper
- 1 pound linguine
- 1/2 cup freshly grated Parmesan cheese

In medium skillet, melt margarine over medium heat. Remove 2 table-spoons and set aside. Add oil and heat. Sauté green onion until tender. Add clam liquor, tomatoes, garlic, parsley, oregano, basil and pepper and simmer 10 to 15 minutes or until clams are tender.

Meanwhile, cook linguine according to package directions. Toss with reserved 2 tablespoons margarine and 1/4 cup Parmesan. Add 2 cups sauce and toss again. Place on serving plates and top with remaining sauce. Sprinkle with 1/4 cup Parmesan. Serves 8 to 10.

Note: Another version can be found on p. 220.

Vermicelli with Shrimp and Tomatoes

- 1 1/2 pounds medium shrimp
- 1/4 cup margarine or butter
- 1/4 cup olive oil
- 1 cup chopped onion
- 4 teaspoons minced garlic
- 1 14 1/2-ounce can chopped tomatoes, undrained
- 6 ounces sliced ripe olives
- 1 tablespoon basil
- 1 teaspoon oregano
- 1/2 teaspoon rosemary
- 1/2 teaspoon ground fennel
- 1/2 teaspoon salt
- 1/4 teaspoon freshly ground black pepper
- 1/2 cup freshly grated Parmesan cheese
- 3/4 pound vermicelli

Cook shrimp in salted or seasoned water. Peel and set aside.

In large skillet melt margarine over medium heat. Add olive oil and heat. Sauté onion and garlic until tender. Add tomatoes, olives, basil, oregano, rosemary, fennel, salt and pepper. Simmer 10 to 15 minutes.

Meanwhile, cook pasta according to package directions.

Add shrimp to sauce mixture. Add 1/4 cup Parmesan and cook until melted. Pour over pasta. Sprinkle with 1/4 cup Parmesan. Serves 6 to 8.

Pasta with Clam-Vegetable Sauce

- 1 1/2 cups cooked clams, chopped and drained, with 1/2 cup liquor reserved
- 1/4 cup margarine or butter
- 1/2 pound sliced fresh mushrooms
- 1/3 cup chopped green pepper
- 1/3 cup chopped onion
- 6 teaspoons minced garlic
- 2 cups freshly grated mozzarella cheese
- 1/2 teaspoon salt
- 1/4 teaspoon freshly ground black pepper
- 1/2 pound fusilli
- 1/4 cup freshly grated Parmesan cheese

In medium skillet, melt margarine over medium heat. Sauté mushrooms, green pepper, onion and garlic until tender. Add clam liquor and 1 cup mozzarella. Cook, stirring constantly until cheese melts. Add clams, salt and pepper. Heat thoroughly.

Cook pasta according to package directions.

Mix sauce with pasta and remaining 1 cup mozzarella. Sprinkle with Parmesan. Serves 4 to 6.

Stir-Fried Noodles with Shrimp

- 3/4 pound medium shrimp, peeled
- 4 ounces thin egg noodles
- 2 tablespoons vegetable oil
- 1 teaspoon minced garlic
- 1 cup Chinese (or green) cabbage, cut in thin strips
- 1/2 cup thinly sliced carrots
- 1 1/4 cups bean sprouts
- 1 cup thinly sliced green onion, including tops
- 2 1/2 tablespoons soy sauce
- 1/4 teaspoon salt
- 1/4 teaspoon freshly ground black pepper

Cook noodles according to package directions. Drain and set aside.

Heat oil in wok or heavy large skillet over medium heat. Add green onion and stir 1 minute. Add shrimp and garlic and stir 2 minutes. Add cabbage and carrots and stir 4 minutes. Add bean sprouts and stir 3 minutes. Add noodles, soy sauce, salt and pepper and stir until noodles are heated. Serves 2 to 3.

Linguine with Shrimp Sauce

- 1 1/2 pounds medium shrimp
- 3/4 pound linguine
- 3 tablespoons olive oil
- 2 teaspoons minced garlic
- 1 cup chicken broth
- 1/2 cup dry white wine
- 3 tablespoons margarine or butter
- 1/4 cup chopped fresh parsley
- 1/4 teaspoon red pepper flakes
- 1/2 teaspoon salt
- 1/4 teaspoon freshly ground black pepper

Cook shrimp in salted or seasoned water. Peel and set aside.

Cook linguine according to package directions. Drain, toss with 2 tablespoons olive oil and set aside. In medium saucepan, heat 1 tablespoon olive oil over medium heat. Lightly sauté garlic. Add broth and bring to boil. Add wine and reheat. Add pasta, shrimp and margarine and reduce heat. Stir in parsley, red pepper, salt and black pepper. Simmer until heated. Serves 6 to 8.

SEAFOOD: A SOUTHERN TRADITION

Early on, Southerners established a tradition of fish and shellfish cookery. No doubt the early settlers took advantage of the indigenous seafood partly due to necessity. Today, however, most of us choose Southern recipes because of the eating pleasure and nutrition they offer.

Southerners can claim a proud heritage of good foods and superior cooking. We remain famous for plantation fare as well as our city hospitality, and are known worldwide for our flair for entertaining and culinary skills.

Southern seafood cooking developed naturally. A diversity of waters — bayous, bays, streams, sounds and the Atlantic Ocean — produced a diversity of foods such as finfish, oysters, blue crabs, shrimp, clams and scallops. Over time, a diversity of cuisines followed.

Centuries ago, early French and Spanish flavors blended. Later the English brought their style. And African-Americans came to infuse the flavors of Africa as well. Legendary Cajun and Creole cooking associated with Louisiana was inspired and enhanced by Native Americans and African-Americans.

The names of Creole and Cajun recipes often come from the native languages, in fact. "Jambalaya," for instance, derives from the French word meaning "ham" and the African word for "rice," connected by the Acadian "a la." "Gumbo," a Cajun soup, comes from the African word for "okra." If it doesn't contain okra, it's not gumbo.

Closer to home, seafood traditions Down East began as Europeans and New Englanders traveled south in the 18th and 19th centuries, establishing places like Fish Towne (now Beaufort), Diamond City, Harker's Island and other Core Banks towns. In the summer and fall, thick schools of mullet, mackerel and bluefish streamed through local waters. By winter, oyster rock and clam and scallop beds put food on the table and money in locals' pockets. Vegetables from the garden and a hot batch of freshly milled cornbread rounded out most meals Down East back then — and still do today.

The recipes in this section reflect a combination of these rich traditions.

In the summer and fall, thick schools of mullet, mackerel and bluefish streamed through local waters. By winter, oyster rock and clam and scallop beds put food on the table and money in locals' pockets. Vegetables from the garden and a hot batch of freshly milled cornbread rounded out most meals Down East back then — and still do today.

For our Creole and Cajun recipes we used moderate amounts of spices. We realize that some people like spicy foods while others prefer milder dishes. Always adjust seasonings to your own tastes.

Carolina Baked Flounder
- 1 3- to 4-pound flounder, dressed (see p. 48 for dressing instructions)
- 4 cups potatoes, sliced crosswise in 1/8-inch slices
- 1 cup sliced onion
- 4 tablespoons margarine or butter, melted
- salt
- freshly ground black pepper
- 3 slices bacon
- 3 tablespoons flour
- 1 cup water

Score by making three diagonal slashes on top of the fish. Place potatoes and onion around fish. Brush fish with melted margarine. Sprinkle fish, potatoes and onion lightly with salt and pepper. Lay bacon over fish. Bake at 400 F for 15 minutes. Lower heat to 350 F. Continue to bake until potatoes are tender and fish flakes easily with a fork, about 30 to 45 minutes. About 15 minutes before fish is done, mix flour and water. Pour around fish. This will thicken. Serves 6 to 8.

Deviled Clams
- 2 cups finely chopped clams
- 1/2 cup clam liquor
- 4 tablespoons margarine or butter
- 2 tablespoons minced onion
- 2 tablespoons minced green pepper
- 2 tablespoons minced celery leaves
- 1/4 cup chopped celery
- 1/8 teaspoon freshly ground black pepper
- 1/2 teaspoon prepared mustard
- 3/4 cup fresh cracker crumbs

Place clams and liquor in medium saucepan and simmer 5 minutes. Melt margarine in small saucepan over medium heat. Add onion, green pepper, celery leaves, celery, pepper and mustard. Cook until vegetables are tender. Add to clam mixture. Stir in crumbs and mix well. Place in individual serving cups or imitation shells. Bake at 350 F for 20 minutes or until crumbs are nicely browned and mixture is bubbly. Serves 6 to 8.

Southern-Fried Oysters
- 1 pint shucked oysters, standard or select
- Bisquick (or similar baking mix)
- oil for deep frying

Drain oysters and pat dry. Roll in baking mix. Deep fry in preheated 375 F oil until golden brown, about 4 or 5 minutes. Drain on paper towels. Serves 4 to 6.

Note: As our long-time newsletter readers know well, we pride ourselves on making most things "from scratch." However, we tried, but couldn't improve on this very Southern recipe!

Fish Chowder
- 1 pound skinless firm fish fillets, cut into 1-inch pieces
- 3 strips bacon
- 1/2 cup chopped onion
- 2 cups hot water
- 1 cup diced potatoes
- 3/4 teaspoon salt
- 1/4 teaspoon freshly ground black pepper
- 2 cups milk
- 2 tablespoons finely chopped fresh parsley

Fry bacon over medium heat until crisp. Remove, crumble and set aside. Put 1 tablespoon bacon drippings in large saucepan, discarding the rest. Add onion and cook over medium heat until slightly brown. Add water, potatoes, salt and pepper; cook until potatoes are partially tender, about 10 minutes. Add fish and cook until potatoes are done and fish can be flaked easily with a fork, about 10 minutes. Add milk and heat. Do not boil. Place in serving bowls. Sprinkle with bacon and parsley. Serves 4 to 6.

Spicy Seafood Gumbo
- 3/4 pound small shrimp, peeled
- 1 pint standard oysters, undrained
- 1/2 pound backfin crabmeat
- 1/2 pound firm skinless fillets, cut into 1-inch pieces
- 1/4 cup vegetable oil
- 1/4 cup flour
- 3/4 cup chopped onion
- 1/2 cup chopped celery
- 2 teaspoons pressed garlic

- 1 14 1/2-ounce can chicken broth
- 1 14 1/2-ounce can diced tomatoes, undrained
- 1 tablespoon Worcestershire sauce
- 3/4 teaspoon Tabasco sauce
- 1 bay leaf
- 2 tablespoons chopped fresh parsley
- 1/4 teaspoon dried thyme
- 1/4 teaspoon dried basil
- 1/4 teaspoon dried oregano
- 1/4 teaspoon freshly ground black pepper
- 1/2 teaspoon salt
- 1 10-ounce package frozen cut okra
- cooked rice (optional)

Remove any shell or cartilage from crabmeat. Heat oil in large pot or Dutch oven over medium heat. Add flour and cook until the mixture, known as "roux," is copper-colored, about 15 to 20 minutes. Add onion, celery and garlic and cook until tender, about 5 minutes. Add broth, tomatoes, Worcestershire, Tabasco, bay leaf, parsley, thyme, basil, oregano, pepper and salt. Bring to boil, reduce heat and simmer 20 minutes. Add okra. Simmer 25 minutes. Add fish, shrimp and oysters. Simmer 5 minutes. Add crabmeat and continue simmering until fish, shrimp and oysters are done, about 5 more minutes. Serve as soup or over rice, if desired. Serves 8 to 10.

Note: If you don't want to make a roux, omit flour. Sauté vegetables lightly in oil, then continue recipe. It will still be a great dish!

Crab Savannah

- 1 pound backfin crabmeat
- 2 cups dry bread crumbs
- 4 tablespoons margarine or butter, melted
- 1 tablespoon Worcestershire sauce
- 1/8 teaspoon Tabasco sauce
- 1/8 teaspoon salt
- 1/8 teaspoon freshly ground black pepper
- 1 1/4 cup light cream
- 1/2 cup dry bread crumbs
- 1 1/2 tablespoons margarine or butter

Remove any shell or cartilage from crabmeat. Mix crab meat with 2 cups bread crumbs. Combine 4 tablespoons of margarine, Worcestershire, Tabasco, salt and pepper in medium bowl. Add crabmeat and mix gently. Add cream and blend well. Turn into lightly greased 1 1/2-quart casserole dish. Combine bread crumbs and 1 1/2 tablespoons margarine. Sprinkle over casserole. Bake at 350 F for 25 to 30 minutes or until bubbly and lightly browned. Serves 6.

Creole Bouillabaisse

- 1 pound skinless snapper fillets
- 1 pound skinless grouper fillets
- 3/4 pound medium shrimp, peeled
- 1 pint standard oysters, undrained
- 1 pound backfin crabmeat
- 2 tablespoons vegetable oil
- 2 tablespoons olive oil
- 1/4 cup flour
- 1 cup chopped onion
- 1/2 cup chopped celery
- 1 teaspoon pressed garlic
- 5 cups water
- 1/4 cup dry white wine
- 1 14 1/2-ounce can diced tomatoes, undrained
- 2 tablespoons chopped fresh parsley
- 1 tablespoon fresh lemon juice
- 1 bay leaf
- 2 teaspoons salt
- 1/4 teaspoon cayenne pepper

Remove any shell or cartilage from crabmeat. Cut fish into serving-size portions. In large pot or Dutch oven, heat vegetable oil and olive oil over medium heat. Blend in flour. Cook, stirring constantly, until light brown. Add onion, celery and garlic and cook until tender. Gradually stir in water. Add wine, tomatoes, parsley, lemon juice, bay leaf, salt and cayenne. Cover and simmer 20 minutes. Add fish and simmer 3 to 5 minutes. Add shrimp, oysters and crabmeat and simmer until shrimp and oysters are done, about 10 minutes. Serves 10 to 12.

Creole Sautéed Mahi-Mahi

- 2 medium mahi-mahi fillets (about 1 1/2 pounds total)
- 2 1/2 tablespoons minced green onion
- 4 tablespoons vegetable oil
- 4 tablespoons margarine or butter

Prepare Creole Seasoning. Cut fillets into serving-size pieces. Sprinkle green onion and Creole Seasoning over them.

Heat oil in large skillet over medium heat. Add margarine and heat. Place fish in pan, seasoning side up, and sauté until golden brown, about 6 minutes, longer if pieces are thick. Turn and repeat on other side. Cook until golden brown and fish flakes easily with a fork, about 6 minutes more. Serve seasoning side up. Serves 6 to 8.

Creole Seasoning:

- 1 teaspoon pressed garlic
- 1/2 teaspoon salt
- 1/4 teaspoon cayenne pepper
- 1/2 teaspoon freshly ground black pepper
- 1/2 teaspoon dried thyme
- 1/2 teaspoon dried oregano
- 1/2 teaspoon dried basil

In small bowl combine garlic, salt, cayenne, pepper, thyme, oregano and basil.

Carolina Fish Stew

- 2 pounds firm fish, cut into 1-inch squares
- 4 slices bacon
- 1 cup chopped onion
- 1 quart boiling water
- 1 14 1/2-ounce can diced tomatoes, undrained
- 2 teaspoons salt
- 1/2 teaspoon dried thyme
- 1/2 teaspoon dried marjoram
- 2 whole dried red pepper pods
- 1 1/2 cups diced potatoes

In large saucepan, cook bacon over medium heat. Remove bacon and set aside. Remove all but 3 tablespoons bacon fat from pan. Add onion and sauté until tender. Add water, tomatoes, salt, thyme, marjoram and pepper. Bring to boil. Add potatoes and cook until about half done, about 15 to 20 minutes. Add fish. Lower heat and cook until fish flakes easily with a fork, about 10 to 15 minutes. Do not allow to boil. Place in soup bowls. Crumble bacon and sprinkle over top just before serving. Serves 8 to 10.

Shrimp and Oyster Jambalaya

- 1 pound small shrimp, peeled
- 1 pint standard oysters
- 1/2 pound Italian sausage, cut into bite-size pieces
- 1 tablespoon margarine or butter
- 1 cup chopped onion
- 1 cup chopped celery
- 1 tablespoon flour
- 1 14 1/2-ounce can diced tomatoes, undrained
- 1 cup uncooked rice
- 1 teaspoon pressed garlic
- 1 14 1/2-ounce can chicken broth
- 1/2 teaspoon crushed red pepper
- 1/2 teaspoon dried thyme
- 1/2 cup chopped green pepper
- 3 tablespoons minced fresh parsley

Melt margarine in large heavy pot over medium heat. Add sausage, onion and celery and cook until sausage is brown and onion and celery are tender. Stir in flour and cook slowly, stirring constantly, until the roux is copper-colored. Add tomatoes. Cover and simmer about 5 minutes. Add rice, garlic, broth, red pepper, thyme, green pepper and parsley. Mix well. Cover and simmer until rice is barely done, about 20 minutes. Return to boil. Stir in oysters and shrimp. Cook until oysters and shrimp are done, about 8 to 10 minutes. Serves 8 to 10.

An easy way to enhance

simply prepared seafood is

to use a sauce, butter or

marinade. Delicious fish can be

made even better by adding a

basic, easy-to-prepare dressing.

Butters and sauces also add

eye appeal, particularly to

steamed or poached fish.

BUTTER, SAUCE UP OR MARINATE YOUR SEAFOOD

An easy way to enhance simply prepared seafood is to use a sauce, butter or marinade. Delicious fish can be made even better by adding a basic, easy-to-prepare dressing. Butters and sauces also add eye appeal, particularly to steamed or poached fish. Remember that you want to bring out natural flavors, not disguise them. Avoid heavy sauces that cover up the true taste of the seafood.

Often we think only of tartar or cocktail sauce or a rich sauce such as Hollandaise for seafood. We did not include these here, since most of you already have favorite recipes for them. Instead, we recommend some quick, easy-to-prepare and flavorful sauces.

Sauces should complement the type of fish served. Delicate flavors such as flounder and snapper need butter or cream sauces that will not overpower the fish. Oilier, more flavorful fish such as mackerel or bluefish can take a stronger lemon, vinegar or tomato-based sauce. Cold fish are best complemented by mayonnaise-based sauces. Fried fish also are often served with a mayonnaise-based sauce such as tartar sauce. And herb butters or sauces bring out the flavor of poached or steamed fish.

Creating a sauce can be as simple as adding margarine or herbs to natural cooking juices. Use your imagination. Make a simple butter sauce and add slivered, toasted almonds for amandine. Or add fresh lemon juice or curry.

Flavored mayonnaise can be easily prepared, too. Just add ingredients such as fresh dill, garlic and Dijon mustard to your favorite mayonnaise. Or for a curry mayonnaise, add fresh lemon juice, curry powder, Dijon mustard, fresh garlic and freshly ground black pepper.

Homemade mayonnaise made with raw eggs should not be used because of the risk of salmonella poisoning. If you make your own mayonnaise, use the American Egg Board's cooked mayonnaise recipe included here.

Butters sometimes classify as sauces since they melt on the food. In these recipes, we use the term "butter" loosely, since margarine can also be used. (Note the butter/margarine discussion in Chapter 5, p. 68.) The flavor of butter definitely enhances seafood more than margarine or other fats.

Like our sauces, herb butters are easy to make. Simply chop your favorite herbs and add to softened butter or margarine, along with fresh garlic or lemon juice. It's a good idea to let prepared butters stand in the refrigerator for several hours or overnight so that flavors can blend. But if you don't have time for this, they are still tasty.

Allow refrigerated butter blends to soften before spreading on the fish. You can also roll the butter into a log, wrap tightly and refrigerate. Then slice it to use on hot fish or place it on the fish while cooking or grilling.

Most of these butters will add just a few calories and little fat to your fish. Try them on other foods such as poultry or vegetables, or spread them on warm French bread.

These recipes are basic and easy. You'll notice that most of them call only for melted butter or margarine, salt, pepper and simple cooking methods.

Marinades are flavored liquids that enhance or add flavor to foods. They usually contain an acidic liquid such as citrus juice, vinegar or soy sauce, along with seasonings. Marinades add variety to seafood. Although the distinctive flavors of fish and shellfish are always delicious when prepared simply, occasionally we like to vary them. However, marinades should be used to enhance the true flavor, not to mask or overcome it. Any seafood can be marinated, but fish, shrimp and scallops are the most popular choices.

Marinating times vary with foods. Because seafood is more tender than other meats, it requires less marinating time, usually about 15 to 30 minutes. If left longer, the seafood begins to appear "cooked" from the acidity of the marinade. Not only is the texture changed, but the flavor of the marinade becomes too intense.

Marinating times also differ among seafood selections. For example, fish such as flounder and snapper require less marinating time than firmer fish such as catfish and grouper. Be sure to adapt marinating time to the species.

Always use a nonreactive container for marinating. Choose glass, stainless steel or a plastic bag. Some metals can combine with ingredients to produce a chemical reaction or an undesirable flavor. Unless the pieces are too large or there is too much quantity, plastic bags are quite convenient for marinating seafood. You can turn them over instead of turning the food. And there's no clean-up.

Always marinate seafood in the refrigerator, never at room temperature. Fillets may be marinated skinless or with the skin on. The choice is a personal preference. Pan-dressed fish take longer to marinate than steaks or fillets and may need to be turned more often. When marinating dressed fish, make several diagonal slits on each side.

You may have noticed that many recipes for marinated food suggest grilling as the cooking method. Some contained here, such as *Citrus-Marinated Fillets*, are easily adapted to the grill.

If you use a marinade that does not contain oil, you may want to brush the seafood lightly with oil or melted butter or margarine when grilling or cooking in the oven.

Never reuse marinades. They may contain harmful bacteria — left by the raw fish — that can cause illness. If you are going to baste the food with marinade, reserve some before you place the seafood in the marinade and use the reserve for basting.

Since butters, sauces and marinades usually contain salt, remember to use less, if any, salt on the seafood itself.

For additional ideas for sauces and butters, see the sections on poaching and steaming.

Cooked Mayonnaise*

- 2 egg yolks
- 2 tablespoons vinegar or lemon juice
- 2 tablespoons water
- 1 teaspoon sugar
- 1 teaspoon dry mustard
- 1/2 teaspoon salt
- 1/8 teaspoon pepper
- 1 cup cooking oil

In small saucepan, stir together egg yolks, vinegar, water, sugar, mustard, salt and pepper until thoroughly blended. Cook over very low heat, stirring constantly, until mixture bubbles in 1 or 2 places. Remove from heat. Let stand 4 minutes. Pour into blender. Cover and blend at high speed. While blending, very slowly add oil. Blend until thick and smooth. Occasionally turn off blender and scrape down sides of container with spatula. Cover and chill if not using immediately. Makes about 1 1/4 cups.

Recipe from the American Egg Board

Cold Poached Bluefish with Dill Mayonnaise

- 6 medium skinless bluefish fillets
- 6 cups water
- 1 cup dry white wine
- 2 lemon slices
- 1 large onion, sliced
- 2 carrots, chopped
- 2 stalks celery, including leaves, sliced
- 3 sprigs fresh thyme
- 3 sprigs fresh parsley
- 1 bay leaf
- 1 teaspoon salt
- 1/4 teaspoon whole black peppercorns

Prepare Dill Mayonnaise and refrigerate.

Bring poaching ingredients to boil in large, shallow pan or fish poacher. Partially cover, reduce heat and simmer 15 to 20 minutes. Gently place fillets in poaching liquid. Reduce heat and cook until fish flakes easily when tested with a fork, about 15 minutes. Do not boil. Refrigerate until thoroughly chilled, overnight if possible. Cut into serving-size pieces. Serve with Dill Mayonnaise. Serves 12.

Dill Mayonnaise:
- 3/4 cup mayonnaise
- 3 tablespoons sour cream
- 3 tablespoons finely chopped fresh dill
- 1 1/2 teaspoons Dijon mustard
- 1 clove garlic, pressed

In small bowl, combine mayonnaise, sour cream, dill, mustard and garlic. Chill for several hours or overnight to develop flavors. Serve over cold poached fish.

Note: Our Dill Mayonnaise recipe came from the kitchen of Mary Dudley Price.

Steamed Flounder with Shrimp Sauce
- 8 small flounder fillets
- 2 1/2 tablespoons margarine or butter, melted
- salt
- freshly ground black pepper

Prepare Shrimp Sauce and keep warm.

Bring water to boil in bottom of steamer. Brush fillets with melted margarine. Sprinkle lightly with salt and pepper. Place in top part of steamer. Cover. Steam until fillets flake easily with a fork, about 8 to 10 minutes. Serve with Shrimp Sauce. Serves 8.

Shrimp Sauce:
- 1/2 pound small shrimp, peeled
- 2 tablespoons margarine or butter
- 2 tablespoons flour
- 1/2 teaspoon salt
- 1 cup milk
- 2 tablespoons chopped fresh parsley

Chop shrimp coarsely. Melt margarine in small saucepan over medium heat. Cook shrimp until golden, about 2 to 3 minutes. Blend in flour and salt. Add milk slowly, stirring constantly. Continue to cook and stir until thick. Stir in parsley. Serve over warm fillets.

Sautéed Spanish Mackerel with Provencal Sauce

- 4 medium Spanish mackerel fillets
- salt
- freshly ground black pepper
- 4 tablespoons margarine or butter.

Prepare Provencal Sauce and keep warm.

Cut fillets into halves. Sprinkle lightly with salt and pepper. Melt margarine in large skillet over medium heat. Sauté fillets until golden brown on one side, about 5 minutes. Turn and repeat on other side. Serve with Provencal Sauce. Serves 8.

Provencal Sauce:

- 2 tablespoons margarine or butter
- 1/4 cup chopped green onion, including tops
- 1 clove garlic, pressed
- 1/2 cup dry white wine
- 1 14 1/2-ounce can chopped tomatoes, drained
- 2 tablespoons chopped fresh parsley
- 1/8 teaspoon salt
- 1/8 teaspoon freshly ground black pepper

Melt margarine in small saucepan over medium heat. Add green onion and garlic. Cook until tender, about 2 to 3 minutes. Add wine. Cook, stirring constantly, until liquid is slightly reduced. Add tomatoes, parsley, salt and pepper. Heat. Serve over sautéed fillets. Makes about 2 cups.

Flounder Fillets with Black Butter Sauce

- 6 small, skinless flounder fillets
- 1 egg, beaten
- 1/4 teaspoon salt
- 1/8 teaspoon freshly ground black pepper
- 3/4 cup flour
- oil for frying

Prepare Black Butter Sauce and keep warm.

In medium bowl, combine egg, salt and pepper. Dip fillets in egg mixture, then roll in flour. Heat oil in large skillet over medium heat. Fry fillets until golden brown on one side. Turn and repeat on other side. Drain on paper towels. Serve with Black Butter Sauce. Serves 6.

Black Butter Sauce:
- 1/2 cup margarine or butter
- 2 tablespoons chopped fresh parsley
- 2 tablespoons fresh lemon juice
- 1/8 teaspoon salt
- 1/8 teaspoon freshly ground black pepper

Melt margarine in small saucepan over low heat. Remove from heat and let stand a few minutes. This allows the solids to settle to the bottom. Skim fat from the top and strain the clear yellow liquid into another saucepan. Heat over low heat until dark, golden brown. Add parsley, lemon juice, salt and pepper. Spoon hot sauce over fish.

Baked Grouper with Lemon-Chive Butter
- 4 medium grouper fillets
- 8 tablespoons margarine or butter, melted
- salt
- freshly ground black pepper

Prepare Lemon-Chive Butter and set aside.

Brush fillets with melted margarine. Sprinkle with salt and pepper. Bake at 400 F until fish flakes easily with a fork, about 15 to 20 minutes. Cut into halves. Serve with Lemon-Chive Butter. Serves 8.

Lemon-Chive Butter:
- 1/2 cup margarine or butter, softened
- 2 tablespoons chopped fresh parsley
- 2 tablespoons snipped fresh chives or 1 tablespoon dried
- 1 teaspoon dried tarragon
- 1/16 teaspoon salt
- 1 teaspoon lemon zest
- 1/2 tablespoon fresh lemon juice

In small bowl, blend together margarine, parsley, chives, tarragon and salt. Add lemon zest and juice and blend thoroughly. Spread over warm fish.

Broiled Mahi-Mahi with Green Onion Butter

- 1 medium mahi-mahi fillet
- 2 tablespoons margarine or butter, melted
- salt
- freshly ground white pepper

Prepare Green Onion Butter and set aside. Cut fillet into serving-size pieces.

Brush fillet with melted margarine. Sprinkle with salt and pepper. Broil about 4 inches from heat source until done, about 12 to 15 minutes. Cut into serving-size portions. Serve with Green Onion Butter. Serves 4.

Green Onion Butter:

- 4 tablespoons margarine or butter, softened
- 1/2 tablespoon minced fresh parsley
- 1/2 tablespoon minced fresh tarragon or 1 teaspoon dried
- 1 tablespoon minced green onion

Combine margarine, parsley, tarragon and green onion in small bowl. Spread over warm fish.

Baked Spotted Trout with Parsley Butter

- 3 medium trout fillets
- 1 tablespoon margarine or butter, melted
- salt
- freshly ground black pepper
- paprika

Prepare Parsley Butter and set aside.

Brush fillets with melted margarine. Sprinkle lightly with salt. Sprinkle with pepper and paprika. Bake at 400 F until done, about 12 to 15 minutes. Cut into serving-size pieces. Serve with Parsley Butter. Serves 6.

Parsley Butter:

- 4 tablespoons margarine or butter, softened
- 1 1/2 tablespoons minced fresh parsley

Cream margarine in small bowl. Blend in parsley. Spread over warm fish.

Broiled Flounder with Garlic-Basil Butter

- 6 small flounder fillets
- 1/4 cup margarine or butter, melted
- salt
- freshly ground black pepper

Prepare Garlic-Basil Butter and set aside.

Place fillets on broiler pan. Brush with melted margarine. Sprinkle lightly with salt and pepper. Broil about 4 inches from heat about 10 to 12 minutes or until fish flakes with a fork. Serve with Garlic-Basil Butter. Serves 6.

Garlic-Basil Butter:

- 1/2 cup margarine or butter, softened
- 1 teaspoon pressed garlic
- 1 teaspoon finely chopped fresh basil
- 1 teaspoon fresh lemon juice
- 1/8 teaspoon salt

In small bowl, combine margarine, garlic, basil, lemon juice and salt. Allow to stand at least 1 hour for flavors to develop. Spread over warm fillets.

Poached Flounder with Herb Butter

- 6 small flounder fillets
- 6 cups water
- 2 cups dry white wine
- 1 large onion, sliced
- 2 carrots, sliced
- 4 celery stalks with leaves, sliced
- 3 sprigs fresh parsley
- 3 sprigs fresh thyme
- 1 bay leaf
- 1 teaspoon salt
- 1 teaspoon black peppercorns, crushed

Prepare Herb Butter and set aside. Combine ingredients for poaching liquid in a fish poacher or large, shallow pan. Bring to boil. Partially cover, reduce heat and simmer 20 minutes.

Gently place fish in liquid, submerging it entirely. Cook, uncovered, until fish flakes easily when tested with a fork, about 10 minutes. Gently remove to serving platter. Serve with Herb Butter. Serves 6.

Herb Butter:
- 1/2 cup margarine or butter, softened
- 2 tablespoons minced fresh chives
- 2 tablespoons minced fresh parsley
- 2 teaspoons minced fresh tarragon
- 1/4 teaspoon salt
- 1/4 teaspoon freshly ground white pepper

In small bowl, cream together margarine, chives, parsley, tarragon, salt and pepper. Allow to stand at least 1 hour to develop flavors. Spread over warm fish.

Baked Fish with Herb-Butter Sauce
- 1 large grouper fillet (about 2 pounds)
- 4 tablespoons melted margarine or butter
- salt
- freshly ground white pepper

Brush fillet with melted margarine. Lightly salt and pepper. Bake at 450 F until fish flakes easily with a fork, about 25 minutes. Cut into serving-size pieces. Serve with Herb-Butter Sauce. Serves 6 to 8

While fish is baking, prepare Herb-Butter Sauce.

Herb-Butter Sauce:
- 1/4 cup fish or chicken broth
- 1/4 cup dry white wine
- 1/2 cup thinly sliced green onion, including tops
- 1/4 teaspoon freshly ground white pepper
- 1/4 pound margarine or butter
- 1 1/2 teaspoons chopped fresh tarragon (or 1/2 teaspoon dried)
- 2 teaspoons chopped fresh basil (or 1 teaspoon dried)
- 2 teaspoons chopped fresh parsley
- 1/2 teaspoon salt
- 1 tablespoon fresh lime juice

In small saucepan, combine broth, wine and onion. Bring to a boil, lower and cook until liquid is reduced to about half. Cut butter into cubes and add it slowly to the sauce, beating with a whisk over low heat. Do not allow to boil.

When all butter is added and heated through, remove from heat and stir in tarragon, basil, parsley and salt. Add lime juice and beat again. Serve over baked fish.

Broiled Fillets with Dill Sauce

- 3 medium flounder fillets
- 1 tablespoon margarine or butter
- salt
- freshly ground black pepper

Prepare Dill Sauce and refrigerate.

Brush fillets with margarine. Lightly salt and pepper. Broil about 4 inches from heat until fish flakes easily with a fork, about 10 minutes. Cut fillets into halves. Pour Dill Sauce over fillets. Serves 6.

Dill Sauce:

- 1/2 cup sour cream
- 1/4 cup mayonnaise
- 1 1/2 tablespoons minced, fresh dill
- 1/4 teaspoon pressed garlic
- 1/2 teaspoon fresh lemon juice
- 1/8 teaspoon salt
- 1/8 teaspoon freshly ground white pepper

In small bowl, combine sour cream, mayonnaise, dill, garlic, lemon juice, salt and pepper. Refrigerate at least 1 hour. Spread over hot fish.

Basil-Parmesan Marinated Flounder

- 4 medium flounder fillets
- 1/3 cup chopped fresh basil
- 2 tablespoons vegetable oil
- 2 tablespoons white wine vinegar
- 8 tablespoons freshly grated Parmesan cheese
- 1/4 teaspoon pressed garlic
- 1/8 teaspoon freshly ground black pepper
- 1/8 teaspoon salt

In small, nonreactive bowl, combine basil, oil, vinegar, 6 tablespoons Parmesan, garlic, pepper and salt. Place fillets in baking dish and pour marinade over them. Marinate in refrigerator for 20 minutes, turning once.

Spoon excess marinade from dish. Sprinkle 2 tablespoons Parmesan over fillets. Bake at 400 F until fish flakes easily with a fork, about 12 to 15 minutes. Cut into halves. Serves 8.

Citrus-Marinated Fillets

- 4 medium snapper fillets
- 1/2 cup fresh orange juice
- 1/4 cup fresh lemon juice
- 1/4 cup fresh lime juice
- 2 tablespoons vegetable oil
- 4 teaspoons fresh rosemary, crushed
- 1/4 teaspoon salt
- 1/8 teaspoon freshly ground white pepper

Combine orange juice, lemon juice, lime juice, oil, rosemary, salt and pepper in small nonreactive bowl. Place fish in baking dish and pour marinade over. Marinate in refrigerator 20 minutes, turning once.

Remove fish from marinade and place on lightly greased broiler pan. Broil about 4 inches from heat source for 10 to 12 minutes, or until fish flakes easily when tested with a fork. Cut into halves. Serves 8.

Italian-Marinated Catfish

- 4 large catfish fillets
- 2 tablespoons extra virgin olive oil
- 1/4 cup white wine vinegar
- 1/2 teaspoon salt
- 1/4 cup chopped fresh parsley
- 1/2 teaspoon chopped fresh oregano
- self-rising yellow cornmeal
- vegetable oil for frying

Mix olive oil, vinegar, salt, parsley and oregano in small, nonreactive bowl. Place fillets in baking dish and pour marinade over them. Marinate in refrigerator for 30 minutes, turning once. Remove fish from marinade.

Dredge fillets in cornmeal. Fry in hot vegetable oil until golden brown on one side, about 4 to 5 minutes. Turn and repeat on other side. Drain on paper towels. Cut into serving-size pieces. Serves 8.

Orange-Marinated Snapper
- 4 medium snapper fillets
- 1/4 cup fresh orange juice
- 3 tablespoons fresh lemon juice
- 1 teaspoon salt
- 1/2 teaspoon freshly ground black pepper
- 3/4 cup dry white wine
- 3/4 teaspoon pressed garlic
- 1/4 cup melted margarine or butter

Cut fillets in half.

In small, nonreactive bowl, combine orange juice, lemon juice, salt, pepper, wine and garlic. Place fillets in baking dish and pour marinade over them. Marinate in refrigerator for 20 minutes, turning once. Remove excess marinade.

Brush fish with melted margarine. Bake at 400 F for 10 to 12 minutes, or until fish flakes easily when tested with a fork. Cut into halves. Serves 8.

Marinated Grilled Shrimp
- 1 pound large shrimp, peeled
- 1/4 cup pineapple juice
- 1/2 teaspoon fresh lemon juice
- 1 1/2 teaspoon soy sauce
- 1/4 teaspoon pressed garlic
- 1/8 teaspoon freshly ground black pepper

In medium, nonreactive bowl, combine pineapple juice, lemon juice, soy sauce, garlic and pepper. Reserve 2 tablespoons marinade. Add shrimp. Marinate in refrigerator for 20 minutes, stirring occasionally. Remove from marinade.

Thread shrimp on skewers. Grill or broil about 4 inches from heat until golden on one side, about 4 to 5 minutes. Brush with remaining marinade. Turn and repeat on other side. Serves 3 to 4.

TURNING FLAKED FISH INTO SALADS, PIZZA AND OTHER GOOD THINGS

One of the Nutrition Leaders' first tasks back in the early 1970s was to create healthy, tasty and low-cost dishes with fresh fish flakes. Back then, that meant using mostly canned tuna and salmon.

Today homemade flaked fish using fresh fillets or shellfish provides a versatile alternative to the popular canned fish we buy. Delicious appetizers, salads, sandwiches, fish cakes and casseroles can be easily prepared with fresh fish flakes. And they can be used in any recipe that calls for canned fish.

Using flaked fish helps vary the use of fish in your menu. Rather than cooking and serving individual pieces of fish, occasionally flaking the fish and combining it with other favorite ingredients can make a great new recipe. And fish flakes provide additional ways to enjoy the nutritious benefits of seafood, too. They are high in protein, but low in calories, cholesterol and sodium.

For flaking, fish is usually poached or steamed. Then the meat is flaked away from the bone with a fork. Leftover fish from an earlier meal can also be used to make flaked fish. It can be the primary ingredient in dishes such as salads or added as an extender in preparations such as deviled crab.

In this section, we actually substituted flaked fish for other seafood in some of our previous recipes. The results were quite satisfactory. For example, in the *Deviled Crab with Fish* recipe we substituted flaked fish for half the crabmeat, extending the crab. In taste tests, few participants noticed the difference and many preferred the extended dish because of the milder flavor.

Basically, a 1-pound, dressed fish yields about 1 3/4 cups of flakes. To avoid the problem of removing small bones, use fish that weigh at least 1 1/2 to 2 pounds.

Flaked fish can be frozen for up to three months. Just measure the amount you will need for recipes and freeze in airtight pouches. Enhance the flavor and improve the quality by adding a small amount of the cooking broth (about 1/2 cup per 1 1/2 cups flakes) to each package. If you have a surplus of fish from a vacation trip, try flaking some of them. Then package and freeze them for later use. You can thaw what you need and prepare a favorite recipe. It's as easy as opening a can of fish. Plus you have the pleasure of using your catch long after the vacation has ended.

It is most economical to use less expensive species for flaking. But if you want to create a dish such as an elegant salad, use a more expensive species. Grouper, for example, costs more, but overall costs still will be less than serving whole fish or fillets.

Any fish can be flaked, but moderately flavored ones, such as porgies, flounder and spotted sea trout are usually preferred. Fish with milder flavors are more versatile than fish such as mullet with more pronounced flavors. However, we have had great success using 1 1/2- to 2- pound bluefish that are moderately flavored. Flakes from a fresh bluefish work well in fish cakes and as an extender in dishes such as deviled crab. Don't use the large bluefish, though. They taste too oily.

You can flake fresh or frozen fish. Dressed whole fish, with the heads left on, give maximum flavor and yield. But you can also use fillets and steaks.

If you decide to poach or steam fish for flaking, you can make a nice court bouillon or simply use lightly seasoned water. We like the following method, which makes delicately flavored fish flakes and broth. A combination of poaching and steaming works well for large fish that cannot be submerged in water.

Use scaled, eviscerated and degilled fish. Leave heads on, but be sure the body cavity and head are free of membranes and blood.

Melt 1/4 cup of margarine or butter in an electric skillet or pan on top of stove. Lightly sauté a bed of cut onions, celery and carrots, adding garlic powder, freshly ground black pepper and a bay leaf.

Place fish on vegetable bed. Add water to half submerge the fish. Cover and bring to a simmer. Cook with just enough heat to produce steam, on simmer or lower. Do not boil. Cook until fish flakes easily with a fork. Cooking time will be determined by the size of the fish.

Remove fish and let cool enough to handle. Remove and discard skin, dark meat and rib portion. Gently flake meat from the backbone with a fork.

You can use the broth as it is. Or to make a richer broth, return backbone and head to skillet, cover and continue to cook until liquid is reduced by half.

You can place the cooked vegetables in a food processor or use a potato masher to squeeze them if you want to add them as a purée to the broth. Or you can serve the delicious vegetables just as they are.

Cool broth in refrigerator until it congeals. Remove solid fat layer from the top. Strain broth before using. You can use the broth in the same way you use chicken or beef broth. (And no, it won't taste "fishy" if you've used fresh fish.)

Over the years we have served our *Fish Flake and Macaroni Salad* to hundreds of workshop participants and received rave reviews. And many kids have tasted our *Seafood Pizza* and decided that they like seafood after all.

Deviled Crab with Fish
- 1/2 pound fish flakes
- 1/2 pound special or claw crabmeat (see section on crabs, p. 191.)
- 2 tablespoons chopped onion
- 2 tablespoons margarine or butter
- 2 tablespoons flour
- 3/4 cup milk
- 1/4 teaspoon salt
- 1/8 teaspoon freshly ground black pepper
- 1/2 teaspoon dry mustard
- 1 teaspoon Worcestershire sauce
- 1/2 teaspoon sage
- 1/16 teaspoon cayenne pepper
- 1 tablespoon fresh lemon juice
- 1/4 teaspoon Tabasco sauce
- 1 egg, beaten
- 1 tablespoon chopped fresh parsley
- 1 tablespoon margarine or butter, melted
- 1/4 cup dry bread crumbs

Remove any shell or cartilage from crabmeat. In medium pan, cook onion in margarine until tender. Blend in flour. Add milk gradually and cook until thick, stirring constantly. Add salt, black pepper, mustard, Worcestershire, sage, cayenne, lemon juice and Tabasco. Stir a little of this sauce into the egg and mix well. Slowly add egg mix back to sauce, stirring constantly.

Gently stir in parsley, crabmeat and fish flakes. Place in greased, individual crab shells or baking dishes. Combine margarine and crumbs; sprinkle over tops. Bake in moderate oven at 350 F for 15 to 20 minutes or until brown and bubbly. Serves 6 to 8.

Fish Flake and Macaroni Salad

- 1 1/2 cups fish flakes
- 4 ounces small shell macaroni
- 1/2 cup chopped celery
- 1/3 cup chopped onion
- 2 tablespoons chopped green pepper
- 1/2 cup mayonnaise (or to desired consistency)
- 1/2 teaspoon salt
- 1/2 teaspoon celery seed
- 1/4 teaspoon freshly ground black pepper
- 1 small jar chopped pimento, drained
- 1 8-ounce can sweet peas, drained
- paprika
- lettuce leaves
- Garnish: tomato wedges

Cook macaroni according to package directions. Drain. Rinse with cold water. Drain while cutting up celery, onion and pepper.

Place mayonnaise in medium bowl. Add salt, celery seed, black pepper and mix well. Add celery, onion, green pepper and pimento and mix. Add macaroni and mix well.

Gently blend in fish flakes and peas. Chill well before serving. Arrange on lettuce leaves. Sprinkle with paprika. Garnish with tomato wedges. Serves 8 to 10. (Excellent when made one day and served the next.)

Fish and Shrimp Casserole

- 1 cup flaked fish
- 1/2 pound cooked small shrimp
- 1/4 cup margarine or butter
- 1/4 cup flour
- 2 cups milk
- 1 teaspoon salt
- 2/3 cup sliced fresh mushrooms
- 3/4 teaspoon finely chopped green pepper
- 1/4 cup chopped green onion, including tops
- 1/4 cup chopped black olives
- 3/4 teaspoon chopped pimento
- 1 teaspoon Worcestershire sauce
- 2 cups freshly grated mild cheddar cheese

Melt margarine in medium saucepan over medium heat. Blend in flour. Stirring constantly, add milk gradually and continue until sauce is smooth and thick. Add salt, mushrooms, green pepper, onion, olives, pimento and Worcestershire. Mix well. Gently stir in flaked fish, shrimp and 1/3 cup of cheese. Continue cooking over low heat until cheese is melted.

Place in greased, medium shallow casserole. Sprinkle top with remaining cheese. Bake at 350 F for 20 to 25 minutes, or until bubbly and cheese is melted. Serves 4 to 6.

Seafood and Vegetable Casserole

- 1 cup flaked fish
- 1/2 pound small shrimp, peeled and deveined
- 2 tablespoons margarine or butter
- 1/4 cup finely chopped green pepper
- 1/2 cup finely chopped onion
- 1/2 cup finely chopped celery
- 1/2 teaspoon salt
- 1/8 teaspoon freshly ground black pepper
- 1/2 teaspoon Worcestershire sauce
- 1/4 cup mayonnaise
- 1/4 cup sour cream
- 2 tablespoons dry sherry
- 1/2 cup fresh bread crumbs
- 2 tablespoons margarine or butter, melted

Melt 2 tablespoons margarine in medium saucepan over medium heat. Sauté green pepper, onion and celery until tender. Add salt, black pepper, Worcestershire, mayonnaise, sour cream and sherry. Mix well. Gently stir in fish and shrimp.

Place in greased individual shells, ramekins or medium casserole dish. Mix crumbs with 2 tablespoons melted margarine. Sprinkle over top. Bake at 350 F for 25 to 30 minutes, or until bubbly and lightly browned. Serves 4 to 6.

Fancy Fish Spread

- 2 cups flaked fish
- 8 ounces cream cheese, softened
- 2 tablespoons grated onion
- 1/2 teaspoon minced garlic
- 1 tablespoon milk
- 1/2 teaspoon salt
- 1/4 teaspoon freshly ground white pepper
- 1 teaspoon prepared horseradish
- 1 tablespoon fresh lemon juice
- paprika
- assorted crackers

Place softened cream cheese in medium bowl. Add onion, garlic, milk, salt, pepper, horseradish and lemon juice. Blend well. Gently stir in fish. Place in 8-inch pie pan. Sprinkle with paprika.

Bake at 350 F for 15 minutes or until bubbly. Serve with assorted crackers.

Choice Fish Cakes

- 2 cups flaked fish
- 4 tablespoons margarine or butter
- 1/2 cup chopped onion
- 1/2 cup chopped celery
- 2 tablespoons chopped fresh parsley
- 1 cup soft bread crumbs
- 1 egg, beaten
- 1 teaspoon salt
- 1/2 teaspoon freshly ground black pepper
- 1/4 teaspoon ground ginger
- 1/4 cup milk
- cracker crumbs
- vegetable oil for frying

Melt margarine in medium saucepan over medium heat. Sauté onion and celery until tender. Remove from heat. Add parsley, bread crumbs, egg, salt, pepper and ginger. Blend well. Stir in milk. Gently fold in flaked fish. Form into 6 or 8 cakes and roll lightly in cracker crumbs.

Fry in hot oil, 375 F, until brown on one side, about 5 minutes. Turn and repeat on other side. Drain on paper towels. Serves 6 to 8.

Note: There is another recipe for fish cakes in our sandwich section, p. 141.

Seafood Pizza
- 1 cup flaked fish
- 1/2 cup chopped shrimp (or crabmeat or clams)
- 2 tablespoons olive oil
- 3/4 cup finely chopped onion
- 3 cups canned, chopped tomatoes, undrained,
- 1 6-ounce can tomato paste
- 1/4 teaspoon garlic powder
- 3/4 tablespoon oregano
- 3/4 teaspoon basil
- 1 small bay leaf
- 1 tablespoon sugar
- 1/2 teaspoon salt
- 1/4 teaspoon freshly ground black pepper
- 1 cup freshly grated mozzarella cheese
- 2 large unbaked pizza crusts

Heat oil in large saucepan over medium heat. Lightly sauté onion. Stir in tomatoes, tomato paste, garlic powder, oregano, basil, bay leaf, sugar, salt and pepper. Simmer 20 minutes. Add shrimp. Continue to simmer 10 minutes longer. Gently stir in flaked fish.

Spread on pizza crusts. Top with cheese. Bake at 450 F until crust is brown and cheese is melted and lightly browned, about 20 to 25 minutes. *(Hint: If you only need one pizza, freeze sauce for later use. Freezes well.)*

DRESSED-UP FISH — SEAFOOD STUFFINGS

How can you add more flavor to an already delicious, fresh fish? Dress it up, of course. Seafood stuffings, or dressings, add variety to fish preparations and can also serve as an additional main food in the meal.

Stuffings can range from simple to elaborate. They can be as easy as a basic bread or vegetable stuffing or as fancy as those with shellfish or other meat. Most stuffings contain celery, onion and spices as the basic ingredients. But add, omit or vary ingredients to suit personal tastes. Just be sure that other flavors do not overwhelm the fish.

Stuffed fish recipes sometimes call for sauces. Although they provide additional variety, they often can be omitted.

To stuff whole fish, use either small fish or those weighing up to six pounds. Either remove the head and tail, or leave them on. If you leave the head on, be sure the fish's gills have been removed. Gently place the stuffing inside the fish cavity. Fasten with toothpicks or sew with heavy thread. After the fish is baked, remove the top skin.

Most recipes for stuffed fish call for whole fish. We tried a number of these. Although they were delicious, we always heard the same complaints. Cutting through the backbone is difficult, especially if the fish is large, and the servings usually look unappealing. Bones in most stuffed fish create an even bigger nuisance.

Because of these problems, we used only skinless, boneless fillets in these recipes. You can still use the stuffing recipes in whole fish if you prefer.

Rolled fillets can be fastened with toothpicks before cooking. Or you can roll them and place them in lightly greased muffin tins. Our *Vegetable-Stuffed Flounder Fillets* look almost too pretty to eat.

If you place stuffing between two fillets, you may want to leave the skin on the top fillet. This holds in moisture. Just remove the skin before serving the fish.

Always prepare stuffings just before cooking. Never stuff fish ahead of time, even if you're going to refrigerate it. And handle stuffings lightly. Place them loosely in the fish rather than packing them. Packing will cause them to be heavy and doughy.

About one-half cup of stuffing per pound of fish is needed. If extra stuffing remains, place it in a lightly greased baking dish and cook it along with the fish. Or freeze it separately from any leftover fish.

As always, remember that you can substitute species. If a recipe calls for flounder and only snapper is available, don't be afraid to switch. Just exchange similar species — white fish for white fish or lean for lean. Our *Baked Grouper with Orange-Rice Stuffing* specifies grouper, but snapper, flounder or other white fish tastes just as delicious.

Most stuffings contain celery, onion and spices as the basic ingredients. But add, omit or vary ingredients to suit personal tastes. Just be sure that other flavors do not overwhelm the fish.

Red Snapper with Bacon-Mushroom Stuffing

- 6 medium skinless snapper fillets
- 1/2 pound small shrimp, coarsely chopped
- 6 slices bacon, diced
- 1/2 cup sliced fresh mushrooms
- 2 cups soft bread cubes
- 1 tablespoon minced onion
- 2 tablespoons fresh lemon juice
- 1 tablespoon chopped fresh parsley
- 1 teaspoon sage
- 1/2 teaspoon salt
- 1/4 teaspoon freshly ground black pepper
- 1 egg, beaten
- 3 tablespoons margarine or butter, melted

In large skillet, cook bacon over medium heat until crisp, then remove from skillet. Sauté mushrooms in bacon drippings until lightly browned. Remove from heat. Add shrimp, bacon, bread cubes, onion, juice, parsley, sage, salt, pepper and egg. Mix well.

Place 3 fillets in lightly greased baking pan, flesh side up. Spread with stuffing. Place other fillets on top, flesh side down. Brush with melted margarine. Salt lightly. Bake at 450 F until fish flakes easily with a fork, about 20 to 30 minutes. Sprinkle with paprika about 5 minutes before cooking time is up. Cut into halves. Serves 12.

Vegetable-Stuffed Flounder Fillets

- 8 small, skinless flounder fillets
- 3/4 cup finely chopped green onion, including tops
- 1/4 cup finely chopped fresh parsley
- 1/4 cup finely chopped fresh dill
- 2 tablespoons margarine or butter, melted
- 2 eggs, beaten
- 1/2 cup dry bread crumbs
- 1/2 teaspoon salt
- 1/4 teaspoon freshly ground black pepper
- vegetable oil for frying

Combine green onion, parsley and dill in small bowl. Brush flesh side of fillets with melted margarine. Spread vegetable mixture evenly over fillets. Roll up and fasten with toothpicks. Mix crumbs, salt and pepper in a small bowl.

Dip rolled fillets in eggs, then in crumbs. Fry in hot oil, 375 F, until golden brown on both sides and cooked through. Drain on paper towels. Serves 8.

Flounder Fillets with Crab Stuffing

- 6 medium, skinless flounder fillets
- 6 tablespoons margarine or butter, melted
- 3 tablespoons fresh lemon juice
- 1/2 teaspoon salt
- paprika

Prepare Crab Stuffing and set aside.

Lightly grease baking dish or pan large enough to hold 3 fillets. Combine margarine, lemon juice and salt. Spread 3 tablespoons of margarine mix on bottom of baking dish. Place 3 fillets in dish, flesh side up. Place equal amounts of stuffing on each fillet. Place remaining 3 fillets on top of stuffed fillets, flesh side down. Brush remaining margarine mix on fillets and sprinkle lightly with salt. Bake at 400 F for 35 to 45 minutes, or until fish flakes easily when tested with a fork and stuffing is hot. Sprinkle with paprika about 10 minutes before end of cooking time. Cut into halves. Serves 12.

Crab Stuffing:

- 1/2 pound crabmeat
- 6 tablespoons margarine or butter
- 1/2 cup chopped onion
- 1/3 cup chopped celery
- 1/4 cup finely chopped green pepper
- 1 teaspoon minced garlic
- 2 cups soft bread cubes
- 3 eggs, beaten
- 1 tablespoon chopped fresh parsley
- 1/2 teaspoon salt
- 1/2 teaspoon freshly ground black pepper

Remove any shell or cartilage from crabmeat. Melt margarine in small saucepan over medium heat. Sauté onion, celery, green pepper and garlic until tender. Remove from heat.

In medium bowl combine bread cubes, eggs, parsley, salt and pepper. Stir in cooked vegetables and crabmeat. Mix thoroughly.

Stuffed Mahi-Mahi with Egg Sauce

- 2 large, skinless mahi-mahi fillets, about 2 pounds
- 2 1/2 cups fresh bread crumbs
- 3/4 cup margarine or butter, melted
- 3/4 teaspoon salt
- 1 1/2 teaspoons sage
- 3/4 cup minced onion
- 1/4 teaspoon freshly ground black pepper
- 2 tablespoons margarine or butter, melted

Trim all dark meat from fillets.

Combine crumbs, 3/4 cup margarine, salt, sage, onion and black pepper in medium bowl. Place one fillet in lightly greased baking pan, flesh side up. Spread with stuffing. Place other fillet on top, flesh side down. Brush with 2 tablespoons melted margarine. Sprinkle lightly with salt.

Bake at 450 F for 10 minutes, reduce heat to 400 F and cook until fish flakes easily when tested with a fork and stuffing is hot, about 30 minutes. Cut into serving-size pieces Serve with Egg Sauce. Serves 6 to 8.

While fish is cooking, prepare egg sauce and keep warm.

Egg Sauce:

- 4 tablespoons margarine or butter
- 4 tablespoons flour
- 2 cups milk
- 1/2 teaspoon salt
- 1/4 teaspoon freshly ground black pepper
- 2 eggs, hard-boiled and chopped

Melt margarine in medium skillet over medium heat. Blend in flour. Add milk gradually, stirring constantly. Cook, stirring, until thick. Add salt and pepper. Cut eggs into small pieces and add to sauce. Spoon over hot fish.

Baked Grouper with Orange-Rice Stuffing

- 2 large, skinless grouper fillets, about 2 pounds total
- 1/2 teaspoon salt
- 2 tablespoons margarine or butter, melted

Prepare Orange-Rice Stuffing and set aside.

Sprinkle 1 fillet with salt. Place in greased baking dish, flesh side up. Place stuffing on top. Place other fillet on top, flesh side down. Brush with melted margarine and sprinkle with salt. Bake at 400 F until fish flakes easily when tested with a fork and stuffing is hot, about 30 to 40 minutes. Cut into serving-size pieces. Serves 6 to 8.

Orange-Rice Stuffing:

- 2 tablespoons margarine or butter
- 1/2 cup chopped celery, including leaves
- 2 tablespoons finely chopped green onion
- 1/2 cup fresh orange juice
- 1 tablespoon fresh lemon juice
- 1 1/2 teaspoons orange zest
- 1/4 teaspoon salt
- 1 cup cooked rice
- 1/3 cup almond slivers, toasted

In medium saucepan, melt margarine over medium heat. Sauté celery and onion until tender. Add juices, zest and salt. Bring to boil. Add rice and stir well. Cover and remove from heat. Allow to stand for 5 minutes, then add almonds.

Red Snapper Fillets with Shrimp Stuffing

- 6 medium, skinless snapper fillets
- 1/2 pound small shrimp, peeled
- 1/4 cup margarine or butter
- 1/4 cup finely chopped onion
- 1/4 cup chopped celery
- 1 egg, beaten
- 2 tablespoons milk
- 2 cups soft bread cubes
- 1/2 teaspoon nutmeg
- 1/2 teaspoon salt
- 1/4 teaspoon freshly ground black pepper

Chop shrimp coarsely. In small skillet, melt margarine over medium heat. Sauté onion and celery until soft. Add shrimp and cook until done, about 3 minutes. Remove from heat.

In medium bowl combine egg, milk, bread cubes, nutmeg, salt and pepper. Add shrimp mixture and mix well.

Place 3 fillets in greased baking dish, flesh side up. Spread stuffing mixture on top. Place remaining fillets on top, flesh side down. Bake at 450 F until fish flakes easily with a fork and stuffing is cooked, about 25 to 30 minutes. Cut into halves. Serves 12.

Flounder Fillets with Parmesan Stuffing
- 6 small, skinless flounder fillets
- salt
- freshly ground black pepper
- 2 tablespoons margarine or butter, melted

Prepare Parmesan Stuffing and set aside.

Sprinkle fillets with salt and pepper. Roll up, lapping small end over larger, leaving space in the middle for stuffing.

Place rolled fillets in greased muffin tin. Spoon Parmesan stuffing into center of each. Baste tops with melted margarine and bake at 450 F until stuffing is lightly browned and fish flakes easily with a fork, about 20 minutes. Serves 6.

Parmesan Stuffing:
- 2 tablespoons margarine or butter
- 1/2 cup chopped onion
- 1/2 cup chopped celery
- 1 1/2 cups fresh bread crumbs
- 1/2 cup freshly grated Parmesan cheese
- 1/4 teaspoon salt
- 1/4 teaspoon freshly ground black pepper
- 3/4 teaspoon chopped fresh basil

Melt margarine in medium skillet over medium heat. Sauté onion and celery until soft. Remove from heat. Combine with crumbs, Parmesan, salt, pepper and basil.

SEAFOOD IN PARCHMENT — POCKETS OF FLAVOR

Food cooked and served in parchment makes an elegant specialty item on many fine restaurants' menus. But you don't have to be a gourmet cook to use this method. It's really quite simple. Just seal the food in parchment packages, place it in the oven, and soon you'll have a great meal.

While the French get credit for introducing the technique of cooking in parchment, or *en papillote*, the theory originated much earlier. Long before pots and pans were invented, people wrapped meat in leaves to protect it from the fire. Today we use other wrappers, such as crepe wraps or won tons, to do the same thing.

Steam fills and inflates the packages as they cook. The flavors mingle and the natural juices are held in. Each packet is an individual serving. Because parchment is cooked in the oven, directions for it will say "bake." But you are really steaming the food.

Cooking in parchment creates a dramatic and easy way to serve a crowd. Packets can be prepared ahead of time and refrigerated. They can go from the refrigerator to the oven. The cooked packets can easily be placed on each person's plate. Then everyone can cut or tear one open.

As the packages open, steam billows out, along with the delightful aromas of the seafood. Your family and friends will enjoy this unusual presentation as well as the delicious food.

Aluminum foil can be used the same way as parchment, but it doesn't create the same visual effect.

Using parchment is a good way to interest children in cooking seafood. And it's also a helpful way to get them to try new foods. They're fascinated by this different way of eating.

At one time, people used brown paper bags for cooking. And children have sometimes been taught how to cook an individual meal in a lunch bag. But since we can't be sure of the composition of such materials, we don't recommend cooking in them. Parchment, on the other hand, is designed for cooking. It comes in rolls or sheets and can be found at cooking supply stores and some supermarkets.

Some cookbooks tell you to precook food, then reheat it about five minutes *en papillote*. But this is an unnecessary step for most preparations. The seafood recipes we prepared were cooked entirely in the parchment. They were attractive, moist and delicious.

Try using skinless fillets in your parchment cooking. They hold together well, and you don't have to worry that they'll break apart when you serve them.

Using parchment is a good way to interest children in cooking seafood. And it's also a helpful way to get them to try new foods. They're fascinated by this different way of eating.

Always feel free to substitute species. Our recipe, *Fillets with Herb Butter in Parchment* calls simply for fillets. A variety of fish will work in this recipe. As always, use the freshest fish you can find. And you can easily adapt favorite seafood recipes to parchment cooking. Don't be afraid to try.

Parchment can be cut into rectangular or oval shapes. But the classic pattern is a heart shape.

Cut a piece of parchment 12 x 18 inches or slightly more than twice as wide as the fillet to be cooked. (The extra allows room for sealing.) Fold in half (12 x 9 inches). Starting at the fold, draw half a heart shape and cut it. Unfold.

Lightly oil all but a 2-inch border of the parchment. Center food on one side of the heart, near the fold. Leave a 2-inch border at the edge.

Fold the paper over the food so the cut edges meet. Starting at one end, fold a small section of parchment together, then fold again. Hold this section down and fold the next section. Continue until edges are completely sealed.

Place on a baking sheet and place in a preheated oven. Cook for the designated time.

The pouch will puff up with steam and brown during cooking.

Although it is difficult, you may want to check for doneness the first time or two that you cook in parchment. Just open one package to check. You can't reseal it well enough for steam to rebuild, but it will continue to cook if you return it to the oven. Don't be afraid to try cooking *en papillote*. It's easy and fun. And you'll have some delicious seafood!

Flounder with Fresh Mushrooms in Parchment

- 1 1/2 pounds flounder fillets
- vegetable oil
- 6 tablespoons margarine or butter
- 2 cups sliced fresh mushrooms
- 1 tablespoon finely chopped green onion, including tops
- 1/4 cup dry vermouth
- 1 1/2 teaspoons finely chopped fresh parsley
- salt
- freshly ground white pepper

Cut fillets into serving sizes. Prepare 4 or 6 pieces of parchment. Lightly oil each piece.

In medium skillet, melt margarine over medium heat. Lightly sauté mushrooms and green onion. Add vermouth and simmer until liquid is almost gone. Add parsley.

Place fish on parchment and sprinkle lightly with salt and pepper. Place equal amount of mushroom mixture over each. Close parchment. Place on baking sheet. Bake at 400 F until puffed and lightly browned, about 12 to 15 minutes. Place on serving plates. Serves 4 to 6.

Parmesan Snapper in Parchment

- 3 medium snapper fillets
- 1/2 cup vegetable oil
- 1/2 teaspoon salt
- 1/2 teaspoon pressed garlic
- vegetable oil for parchment
- 1 cup freshly grated Parmesan cheese
- 1 cup toasted fresh bread crumbs

In long glass baking dish, combine oil, salt and garlic. Cut fish into 6 portions. Place in mixture and marinate 10 minutes. Turn and marinate 10 minutes longer.

While fish is marinating, prepare 6 pieces of parchment. Lightly oil each. Place on baking sheet.

Remove fish from marinade. Roll in cheese, then in crumbs. Place each on a piece of parchment. Close parchment. Bake at 400 F until puffy and lightly browned, about 15 minutes. Place on individual plates. Serves 6.

Savory Shrimp in Parchment

- 1 pound medium or large shrimp, peeled and deveined
- vegetable oil for parchment
- 3 tablespoons vegetable oil
- 1 tablespoon finely chopped green onion, including tops
- 1/2 teaspoon pressed garlic
- 1 tablespoon chopped fresh parsley
- 1/4 teaspoon savory
- 1 1/2 teaspoons fresh lemon juice
- 1/2 cup dry bread crumbs
- 3 or 4 tablespoons freshly grated Parmesan cheese
- 3 or 4 tablespoons dry white wine

Prepare 3 or 4 pieces of parchment. Lightly oil each. Place on baking sheet.

In small saucepan, heat 3 tablespoons oil over medium heat. Sauté onion and garlic until tender. Remove from heat and add parsley, savory, lemon juice, crumbs and Parmesan.

Divide shrimp evenly on parchment. Sprinkle with crumb mixture. Pour 1 tablespoon wine over each. Close parchment. Bake at 400 F until shrimp are done, about 10 to 12 minutes. Place on serving plates. Serves 3 to 4.

Fillets with Herb Butter in Parchment

- 6 small fish fillets
- vegetable oil
- 1/2 cup margarine or butter, softened
- 1/2 cup finely chopped green onion, including tops
- 2 tablespoons finely mined fresh parsley
- 1 teaspoon finely minced fresh tarragon (or 1/2 teaspoon dried)
- 1 tablespoon finely minced fresh chervil (or 1 1/2 teaspoons dried)

Prepare 6 pieces of parchment. Lightly oil each.

In small bowl, combine margarine, green onion, parsley, tarragon and chervil. Place a fillet on each piece of parchment and spread evenly with the herbed margarine. Close parchment and place on baking sheet. Bake at 400 F until done, about 12 to 15 minutes. Place on individual plates. Serves 6.

Flounder with Fine Herbs in Parchment

- 4 small flounder fillets
- vegetable oil
- 4 tablespoons margarine or butter
- 2 tablespoons finely chopped onion
- 2 tablespoons finely chopped fresh mushrooms
- 1 teaspoon finely chopped fresh parsley
- 1 teaspoon finely chopped green onion tops
- 1 teaspoon finely chopped celery leaves
- 1 teaspoon finely chopped fresh tarragon
- 1 teaspoon pressed garlic
- 1/2 teaspoon salt
- 1/2 teaspoon freshly ground black pepper
- 1/4 cup dry white wine

Prepare 4 pieces of parchment. Lightly oil each and place on baking sheet.

In small saucepan, melt margarine over medium heat. Lightly sauté onion and mushrooms. Add parsley, green onion, celery, tarragon, garlic, salt and pepper. Stir in wine and mix thoroughly.

Place fillets on parchment. Spread vegetable mixture evenly over fillets. Close parchment. Bake at 400 F until done, about 12 to 15 minutes. Place on individual plates. Serves 4.

Parmesan Flounder in Parchment

- 6 small flounder fillets
- vegetable oil
- 3 tablespoons freshly grated Parmesan cheese
- 1 teaspoon dried basil
- 1/2 teaspoon salt
- 1/2 teaspoon garlic powder
- 1/2 teaspoon freshly ground black pepper
- 3 chopped canned tomatoes
- 3 tablespoons minced green onion, including tops
- 3 tablespoons minced green pepper

Prepare 6 pieces of parchment. Lightly oil each.

Place a fillet on each piece. In a small bowl, combine Parmesan, basil, salt, garlic powder and pepper. Sprinkle evenly over fish. Place equal amounts of tomato, onion and green pepper on top.

Close parchment. Place on baking sheet. Bake at 400 F until puffed and lightly browned, about 12 to 15 minutes. Place on individual plates. Serves 6.

Orange-Nutmeg Flounder in Parchment

- 6 small flounder fillets
- vegetable oil
- 3/4 cup fresh orange juice
- 1 teaspoon orange zest
- 1/4 teaspoon freshly grated nutmeg
- 1/4 teaspoon salt
- 1/4 teaspoon freshly ground white pepper

Prepare 6 pieces of parchment. Lightly oil each.

In small bowl, mix juice, zest, nutmeg, salt and pepper. Lay 1 fillet on each piece of parchment and sprinkle with equal amounts of the orange mixture. Close parchment. Place on baking sheet. Bake at 400 F until puffy and lightly browned, about 12 to 15 minutes. Place on individual plates. Serves 6.

Herbed Shrimp in Parchment

- 2 pounds medium or large shrimp
- vegetable oil
- 2 tablespoons fresh lime juice
- 1 tablespoon olive oil
- 3/4 teaspoon freshly ground black pepper
- 1/2 teaspoon salt
- 1/4 teaspoon dill weed
- 1/4 teaspoon sugar
- 1/2 teaspoon ground cumin
- 1/2 teaspoon basil
- 1 1/2 teaspoons pressed garlic
- 2 teaspoons minced green onion tops

Prepare 6 or 8 pieces of parchment. Lightly oil each with vegetable oil.

Peel shrimp and devein, if desired. Combine juice, olive oil, pepper, salt, dill, sugar, cumin, basil, garlic and green onion in a wide, shallow dish. Lay shrimp flat in mixture, then turn.

Divide shrimp evenly among parchment. Close parchment. Bake at 400 F until puffy and lightly browned, about 10 to 12 minutes. Place on individual plates. Serves 6 to 8.

COOKING
Shellfish

Nutrition Leader Valaree Stanley remembers clambakes and oyster roasts

so plentiful they seemed to never end. Dolena Bell grew up shucking and

roasting shellfish by the sea, too. And each year, Betty Motes throws a huge

family oyster bash in her garage. Here the Nutrition Leaders share the right

CHAPTER EIGHT RECIPES:

- Crab Meat and Mushrooms in Wine Sauce
- She-Crab Soup
- Crab Salad
- Deluxe Crab Cakes
- Deviled Crab
- Crab Newburg
- Crab Imperial
- Deluxe Deviled Crab
- Boiled Hard Crabs
- Steamed Hard Crabs
- Sautéed Soft-Shell Crabs
- Golden-Fried Soft-Shell Crabs
- Broiled Soft-Shell Crabs
- Sautéed Soft Crabs with Fresh Lime
- Stuffed Soft-Shell Crabs
- Grilled Soft-Shell Crabs
- Baked Soft-Shell Crabs
- Pan-Fried Soft Crabs with White Wine Sauce
- Soft-Shell Crabs with Garlic Sauce
- Soft Crabs Amandine
- Savory Baked Shrimp
- Shrimp Newburg
- Individual Shrimp Casseroles
- Shrimp Scampi
- Shrimp Curry
- Shrimp Creole
- Shrimp Salad
- Marinated Charcoal-Grilled Shrimp
- Shrimp au Gratin

- Carolina Shrimp Boil
- Crab-Stuffed Shrimp
- Oyster Stew
- Oysters Rockefeller
- Oysters and Mushrooms au Gratin
- Golden-Brown Fried Oysters
- Broiled Oysters
- Broiled Oysters with Fine Herbs
- Oysters Casino
- Garlic Butter Oysters
- Baked Clams with Garlic Butter
- Broiled Garlic Clams
- Fried Clams
- Baked Stuffed Clams
- Linguine with Clam Sauce
- Steamed Clams in Wine Broth
- Clams Casino
- Hearty Clam Chowder
- Deviled Clams
- Old-Fashioned Clam Chowder
- Down East Clambake
- Swiss Baked Scallops
- Rich Scallop Soup
- Scallops with Green Onion Butter
- Baked Scallops
- Broiled Scallops
- Coquilles St. Jacques
- Scallop Cheese Bake
- Fried Scallops

COOKING

TAKE A CRAB TO LUNCH — OR DINNER

When we talk about food, we're usually not concerned with scientific names. But in the case of the blue crab. Its scientific name, *Callinects sapidus,* means "beautiful swimmer" and appropriately describes this shellfish. It belongs to the family of swimming crabs that usually have the last pair of legs flattened into paddles for swimming.

Blue crabs may be bought live or cooked. Or you can catch your own. But because of the difficulty in picking the meat from the shell, most of us buy crabmeat that is cooked, picked and ready to eat.

Fresh picked crabmeat comes in several forms. The four most common are lump, backfin, special and claw. *Lump*, or *jumbo lump*, is the large white lumps of meat that come from the area of the body adjacent to the back fin appendage. *Backfin* consists of some lumps plus other meat from the body. *Special*, also called *regular* or *flake*, is the white meat without any lumps. Meat from the *claw* is brownish in color and is used in recipes where a white appearance is not important. Many people think that the claw meat has the most flavor.

Picked crabmeat is also available in pasteurized form, which extends its storage life. And you can buy canned crabmeat in the supermarket, but don't expect the same results you get from fresh or pasteurized.

Always be sure that seafood is fresh. If you buy whole crabs, be sure that they are alive. Live crabs show movement of the legs. Cooked crabs look bright red and should have no disagreeable odor. Cooked, picked meat should have good color and no disagreeable odor.

Be especially careful in handling crabmeat. Keep live crabs alive until ready to cook. Discard any that die. When storing cooked crabmeat, place the container in ice and refrigerate it. Pasteurized crabmeat may be kept unopened in the refrigerator for up to six months or a year. Canned crabmeat needs no refrigeration as long as it remains unopened.

Picked crabmeat does not freeze well, primarily due to texture changes. It is best to freeze the whole cooked, cleaned body of the crab, along with the

Blue crabs may be bought live or cooked. Or you can catch your own. But because of the difficulty in picking the meat from the shell, most of us buy crab meat that is cooked, picked and ready to eat.

claws. For maximum quality, use frozen crabs within three months.

Before using picked crabmeat, always examine it for shell fragments and cartilage. Pick up a small amount of meat at a time and feel it carefully. Handle it gently so that you don't break the pieces apart. (Picking instructions, pp. 51-54)

You may sometimes want to serve a dish such as deviled crab or crab imperial in crab shells. Since it's almost impossible to clean them properly at home, we recommend that you buy cleaned or artificial shells in a cooking supply store.

You can often substitute one type of crabmeat for another. For instance, most recipes that call for backfin can be made with special. They taste the same. The only difference is the size of the pieces. You can substitute claw meat if you don't mind the color.

Remember that picked crabmeat you buy has been cooked. When using it in recipes, be sure not to overcook it. You'll usually need to cook the casserole or other dish just long enough to heat it thoroughly. In our recipe for she-crab soup, the crabmeat is heated for a longer time but is not allowed to simmer or boil.

Notice, too, that you can make she-crab soup even if you don't have roe (crab eggs). Just use the yolks of hard-cooked eggs.

If you are going to serve boiled or steamed hard crabs, a coastal favorite, you can dress them before or after cooking. It's a matter of personal preference.

Either way you cook them, it is important for the temperature of the meat to reach 158 F and remain there for at least one minute. Depending upon how many crabs you place in the pot, you'll probably need to boil them 15 minutes or steam them for 30 minutes. If you are cooking a large amount, it will take longer. The safest way to know that the crabs are done and safe to eat is to use a meat thermometer to check the temperature of the meat.

When preparing live crabs, remember to handle them carefully so that you don't get pinched. Pick them up in one hand by one or both of their last two legs.

This savory swimmer is high in protein, low in fat, calories and cholesterol.

This prized crustacean, the blue crab, is one of the most versatile seafoods. Try our recipes but don't hesitate to create your own.

Crab Meat and Mushrooms in Wine Sauce
- 1 pound backfin crabmeat
- 2 tablespoons margarine or butter
- 1/4 pound sliced fresh mushrooms
- 2 tablespoons flour
- 1/2 cup milk
- 1/2 cup dry white wine
- 1/2 teaspoon dry mustard
- 1/4 teaspoon dried tarragon
- 1/2 teaspoon salt
- 1/4 teaspoon freshly ground white pepper
- 1/4 teaspoon Tabasco sauce
- 3/4 cup dry bread crumbs
- 2 tablespoons melted margarine or butter

Melt 2 tablespoons margarine in large skillet over medium heat. Sauté mushrooms until tender. Blend in flour. Add milk, stirring constantly. Add wine, mustard, tarragon, salt, pepper and Tabasco. When heated, add crabmeat. Place in lightly greased casserole. Sprinkle with bread crumbs and drizzle with 2 tablespoons melted margarine. Bake, uncovered, at 350 F for 30 minutes or until lightly browned and bubbly. Serves 4 to 6.

She-Crab Soup
- 1 pound lump crabmeat
- 6 tablespoons margarine or butter
- 3 tablespoons flour
- 2 cups light cream
- 2 cups milk
- 1 teaspoon Worcestershire sauce
- 1/4 teaspoon salt
- 1/4 teaspoon lemon zest
- 1/4 teaspoon mace
- 1/4 teaspoon freshly ground white pepper
- yolks of 4 hard-cooked eggs
- 2 tablespoons dry sherry
- paprika

In top of double boiler, melt margarine. Blend in flour. Stirring constantly, add cream and milk, then Worcestershire, salt, lemon zest, mace and pepper. Add crabmeat and cook slowly for 20 minutes. Do not allow to boil; cook just below the simmer temperature level. Remove from heat.

Crumble egg yolks and sprinkle in bottom of individual soup bowls. Stir sherry into soup. Pour into bowls, then sprinkle with paprika. Serves 6 to 8.

Crab Salad

- 1 pound backfin crabmeat
- 1 cup chopped celery
- 2 tablespoons chopped sweet pickle
- 2 tablespoons finely chopped red onion
- 1/2 cup mayonnaise
- 1 tablespoon fresh lemon juice
- 1/8 teaspoon freshly ground white pepper
- 2 hard-cooked eggs, chopped
- lettuce leaves
- tomato wedges for garnish

Combine celery, pickle, onion, mayonnaise, lemon juice and pepper in medium bowl. Mix well. Gently blend in crabmeat and eggs, being careful not to break pieces apart. Chill thoroughly. Serve on lettuce leaves. Garnish with tomato wedges. Serves 6.

Deluxe Crab Cakes

- 1 pound claw or special crabmeat
- 1 egg, beaten
- 2 tablespoons mayonnaise
- 1/2 teaspoon dry mustard
- 1/8 teaspoon cayenne pepper
- 1/8 teaspoon Tabasco sauce
- 1/2 teaspoon freshly ground white pepper
- 3 tablespoons finely chopped fresh parsley
- 1 1/2 tablespoons fresh cracker crumbs
- vegetable oil for frying
- lemon wedges (optional)

In medium bowl, place egg, mayonnaise, mustard, cayenne, Tabasco and pepper, and whisk until smooth. Add crabmeat, parsley and crumbs and toss together lightly with a fork. Shape into 6 to 8 patties. Wrap in wax paper and chill for 30 minutes.

Fry in hot oil until golden brown on one side, about 4 to 5 minutes. Turn and repeat on other side. Drain on paper towels. Serve with lemon wedges. Serves 6.

Deviled Crab

- 1 pound special or claw crabmeat
- 2 tablespoons margarine or butter
- 1/2 cup finely chopped onion
- 1/2 cup fine, soft bread crumbs
- 1 cup heavy cream
- 1/4 teaspoon cayenne pepper
- 1/2 teaspoon dry mustard
- 1/2 teaspoon salt
- 1/8 teaspoon Tabasco sauce
- 1 egg, beaten
- 1/4 cup fine, soft bread crumbs
- 2 tablespoons margarine or butter, melted

Melt 2 tablespoons margarine in large skillet over medium heat. Sauté onion until tender. Add 1/2 cup bread crumbs. Add cream, stirring constantly. Add cayenne, mustard, salt and Tabasco. Stir in egg. Gently fold in crabmeat. Place in 6 lightly greased shells or ramekins. Sprinkle with 1/4 cup crumbs and drizzle with 2 tablespoons melted margarine. Bake at 350 F for 15 to 20 minutes, or until golden brown and bubbly. Serves 6.

Crab Newburg

- 1 pound backfin crabmeat
- 1/4 cup margarine or butter
- 1/4 cup finely chopped green pepper
- 2/3 cup sliced fresh mushrooms
- 1/4 cup flour
- 1/4 teaspoon salt
- 1/2 teaspoon dry mustard
- 1/8 teaspoon cayenne pepper
- 2 cups milk
- 1/4 cup dry white wine
- 2 tablespoons freshly grated Parmesan cheese
- paprika
- 3 tablespoons chopped fresh parsley

      Melt margarine in medium saucepan over medium heat. Sauté green pepper and mushrooms until soft. In small bowl, combine flour, salt, mustard and cayenne. Blend into melted margarine. Add milk gradually, stirring constantly, then add wine. Cook, continuing to stir, until thick, about 8 to 10 minutes.

      Place crabmeat in 6 lightly greased individual shells or ramekins. Spoon sauce over each. Sprinkle with Parmesan, paprika and parsley. Bake at 350 F until lightly browned and bubbly, about 10 to 12 minutes. Serves 6.

Crab Imperial
- 1 pound backfin crabmeat
- 5 tablespoons mayonnaise
- 1 egg, beaten
- 1/2 teaspoon dry mustard
- 1/8 teaspoon salt
- 1/16 teaspoon freshly ground black pepper
- 1/8 teaspoon Tabasco sauce
- 1/2 tablespoon minced green pepper
- 1/2 tablespoon minced red onion

      Combine mayonnaise, egg, mustard, salt, pepper and Tabasco in large bowl. Add green pepper and onion. Gently stir in crabmeat. Place in 6 lightly greased individual shells or ramekins. Bake at 350 F for 15 to 20 minutes, or until thoroughly heated and bubbly. Serves 6.

Deluxe Deviled Crab
- 1 pound special or claw crabmeat
- 2 tablespoons margarine or butter
- 1/2 cup finely chopped onion
- 2 tablespoons finely chopped green pepper
- 1/4 cup flour
- 1 tablespoon dry mustard
- 1 teaspoon Worcestershire sauce
- 1/4 teaspoon Tabasco sauce
- 1/4 teaspoon freshly ground black pepper
- 1/8 teaspoon cayenne pepper
- 1 1/4 cups light cream
- 1 egg, beaten
- 1/2 cup fresh bread crumbs
- 1/2 teaspoon paprika
- 1 tablespoon margarine or butter, melted
- lemon wedges (optional)

Melt 2 tablespoons margarine in large skillet over medium heat. Sauté onion and green pepper until tender. Stir in flour, mustard, Worcestershire, Tabasco, pepper and cayenne. Add cream gradually, stirring, and cook over low heat until thickened, stirring constantly. In small bowl, add a little of the mixture to the egg. Add egg mixture back to skillet and mix thoroughly. Gently stir in crabmeat.

Place in 6 lightly greased shells or ramekins. Combine crumbs, paprika and melted margarine. Sprinkle on top of each. Bake at 350 F until hot and crumbs are brown, about 15 to 20 minutes. Serve with lemon wedges. Serves 6.

Boiled Hard Crabs

- 3 dozen live blue crabs
- 6 quarts water
- Old Bay Seafood Seasoning (or other)
- salt

Season and salt water according to seasoning package directions. Bring to rolling boil. Place crabs in water. Cover and boil until crabs reach an internal temperature of 158 F and remain there for at least 1 minute, about 15 minutes. Serves 3 to 4.

Steamed Hard Crabs

- 3 dozen live hard crabs
- water
- Old Bay Seafood Seasoning (or other)

You'll need a steamer or other large pot with a rack and a lid (see section on steamers, pp. 90-92). Place water in the bottom of the pot and place the rack over it. When the water comes to a boil, add a layer of crabs on the rack. Sprinkle with seasoning. Repeat, seasoning each layer. Cover with lid and steam until crabs reach an internal temperature of 158 F and remain there for at least 1 minute, about 30 minutes. (The more crabs you have in the pot, the longer the cooking time.) Serves 3 to 4.

No matter where you live,

you can cook and enjoy

soft crabs in a variety of ways.

They taste absolutely

delicious sautéed, baked,

broiled and grilled.

For additional flavors, serve

them stuffed or with sauces.

THE CRAB THAT LOST ITS SHELL

What could be tastier than a hard blue crab with its hidden bits and chunks of sweet, white meat? For many people, the ultimate delicacy is a soft crab that can be eaten almost whole — claws, flipper and a new shell included.

Soft-shell crabs are blue crabs that have shed their hard outer shells as they grow. They are not a separate species as some think.

Soft crabs come live and fresh-frozen. If you purchase them live, often the dealer will clean them for you. Or you can quickly and easily dress them yourself (see section on dressing, p. 51). But handle them carefully to preserve large pieces of meat.

Graded by size, soft-shell crabs range from mediums, 3 1/2 to 4 inches wide, to primes, more than 5 1/2 inches. Markets price them by size.

Natives of New Orleans often claim that they prepare the best soft crabs because they are not afraid to fry them. Many cooks feel that deep frying brings out the best flavor. When cooked this way, they traditionally come with tartar sauce.

In coastal North Carolina, most people pan-fry them. The ultimate Down East sandwich consists of a fried soft crab served with mayonnaise on a soft white bun.

No matter where you live, you can cook and enjoy soft crabs in a variety of ways. They taste absolutely delicious sautéed, baked, broiled and grilled. For additional flavors, serve them stuffed or with sauces.

Our soft-crab recipes are simple and easy to prepare. Cooking times are for average-size crabs. Adjust time for smaller or larger crabs.

The soft-shell crab is low in calories, fat and cholesterol.

Sautéed Soft-Shell Crabs
- 8 soft-shell crabs
- salt
- freshly ground black pepper
- flour
- 1/2 cup margarine or butter

Sprinkle crabs with salt and pepper. Dust with flour. Heat margarine in large skillet over medium heat. Place crabs upside down in skillet when margarine sizzles. Sauté until crisp and nicely browned, about 4 to 5 minutes. Turn and repeat on other side. Serves 4.

Golden-Fried Soft-Shell Crabs

- 6 soft-shell crabs
- 2 tablespoons fresh lemon juice
- 2 tablespoons soy sauce
- salt
- freshly ground black pepper
- flour
- 1 egg, beaten
- 2/3 cup fresh bread crumbs
- oil for frying

Combine lemon juice and soy sauce. Brush on crabs. Season with salt and pepper. Refrigerate for 1 hour.

Roll crabs in flour, dip in egg and coat lightly with crumbs. Deep-fry at 375 F until crisp and golden brown, about 4 to 5 minutes. Serve with tartar sauce (recipe, p. 235). Serves 3.

Broiled Soft-Shell Crabs

- 12 soft-shell crabs
- 1/2 cup margarine or butter, softened
- 2 teaspoons paprika
- 1/2 teaspoon salt
- 1/2 cup chopped fresh parsley
- flour

Blend margarine, paprika and salt in small bowl. Gently mix in parsley. Dust crabs lightly with flour. Place on broiler pan. Spread with half of margarine. Broil about 4 inches from heat until crisp and brown, about 4 to 5 minutes. Turn, spread with remaining margarine and cook until crisp and brown, about 3 to 4 minutes. Remove to serving dish. Pour juices from pan over crabs. Serves 6.

Sautéed Soft Crabs with Fresh Lime

- 8 soft-shell crabs
- 1 cup flour
- 1 teaspoon paprika
- 1/2 teaspoon salt
- 1/4 teaspoon freshly ground black pepper
- 8 tablespoons margarine or butter
- 8 tablespoons fresh lime juice

Combine flour, paprika, salt and pepper in shallow dish. Lightly coat crabs and shake off excess.

Melt margarine in large skillet over medium heat. Place crabs upside down in pan and sauté until golden brown, about 4 to 5 minutes. Turn and repeat on other side. Remove to warm serving platter. Add lime juice to skillet. Scrape up pan deposits and mix well. Remove from heat immediately. Pour over crabs. Serves 4.

Stuffed Soft-Shell Crabs

- 12 soft-shell crabs
- 1/4 cup margarine or butter
- 1/4 cup finely chopped onion
- 1/4 cup finely chopped celery
- 1/4 teaspoon pressed garlic
- 3/4 cup fresh cracker crumbs
- 2 tablespoons milk
- 1 egg, beaten
- 1/2 teaspoon Worcestershire sauce
- 1/2 teaspoon dry mustard
- 1/4 teaspoon salt
- 1/8 teaspoon cayenne pepper
- 1 tablespoon chopped fresh parsley
- 1/4 cup melted margarine or butter

Melt 1/4 cup margarine in small skillet over medium heat. Cook onion, celery and garlic until tender, about 5 minutes. In medium bowl, combine this mixture with crumbs, milk, egg, Worcestershire, mustard, salt, cayenne and parsley. Place crabs in shallow, well-greased baking pan. Lift each side of top shell from crabs and fill cavity with stuffing mixture. Replace shell. Brush crabs with melted margarine. Bake at 400 F until shells turn red and crabs brown slightly, about 15 minutes. Serves 6.

Grilled Soft-Shell Crabs
- 12 soft-shell crabs
- 1/2 cup vegetable oil
- 1/2 cup chopped fresh parsley
- 1 teaspoon fresh lemon juice
- 1/4 teaspoon nutmeg
- 3 tablespoons soy sauce
- 1/4 teaspoon Tabasco sauce

In small bowl, combine oil, parsley, lemon juice, nutmeg, soy sauce and Tabasco. Brush both sides of crabs with sauce. Place upside down on grill about 4 inches over moderately hot coals. Cook until lightly browned, about 5 to 6 minutes. Turn and repeat on other side. Serves 6.

Baked Soft-Shell Crabs
- 12 soft-shell crabs
- 2 eggs, beaten
- 1/4 cup milk
- 1/2 teaspoon salt
- 1/4 teaspoon freshly ground black pepper
- 1/4 teaspoon paprika
- 3/4 cup flour
- 3/4 cup dry bread crumbs
- 4 tablespoons margarine or butter

Combine eggs, milk, salt, pepper and paprika in shallow dish. Combine flour and crumbs in another shallow dish. Dip crabs in egg mixture, then in flour mixture. Place in lightly greased baking pan. Dot with margarine. Bake at 400 F until crabs are browned and tender, about 10 to 12 minutes. Serves 6.

Pan-Fried Soft Crabs with White Wine Sauce
- 6 soft-shell crabs
- 6 tablespoons flour
- 6 tablespoons yellow cornmeal
- 1/2 teaspoon salt
- 1/2 teaspoon freshly ground black pepper
- 3 tablespoons vegetable oil
- 3 tablespoons margarine or butter

Prepare White Wine Sauce and keep warm.

Mix flour, meal, salt and pepper in shallow dish. Turn each crab in the flour mix to coat completely. Gently shake off excess. Heat oil in large skillet over medium heat. Add margarine. When skillet is heated, lay crabs upside down in oil. Sauté until crisp and golden brown, about 4 to 5 minutes. Turn and repeat on other side. Remove to warm platter. Pour wine sauce over crabs. Serves 3.

White Wine Sauce:
- 1/4 cup dry white wine
- 1/4 cup finely chopped green onion, including tops
- 2 tablespoons white wine vinegar
- 1/4 teaspoon cayenne pepper
- 6 tablespoons margarine or butter, melted

Combine wine, onion, vinegar and cayenne pepper. Bring to boil. Cook until reduced by half. Stir in margarine and reheat. Remove from heat. Serve over cooked crabs.

Soft-Shell Crabs with Garlic Sauce
- 12 soft-shell crabs
- 1 cup Bisquick or other baking mix
- 1/8 teaspoon cayenne pepper
- 1/4 teaspoon freshly ground black pepper
- 3/4 cup margarine or butter
- 1 teaspoon pressed garlic
- 4 tablespoons fresh lemon juice
- 2 tablespoons finely minced, fresh parsley

Mix Bisquick, cayenne and black pepper in shallow dish. Dredge crabs until coated. Gently shake off excess. Heat margarine in large skillet over medium heat. Place crabs upside down in pan and cook until golden brown, about 4 to 5 minutes. Turn and repeat on other side. Remove to warm platter.

Add garlic to skillet and stir quickly. Add lemon juice. Scrape up pan deposits. Pour sauce over crabs and sprinkle with parsley. Serves 6.

Soft Crabs Amandine
- 6 soft-shell crabs
- salt
- pepper
- flour
- 3 tablespoons vegetable oil
- 4 tablespoons margarine or butter
- 1/4 cup almond slivers
- 2 tablespoons fresh lemon juice

Sprinkle crabs with salt and pepper. Dredge in flour and shake off excess. Heat oil in large skillet over medium heat. Add 3 tablespoons margarine. When it sizzles, place crabs upside down in skillet. Sauté until crisp and golden, about 4 to 5 minutes. Turn and repeat on other side. Remove to warm platter.

Heat remaining tablespoon margarine in same skillet. Add almonds and sauté until golden brown. Stir in lemon juice. Pour over crabs. Serves 3.

SHRIMP — A FAVORITE CATCH

Ask most people to name their favorite seafood, and chances are they'll answer "shrimp." This tasty crustacean is the most popular seafood in the nation.

But this has not always been the case. Until the late 1920s, fishermen thought of shrimp as pests that fouled their nets and they threw them aside. John Maiolo, a retired sociology professor from East Carolina University reports: "North Carolina fishermen were paid about three cents a pound for their catches. Others were paid five cents a bucket to head them."

Back then, people often called shrimp "bugs." Many of the Nutrition Leaders remember calling them that, and pitching them back in the water when caught. Even today, many fishers going out after the valuable catch will say that they are "going bugging."

Brown, pink and white shrimp, "local" to us, are found along the southeast U. S. coast and in the Gulf of Mexico. Shrimpers catch these favorites in large mesh nets. Many of the shrimp you buy in restaurants and supermarkets are imported from Asian countries. And many of them are cultivated in ponds, which makes a steady supply available. Shrimp are low in calories and fat and high in protein. They contain a moderate amount of cholesterol, depending on the species. (See nutrition section, p. 30.)

Markets price shrimp according to size, based on the number of headless shrimp per pound. Counts are not always uniform, but generally jumbo shrimp

Brown, pink and white shrimp, "local" to us, are found along the southeast U. S. coast and in the Gulf of Mexico. Shrimpers catch these favorites in large mesh nets.

contain about 21 to 25 per pound; large, 31 to 40; medium 41 to 50; and small, 51 to 60. You will see some labeled "jumbo" and "colossal." There are no official standards for labeling the sizes and different markets may use different terms.

Generally, shrimp drop one count in shelling and another in cooking. After peeling and cooking, raw, headless shrimp will yield about three-fourths their weight.

I'm often asked if it's more economical to buy shrimp with the heads on. To determine this, you need to calculate what the headed price is. If heads-on shrimp are below 40 count, divide the price by .63. If they are above 40 count, divide by .55. For example, if large shrimp with heads on are $5 per pound, divide $5 by .63. The answer is $7.94. If this is less than the market price for headed shrimp, it is a better buy.

Use smaller shrimp for casseroles, salads, sandwiches and in spreads and dips. Medium shrimp make good additions in soups and some entrees such as shrimp creole. They also can be steamed or grilled. Use large shrimp for grilling, steaming and other entrees where size matters.

Fresh shrimp smell like sea water. There should be no off-odors, mustiness or chemical smells. Occasionally shrimp will smell and taste like iodine. This is not related to spoilage and is not harmful, but makes them unacceptable for eating. Certain organisms on which shrimp sometimes feed can cause this iodine effect. If you buy shrimp that smell this way, return them to your market for a refund or replacement.

When shopping for shrimp, look for those that are firm and not slippery. Beware of shrimp that are bright pink or red. They have a "cooked" appearance due to not being properly iced.

Look for uniform size and lack of defects such as black spots, yellowing or a bleached appearance. Check for extraneous material such as legs or shell fragments.

Shrimp may be peeled before or after cooking. If they are boiled, steamed or pre-cooked for a recipe, they are much more flavorful if cooked in the shells. If you don't believe this, give it a try. You'll be surprised!

Shrimp must be headed and peeled; deveining them is optional. People often ask if it's necessary. In many shrimp, the "sand vein," as it is commonly called, is small and can be left. It is not necessary to remove it to clean the shrimp, since most of the digestive organs are in the head and thorax and are removed when the shrimp is headed. If the vein is large, it may be gritty and you'll want to remove it. And dishes such as shrimp cocktail, salads and soups are more aesthetically pleasing if the vein is removed.

When precooking for further use in a recipe, shrimp should be cooked in salted or seasoned water.

To cook 1 pound, combine 1 quart of water and 1/2 teaspoon salt in a medium saucepan. Bring to a boil. Add shrimp. Simmer until pink and tender, about 3 to 5 minutes, depending on size of the shrimp. Pour into a colander to drain.

You can add celery leaves, lemon slices, a bay leaf or other favorite seasonings to the water. If you do, boil about 10 minutes before adding shrimp. This will allow the flavors to blend. Also, most markets and stores have seasoning mixes. Some of them, such as Old Bay, are quite good.

If you're hungry for a *Carolina Shrimp Boil*, don't be intimidated by the recipe. You can easily cook it for two or even one. I've done it many times — and it works!

Savory Baked Shrimp

- 1 pound cooked small shrimp, peeled
- 3 tablespoons vegetable oil
- 1 tablespoon finely chopped green onion
- 1/2 teaspoon pressed garlic
- 1 tablespoon chopped fresh parsley
- 1/4 teaspoon savory
- 1 1/2 tablespoons fresh lemon juice
- 1/4 cup dry bread crumbs
- 1 tablespoon freshly grated Parmesan cheese
- 2 tablespoons dry white wine

Heat oil in small saucepan over medium heat. Sauté onion and garlic until tender. Add parsley, savory, lemon juice, crumbs and cheese.

Arrange shrimp in lightly greased medium baking dish. Sprinkle crumb mixture over top. Pour wine over this. Bake at 350 F until heated through and lightly browned, about 10 to 15 minutes. Serves 3 to 4.

Shrimp Newburg

- 1 pound cooked small shrimp, peeled
- 6 tablespoons margarine or butter
- 2 tablespoons flour
- 1/2 teaspoon salt
- 1/8 teaspoon nutmeg
- 1/16 teaspoon cayenne pepper
- 2 cups light cream
- 2 egg yolks, beaten
- 2 tablespoons dry sherry
- 4 slices bread, toasted and cut into points

Cook shrimp in salted or seasoned water.

Melt margarine in medium saucepan over medium heat. Blend in flour. Add salt, nutmeg and cayenne. Add cream gradually, stirring constantly. Cook, stirring constantly, until thick and smooth. In small bowl, stir a little sauce into the beaten egg yolks. Add back to sauce slowly, stirring. Add shrimp and continue to cook until heated through. Remove from heat and add sherry. Serve on toast points. Serves 4.

Individual Shrimp Casseroles

- 1 pound cooked small shrimp, peeled
- 1/4 cup margarine or butter
- 1/2 cup sliced fresh mushrooms
- 1/4 cup flour
- 1/4 teaspoon salt
- 1/2 teaspoon dry mustard
- 1/16 teaspoon cayenne pepper
- 3/4 cup milk
- 1/2 cup freshly grated Parmesan cheese
- paprika

Cook shrimp in salted or seasoned water.

Melt margarine in medium saucepan over medium heat. Sauté mushrooms until tender. Blend in flour, salt, mustard and cayenne. Add milk gradually and cook until thick, stirring constantly. Stir in shrimp. Place in 4 greased individual shells or ramekins. Sprinkle with Parmesan and paprika. Bake at 400 F for 10 minutes, or until cheese is lightly browned. Serves 3 to 4.

Shrimp Scampi

- 1 pound large shrimp, peeled
- 1/2 teaspoon Worcestershire sauce
- 1/4 teaspoon salt
- 1/8 teaspoon freshly ground white pepper
- 1 teaspoon paprika
- 1/4 cup margarine or butter
- 1/3 cup finely chopped green onion, including tops
- 2 tablespoons softened margarine or butter
- 1 teaspoon pressed garlic
- 2 teaspoons finely chopped fresh parsley
- 1/2 cup dry white wine
- cooked rice (optional)

Cook rice according to package directions.

In medium bowl, toss shrimp with Worcestershire. Combine salt, pepper and paprika and sprinkle on shrimp. Melt 1/4 cup margarine in large skillet over medium heat. Add green onion and shrimp. Cook until shrimp are browned, about 5 to 6 minutes, turning once. Stir in softened margarine, garlic, parsley and wine. Simmer 3 to 4 minutes. Serve with rice, if desired. (You'll enjoy it with rice — the broth is delicious.) Serves 3 to 4.

Shrimp Curry

- 1 1/2 pounds cooked small shrimp, peeled
- 4 tablespoons margarine or butter
- 1/2 cup finely chopped onion
- 1 1/2 teaspoons pressed garlic
- 7 tablespoons flour
- 3 tablespoons curry powder (or more to taste)
- 1/2 teaspoon ground ginger
- 1/2 teaspoon salt
- 1 14 1/2-ounce can chicken broth
- 1 cup light cream
- 2 tablespoons fresh lemon juice
- cooked rice

Prepare rice according to package directions.

In large saucepan, melt margarine over medium heat. Sauté onion and garlic until tender. Stir in flour, curry powder, ginger and salt. Add chicken broth and blend. Stir in cream and cook until thickened, stirring constantly. Add shrimp and lemon juice. Continue cooking until shrimp are heated. Do not allow to boil. Serve over hot rice. Serves 6.

Shrimp Creole
- 1 pound small shrimp (or larger, cut in pieces)
- 1/8 cup olive oil
- 1/2 cup chopped onion
- 1/4 cup chopped green onion, including tops
- 1/2 cup chopped celery
- 2 teaspoons finely chopped garlic
- 1 14 1/2-ounce can chopped tomatoes, undrained
- 1 cup fish or chicken broth
- 2 tablespoons red wine
- 1/2 teaspoon salt
- 1 bay leaf
- 1/4 teaspoon freshly ground black pepper
- 1/8 teaspoon cayenne pepper
- 1/4 teaspoon dried thyme leaves
- 2 tablespoons flour mixed with 1/4 cup water
- 1 cup uncooked rice

   Heat oil in large saucepan over medium heat. Sauté onion, green onion, celery and garlic. Add tomatoes, broth, wine, salt, bay leaf, black pepper, cayenne and thyme. Bring to boil. Cover, reduce heat and simmer 30 minutes. Slowly stir in flour mixture to thicken. Continue to simmer for another 10 minutes.

   Meanwhile, cook rice according to package directions.

   Add shrimp to sauce and simmer until they are done, about 10 minutes. Remove bay leaf. Serve over cooked rice. Serves 6.

Shrimp Salad
- 1 pound cooked small shrimp
- 2 tablespoons fresh lemon juice
- 1/2 cup finely chopped celery
- 2 hard-cooked eggs, chopped
- 1/2 cup mayonnaise
- 1/8 teaspoon Tabasco sauce
- 1/8 teaspoon freshly ground white pepper
- lettuce
- tomato wedges

Cook shrimp in salted or seasoned water. Peel and devein.

Mix shrimp with lemon juice. Add celery, eggs, mayonnaise, Tabasco and pepper. Mix well. Chill thoroughly. Serve on lettuce leaves. Garnish with tomato wedges. Serves 3 to 4.

Marinated Charcoal-Grilled Shrimp

- 1 1/2 pounds medium or large shrimp, peeled, with tails left on
- 2 tablespoon fresh lime juice
- 3/4 teaspoon freshly ground black pepper
- 1/2 teaspoon salt
- 1/8 teaspoon dill weed
- 1/4 teaspoon sugar
- 1/2 teaspoon ground cumin
- 1/2 teaspoon basil
- 1 1/2 teaspoons pressed garlic
- 2 teaspoons finely chopped green onion tops
- 1 tablespoon vegetable oil

In wide, shallow dish combine lime juice, pepper, salt, dill, sugar, cumin, basil, garlic, onion and oil. Mix thoroughly. Lay shrimp flat in mixture and marinate in refrigerator for 20 minutes, turning once. Remove shrimp from marinade and thread on skewers or place in hinged wire grill. Cook about 4 inches over medium coals, about 6 to 7 minutes on each side. Serves 6.

Shrimp au Gratin

- 1 pound small or medium shrimp
- salt
- 2 tablespoons margarine or butter
- 1/2 cup soft bread crumbs combined with 3 tablespoons melted margarine or butter
- 1/3 cup freshly grated medium cheddar cheese

Make sauce and keep warm.

Lightly salt shrimp. In medium saucepan, melt margarine over medium heat. Add shrimp and sauté lightly, about 2 minutes. Remove shrimp with slotted spoon.

Add shrimp to sauce mixture and mix well. Pour into greased casserole dish. Sprinkle top with crumb mixture and cheese. Bake at 400 F until lightly browned and bubbly, about 20 minutes. Allow to stand 10 minutes before serving. Serves 3 to 4.

Sauce:
- 3 tablespoons margarine or butter
- 3 tablespoons finely chopped green onion
- 3 tablespoons flour
- 1 cup light cream
- 1/2 teaspoon salt
- 1/4 teaspoon freshly ground white pepper
- 1/8 teaspoon nutmeg
- 1 teaspoon fresh lemon juice

In medium saucepan, melt margarine over medium heat. Lightly sauté onion. Stir in flour. Add cream gradually, stirring constantly, and cook over low heat until thickened. Add salt, pepper, nutmeg and lemon juice.

Carolina Shrimp Boil
- 8 pounds large unpeeled shrimp
- 8 quarts water
- 8 rounded tablespoons Old Bay Seasoning (more to taste)
- 30 small new potatoes (or larger ones, halved or quartered)
- 5 large onions, halved
- 15 ears corn, shucked and cut into thirds

In large cooker, bring water to rolling boil. Add seasoning. Add potatoes and onions. Continue to boil until potatoes are almost done, about 10 minutes. Add corn and cook until done, about 3 minutes. Add shrimp and cook until done, about 3 to 5 minutes. Drain and serve. Serves 12 to 15.

Note: Many people like to shake additional Old Bay over the food after draining it. Also, you can add smoked sausage to the pot. Cut into pieces about 1 1/2-inches long and add after the potatoes. Other seafood seasonings can be used for flavor. Follow package instructions for amounts and cooking methods.

Crab-Stuffed Shrimp

- 1 pound large shrimp
- 1/2 pound backfin crabmeat
- 4 tablespoons melted margarine or butter
- 1/3 cup finely chopped celery
- 1/4 cup finely chopped green onion
- 2 tablespoons mayonnaise
- 1 teaspoon Tabasco sauce
- 1 teaspoon Worcestershire sauce
- 1/2 teaspoon salt
- 1/4 teaspoon freshly ground white pepper
- 2 slices fresh white bread

Shell shrimp, leaving tails on. Split lengthwise until almost cut through, then spread apart in butterfly shape.

Remove any shell or cartilege from crabmeat.

In 2 tablespoons margarine, lightly sauté celery and green onion in small saucepan. In medium bowl, combine mayonnaise, Tabasco, Worcestershire, salt and pepper. Add celery and green onion. Add bread cubes and mix. Gently stir in crabmeat.

Stuff the butterfly shrimp with the crab mixture. Place on a lightly greased baking sheet and brush with the remaining 2 tablespoons margarine. Bake at 400 F until tops are lightly browned and shrimp are done, about 15 minutes. Serves 3 to 4. As an appetizer serves about 10.

A LOVE AFFAIR WITH OYSTERS

Oysters have probably been eaten since before recorded history. Ancient myths tell the story of the goddess Venus rising from the sea and popping out of an oyster. Roman feasts were not complete without the shellfish delicacy harvested in England, other parts of Europe and the Mediterranean.

Written records indicate the establishment of artificial oyster beds 100 years before the birth of Christ. Oriental accounts of oysters as food date much earlier. Oyster shell reefs indicate that they have been in existence for 50 million years.

Oysters provided a staple part of the diet of Native Americans and early settlers in the New World. By the mid-19th century, Americans were engaged in an unending love affair with the oyster. "Oyster expresses" and "oyster caravans" carried the shellfish to inland regions. Almost every town had an "oyster parlor." And the fame of Southern oyster roasts continues to this day — where large groups of family and friends gather to eat oysters cooked over an open fire.

The subject of literature and art for centuries, oysters have also been the basis for a few interesting myths.

We've all heard the phrase: "Eat oysters, love longer." But no one seems to know exactly how or when this idea began. Lord Byron's Don Juan described oysters as "amatory food" more than 150 years ago.

Perhaps people assumed that the oyster's own fruitfulness could be transferred to those who ate it. After all, one oyster is capable of producing about 500 million eggs in a single spawning season.

Another possible explanation may be related to cholesterol. At one time oysters were labeled high in cholesterol. Because cholesterol is a basic building block for male and female hormones, some thought that oysters acted as an aphrodisiac.

Now we know that oysters are not high in cholesterol, and we realize that cholesterol intake does not stimulate sexual prowess. We also know that oysters are low in calories and fat. Oysters contain high-quality protein, minerals and vitamins, too. Easily digested, they are often recommended for special diets.

So, enjoy oysters for their wonderful fresh-ocean flavor and forget about any added bedroom benefits. And while we're talking about oysters, toss out that adage about eating the mollusks only in months with an "r" in the name.

Two possible explanations for this myth come to mind. Oysters, like other seafood, are very perishable. Before the advent of refrigeration, they spoiled quickly in summer months — those without an "r." Also, from May to September, when oysters spawn, they are more watery and have less flavor than the typical "fat" oysters we prefer.

A frequently asked question about oysters concerns red, green or mottled

By the mid-19th century,

Americans were engaged in

an unending love affair with the

oyster. "Oyster expresses"

and "oyster caravans" carried

the shellfish to inland regions.

Almost every town had

an "oyster parlor." And the fame

of Southern oyster roasts

continues to this day —

where large groups of family

and friends gather to eat

oysters cooked over

an open fire.

oysters. These colors are harmless, usually associated with the oyster's diet. The red color disappears when the oyster liquid is warmed. Do beware, though, of any pink color accompanied by a sour odor. This is caused by a spoilage yeast, and the oysters should not be eaten.

Oysters purchased in the shell should be alive. Shells should be closed or should close tightly when tapped. Maintain a temperature of 30 F to 41 F for live oysters. Limit holding time to two to three days. Discard any that die or open. Shucked oysters should be plump with a natural creamy color and clear or slightly opalescent liquid. They should not contain more than 10 percent liquid and should have a mild odor.

Before shucking oysters, rinse them thoroughly with cold, running water, removing mud and grit. You can rinse them easily in the yard, using water from your garden hose with plenty of pressure. Remember to wear heavy gloves when handling oyster shells.

For all recipes that call for shucked oysters, you'll find it much more convenient to buy them already shucked, of course. And you can use them also for many recipes in the shell, such as *Broiled Oysters with Fine Herbs*. Most kitchen and specialty stores sell plastic or glass shells that can substitute for the real thing.

You'll notice that our recipes tell you to use rock salt in the pan when cooking oysters in their shells. A deep layer allows you to level the oysters in the salt, making them steady and also keeping the contents from spilling out of the uneven shells.

Remember to use caution when eating raw or partially cooked oysters. (See chapter on seafood safety, pp. 35-37.)

Oyster Stew
- 1 pint standard oysters, undrained
- 4 tablespoons margarine or butter
- 1 quart milk
- 1 1/2 teaspoons salt
- 1/8 teaspoon freshly ground white pepper
- 1/16 teaspoon paprika
- 4 tablespoons finely chopped fresh parsley
- oyster crackers (optional)

In medium saucepan, melt margarine over medium heat. Add oysters and cook just until edges begin to curl, about 5 minutes. Add milk, salt, pepper and paprika. Cook over medium heat until thoroughly heated and oysters are done, about 8 to 10 minutes. Do not boil. Pour into serving bowls and sprinkle with parsley. Serve with oyster crackers. Serves 4 to 6.

Oysters Rockefeller
- 48 oysters
- 1 1/2 sticks margarine or butter
- 1 10-ounce package frozen chopped spinach, thawed
- 4 tablespoons minced onion
- 4 tablespoons chopped fresh parsley
- 1/2 cup minced celery
- 1/4 teaspoon dried tarragon leaves
- 1/4 teaspoon cayenne pepper
- 1/4 teaspoon garlic powder
- 1/2 teaspoon salt
- 1/4 teaspoon Tabasco sauce
- 2/3 cup toasted, fresh bread crumbs
- 3 tablespoons margarine or butter, melted
- rock salt

Scrub oysters with stiff brush under cold running water. Shuck and drain.

Melt 12 tablespoons margarine in small saucepan. Add spinach, onion, parsley, celery, tarragon, cayenne, garlic powder, salt and Tabasco. Simmer about 5 minutes.

Spread layer of rock salt in baking pan. Place deep halves of oyster shells level on rock salt. Place oyster in each. Spread spinach mixture over each oyster. Combine bread crumbs and 3 tablespoons melted margarine. Sprinkle over tops. Bake at 450 F until oysters are done, about 10 to 15 minutes. Serves 8.

Oysters and Mushrooms au Gratin
- 1 pint standard oysters, liquor reserved
- 2 tablespoons margarine or butter
- 5 tablespoons flour
- 1/2 cup heavy cream
- 3/4 teaspoon salt
- 1/8 teaspoon paprika
- 1/4 teaspoon dry mustard
- 1/8 teaspoon freshly ground black pepper
- 1 cup sliced fresh mushrooms, sautéed in margarine or butter, drained
- 1 teaspoon fresh lemon juice
- 1 teaspoon Worcestershire sauce
- 1/2 cup fresh bread crumbs
- paprika

Drain and dry oysters. Melt margarine in medium saucepan over medium heat. Add flour and stir until blended. Slowly stir in 1/2 cup oyster liquor and cream. Add salt, paprika, mustard and pepper. Cook, stirring, until mixture comes to a boil and thickens. Reduce heat and add cooked mushrooms, lemon juice, Worcestershire and oysters. Heat, stirring until edges of oysters begin to curl, but do not boil. Place in 6 individual shells or ramekins. Sprinkle with bread crumbs and paprika.

Broil about 4 inches from heat until lightly browned, about 5 to 8 minutes. Serves 6.

Golden-Brown Fried Oysters
- 1 pint select oysters
- 1/2 tablespoon sake (rice wine)
- 1/2 teaspoon salt
- freshly ground black pepper
- flour
- 2 eggs, beaten
- vegetable oil for frying

Drain oysters. Place in bowl and mix with sake; let stand about 5 minutes. Remove and pat dry with paper towels. Sprinkle with salt and pepper. Roll in flour, shaking off excess.

Dip oysters in egg and place in oil in large heavy skillet. Cook at 375 F until golden brown on one side, about 1 to 2 minutes. Turn and repeat on other side. Drain on paper towels. Serves 4 to 6.

Broiled Oysters
- 1 quart oysters, drained
- 1 cup margarine or butter, melted
- 1/2 teaspoon salt
- 1/4 teaspoon freshly ground black pepper
- 3 eggs, beaten
- 4 cups fresh bread crumbs

Pat oysters dry. Add salt and pepper to melted margarine. Dip each oyster in margarine, then in eggs, then in bread crumbs. Broil about 4 inches from heat until golden brown on one side, about 5 minutes. Turn and repeat on other side. Serves 8 to 10.

Broiled Oysters with Fine Herbs

- 3 dozen select oysters
- 1/4 pound margarine or butter, softened
- 3/4 cup green onion, including tops, finely chopped
- 1/4 cup finely chopped fresh parsley
- 1/4 cup finely chopped fresh tarragon
- 1/4 cup fresh cracker crumbs
- 2 teaspoons fresh lemon juice
- rock salt

   Shuck oysters and place the deep half of the shells level on a bed of rock salt on baking pan. Mix together margarine, onion, parsley, tarragon, crumbs and lemon juice. Divide evenly over oysters. Broil about 4 inches from heat until done, about 5 to 8 minutes. Serves 6.

Oysters Casino

- 1 pint oysters, drained
- 3 slices bacon
- 4 tablespoons chopped onion
- 2 tablespoons chopped green pepper
- 3 tablespoons chopped celery
- 1 teaspoon fresh lemon juice
- 1/2 teaspoon salt
- 1/4 teaspoon freshly ground black pepper
- 1/2 teaspoon Worcestershire sauce
- 1/8 teaspoon Tabasco sauce

   Chop bacon and fry until brown. Drain on paper towels. Discard all but 1 1/2 tablespoons bacon grease. Sauté onion, green pepper and celery until tender. Add lemon juice, salt, black pepper, Worcestershire and Tabasco. Add bacon and mix well. In lightly greased baking dish, arrange oysters and spread mixture over top. Bake at 350 F until oysters are done and topping is browned, about 10 to 15 minutes. Serves 4 to 6.

Garlic Butter Oysters

- 24 oysters in shell
- 2 teaspoons pressed or minced garlic
- 4 tablespoons chopped fresh parsley
- 2 tablespoons butter
- 4 tablespoons fresh bread crumbs

Shuck oysters and reserve deeper shells. Combine garlic and parsley. Place oysters in reserved shells in a bed of rock salt. Place 1/2 teaspoon garlic/parsley mix on top of each oyster. Place 1/2 teaspoon crumbs over each. Top each with 1/4 teaspoon butter. Broil about 4 inches from heat source until oysters are done and crumbs are brown, about 8 to 10 minutes. Serves 4.

TIME TO CLAM UP

Available year-round, the native hard clam, or quahog, has always been a coastal favorite. Its scientific name, *Mercenaria mercenaria*, comes from the Latin word for "wages." Native Americans once used quahog shells to make beads that were used as wampum, or money.

Today clams may be bought in the shell or shucked. Those in the shell should be heavy and tightly closed, or should close when tapped lightly. They should have a pleasant, briny odor. Discard any with open or broken shells.

Clam meat is translucent. Its color ranges from ivory to golden brown. The liquid should be clear or slightly opaque.

Markets classify hard clams by size. The smallest, under 2 inches, is called the littleneck, after Little Neck Bay on Long Island, where they were once plentiful. Cherrystones are 2 to 3 inches and are named after Cherrystone Creek in Virginia. Topnecks are 3 to 3 1/2 inches. Any quahog larger than 3 1/2 inches is called a chowder clam.

The smaller clams, littlenecks and small cherrystones, are firm but tender with a mild flavor. They can be steamed, broiled, baked, grilled, used in clambakes or other cooked dishes, or on the half-shell. (Be sure to read the chapter on seafood safety before eating raw shellfish, p. 31.) Large clams are less tender, so it's best to chop them for chowders, fritters or stuffed clams. In addition to their great taste and versatility, clams are low in calories, fat and cholesterol.

If you enjoy steamed clams, oysters and mussels, you may want to buy a shellfish steamer. It's a large two-section pot (much like a double boiler). The bottom part holds water. The top part is much bigger, usually more than twice the height of the bottom pot. It has holes in the bottom that allow steam to rise and surround the shellfish. You can buy an inexpensive, enamel one at specialty shops, large general merchandise stores and many hardware stores.

Many of you will buy your clams already shucked. For recipes calling for cooking clams in the shell, you can buy imitation shells at many specialty or kitchen stores. You can also use individual ramekins, dividing the clams into

Today clams may be bought in the shell or shucked. Those in the shell should be heavy and tightly closed, or should close when tapped lightly. They should have a pleasant, briny odor. Discard any with open or broken shells.

serving portions, but the effect is not the same. If you do this, increase the cooking time as necessary.

Remember to cook clams only until tender. Overcooking toughens them. Also, watch the amount of salt you add to clam dishes. Many clams taste salty naturally, and any additional salt will be too much.

You'll notice that our two chowder recipes have a big difference in cooking times. This occurs frequently in books and is confusing when there is no explanation. Our *Hearty Clam Chowder* is made with littleneck clams. They are small and cook in just a few minutes. Our *Old-Fashioned Clam Chowder* is made with chowder clams, which are large and quite tough. They require a longer cooking time, about 1 1/2 to 2 hours.

Baked Clams with Garlic Butter

- 36 littleneck clams
- 1/4 pound margarine or butter, softened
- 2 tablespoons coarsely chopped garlic
- 3 tablespoons coarsely chopped green onion, including tops
- 1/2 cup coarsely chopped fresh parsley
- 1/4 cup dry white wine
- 1/4 cup fresh bread crumbs
- 1/4 teaspoon salt
- 1/4 teaspoon freshly ground black pepper
- 4 tablespoons freshly grated Parmesan cheese
- rock salt

Scrub clams thoroughly with a stiff brush under cold, running water. Open clams and discard top shell.

Combine margarine, garlic, green onion, parsley, wine, crumbs, salt, pepper and half the Parmesan. Blend until smooth.

Place clams on the half shell in a bed of rock salt in a cooking pan. Spoon margarine mixture evenly over clams. Sprinkle with remaining Parmesan and bake at 450 F until clams are done and cheese is melted, about 6 to 8 minutes. Serves 6.

Broiled Garlic Clams
- 36 littleneck clams
- 1/4 cup olive oil
- 1/2 cup freshly grated Parmesan cheese
- 1 teaspoon pressed garlic
- 1 tablespoon finely chopped fresh parsley
- rock salt

Scrub clams thoroughly under cold, running water. Open and discard top shell. Place clams on the half shell in a thick bed of rock salt in a cooking pan. This will keep them level so that no broth is lost.

In a small bowl, mix oil, 3 tablespoons of Parmesan and garlic. Drizzle clams with mixture. Broil about 4 inches from heat until cheese melts and clams are done, about 6 to 8 minutes. Top with parsley and remaining cheese. Serves 6.

Fried Clams
- 36 littleneck clams
- freshly ground white pepper
- 3/4 cup flour
- 2 eggs, well beaten with 1 teaspoon milk or light cream
- 1 cup fine fresh cracker crumbs
- 1/4 cup margarine or butter
- 1 tablespoon vegetable oil
- lemon wedges (optional)

Scrub clams thoroughly under cold, running water. Open clams and discard shells.

Sprinkle clams with pepper, then coat well with flour. Dip in egg mixture. Dip in crumbs and coat well.

Heat margarine and oil in large, heavy skillet. Fry clams until golden brown on one side, about 2 to 3 minutes. Turn and repeat on other side. Drain on paper towels. Serve with lemon wedges. Serves 6.

Baked Stuffed Clams

- 2 cups coarsely chopped clams
- 3/4 cup clam liquor
- 2 cups fresh bread crumbs
- 1 cup freshly grated Parmesan cheese
- 2 tablespoons minced fresh parsley
- 1/4 teaspoon pressed garlic
- 1 teaspoon oregano
- 1/2 teaspoon thyme
- 1/2 teaspoon basil
- 1/2 cup dry white wine
- freshly ground black pepper
- 2 tablespoons olive oil
- rock salt

    Scrub clams thoroughly under cold, running water. Open clams, reserving 3/4 cup of clam liquor. Discard top shell. Chop clams.

    In medium bowl, combine clam liquor, crumbs, Parmesan, parsley, garlic, oregano, thyme, basil, wine, pepper and olive oil.

    Place clams on the half shell in a bed of rock salt in cooking pan. Top each with crumb mixture. Bake at 450 F until browned and clams are done, about 10 to 15 minutes. Serves 6 to 8.

Linguine with Clam Sauce

- 30 cherrystone clams, shucked, coarsely chopped, liquid reserved
- 1/4 cup olive oil
- 1 cup chopped onion
- 3/4 teaspoon pressed garlic
- 2 14 1/2-ounce cans chopped tomatoes, drained
- 1/2 teaspoon freshly ground black pepper
- 1/2 teaspoon red pepper flakes
- 1 teaspoon oregano
- 1/2 pound linguine
- freshly grated Parmesan cheese

    Heat oil in large, heavy saucepan. Sauté onion and garlic until soft. Add tomatoes and simmer, uncovered for 5 minutes. Add black and red pepper and oregano. Cover and simmer gently for 15 minutes, stirring occasionally. Add clams and 3/4 cup reserved liquid. Simmer, uncovered, for 3 to 5 minutes, stirring frequently, until clams are done, about 5 to 10 minutes.

Meanwhile, cook linguine according to package directions. Drain and put in a large, heated bowl. Add half the clam sauce, toss well, dish into heated soup bowls, and top with the remaining sauce. Sprinkle with Parmesan. Serves 4 to 6. *(Note: Another version can be found on p. 150.)*

Steamed Clams in Wine Broth

- 36 littleneck clams in the shell
- 1/2 cup dry white wine
- 2 tablespoons margarine or butter
- 6 tablespoons margarine or butter, melted
- lemon wedges (optional)

Scrub clams thoroughly with stiff brush under cold, running water. Using a steamer or large pot with rack, place wine and 2 tablespoons margarine in bottom of pot. Place rack in pot. Arrange clams on rack. Cover. Place over high heat and bring to boil. Reduce heat and steam for 6 to 10 minutes or until clams open. Arrange clams in their shells in shallow soup bowls and pour steaming broth over them. Add 1 tablespoon melted margarine to each bowl. Serve with lemon wedges. Serves 6.

Clams Casino

- 24 littleneck clams, shucked and drained
- 24 1-inch pieces of bacon (about 3 slices)
- 2/3 cup thinly sliced green onion, including tops
- 1/2 teaspoon freshly ground black pepper
- 1/2 teaspoon thyme leaves
- 2 teaspoons fresh lemon juice
- 1/8 teaspoon Tabasco sauce
- 2 tablespoons dry bread crumbs
- 4 tablespoons finely chopped fresh parsley
- 1 cup dry bread crumbs
- rock salt

In medium saucepan, cook bacon until lightly browned. Remove and reserve. Remove all but 4 tablespoons of bacon grease. Stir in green onion. Add pepper, thyme, lemon juice, Tabasco and 2 tablespoons crumbs. Mix well. Remove from heat.

Place clam shells on bed of rock salt in cooking pan. Place each clam on a half shell. Spoon sauce evenly over clams. Place bacon pieces on top. Sprinkle each with crumbs. Bake at 475 F until browned and liquid is absorbed, about 8 to 10 minutes. Serves 4.

Hearty Clam Chowder

- 2 cups shucked littleneck clams, liquid reserved
- 4 slices bacon, diced
- 1/3 cup thinly sliced green onion, including tops
- 2 cups peeled and diced potatoes
- 1/2 cup thinly sliced celery
- 2/3 cup thinly sliced carrot
- 1/2 teaspoon pressed garlic
- clam liquid plus enough water to make 2 cups
- 1 teaspoon salt* (see note below)
- 1/2 teaspoon freshly ground white pepper
- 1 teaspoon Worcestershire sauce
- 1/4 teaspoon Tabasco sauce
- 2 cups light cream

In a large, deep pan, cook bacon over medium heat, stirring occasionally, until crisp. Remove bacon and reserve. Add onion, potatoes, celery, carrot, garlic, liquid, salt, pepper, Worcestershire, and Tabasco to pan. Bring to boil. Reduce heat, cover and simmer gently until potatoes are tender, about 15 minutes. Add clams and cook until done, about 5 minutes.

Stir in cream. Heat just until steaming. Do not boil. Top with reserved bacon. Serve immediately. Serves 6 to 8.

Note: Taste heated clam liquid for salt content. To taste the liquid, bring a few tablespoons to a boil in the microwave or on the stove top. Do NOT taste the raw liquid. If it is very salty, reduce or eliminate the amount. We've found this step to be essential; many clams are very salty.

Deviled Clams

- 2 cups finely chopped clams
- 1/2 cup clam liquid
- 4 tablespoons margarine or butter
- 2 tablespoons minced onion
- 2 tablespoons minced green pepper
- 1/4 cup chopped celery
- 2 tablespoons minced celery leaves
- 1/8 teaspoon freshly ground black pepper
- 1/2 teaspoon prepared mustard
- 3/4 cup fresh cracker crumbs
- rock salt

Place clams and liquid in medium saucepan and simmer 5 minutes. Melt margarine in small saucepan over medium heat. Add onion, green pepper, celery and leaves, pepper and mustard and cook until vegetables are tender, about 5 minutes. Add to clam mixture. Stir in crumbs and mix well.

Grease clam shells or individual serving cups and place on bed of rock salt in cooking pan. Bake at 350 F for 20 minutes or until crumbs are nicely browned and mixture is bubbly. Serves 6 to 8.

Old-Fashioned Clam Chowder

- 2 cups coarsely chopped chowder clams
- 4 slices bacon
- 2 cups water
- 1/2 cup chopped onion
- 2 teaspoons salt
- 1 teaspoon freshly ground black pepper
- 4 cups diced potatoes
- 1/2 cup instant potato flakes to thicken (optional)

In large saucepan, cook bacon over medium heat until crisp. Remove bacon and set aside. Add clams, water, onion, salt and pepper to pan. Bring to boil. Reduce heat and cook slowly until clams are tender, about 1 1/2 to 2 hours. Add potatoes and cook until done, about 20 minutes. Add potato flakes and simmer until thickened, about 5 minutes. Crumble bacon and sprinkle over chowder. Serves 8 to 10.

Down East Clambake

Per serving:

- 8 to 12 cherrystone clams
- 6 to 8 large shrimp, in shells
- 1 medium sweet potato
- 1 ear sweet corn, in husk
- 2 small onions
- 1 chicken thigh
- salt
- freshly ground black pepper
- mesh bag or 18 x 24-inch piece of cheesecloth

Scrub clams with stiff brush under cold, running water. Rinse shrimp. Scrub potatoes with stiff brush. Pull husks back on corn but do not remove husks. Remove silks and replace husks. Peel onions. Rinse and dry chicken. Sprinkle with salt and pepper.

Place ingredients in bags or cheesecloth. Use ties for bags or tie opposite ends of cheesecloth together. Place on steamer rack over boiling water. Cover and steam until potato is done, about 50 minutes to 1 hour. Serve with bowls of melted margarine, salt and pepper.

Note: You can add dressed hard crabs, if you like, or substitute them for shrimp. Obviously, shrimp are always overcooked in a clambake. Regular attendees at clambakes don't object. You can, however, avoid the problem by steaming the shrimp separately and serving them along with the clambake. Most clambake recipes call for 1/4 of a chicken, but since this is such a large meal, we substituted chicken thighs. This provided plenty of seasoning for the other ingredients.

THE SWEET TASTE OF SCALLOPS

In Greek mythology, the love goddess Aphrodite rose from the sea and was borne across the water on a scallop shell. The Roman goddess Venus was born from a scallop shell. Since that time, artists and poets have paid tribute to the scallop.

The apostle St. James wore the scallop shell as his emblem. And pilgrims who visited what was believed to be his tomb received a scallop shell. The graceful shell is still known to the French as "*coquille St. Jacques,*" or "St. James shell."

Three species of scallops are commercially important to the Mid-Atlantic and South Atlantic. The bay scallop shell grows up to four inches wide and is found in bays and estuaries from New England through North Carolina. The edible meat is the adductor muscle, which is about one-half to three-fourths of an inch in size.

Growing twice as large, the sea scallop comes from the deep waters of the North and Mid-Atlantic. Its meat is one to two inches wide. The plentiful calico scallop, much smaller than the bay, is caught primarily off the Florida coast.

Unlike other mollusks, scallops are not sold in the shell. They are highly perishable and are shucked immediately after capture. Markets sell them fresh or frozen.

Bay scallops yield 70 to 90 shucked scallops per pound, while the larger sea scallops have 20 to 30. The tiny calico has from 150 to 200 scallops in each pound.

The meat of scallops is creamy white, tan or creamy pink.

The bay scallop tastes best — its sweet, mild flavor is the gourmet's favorite. Sea scallops also are mild and briny. The nutty flavor of the calico is slightly more pronounced.

Unlike other mollusks, scallops are not sold in the shell. They are highly perishable and are shucked immediately after capture. Markets sell them fresh or frozen.

Fresh scallops have a sweet smell. Though they have a stronger odor than most seafood when the container is opened, it dissipates quickly. There should not be any iodine, sulfur or ammonia odor. Fresh scallops have an ivory translucence and firm texture with elastic springiness. They should be free of excess liquid. They are not soft and droopy, and they don't settle into each other. These conditions reflect aging.

Scallops in a milky liquid have either been soaked or are old. Scallops that have been soaked are artificially shiny, opaque and flabby. They release more liquid and shrink greatly when cooked.

We're frequently asked if many scallops on the market are not real but rather are cut from the wings of skates, rays or sharks. The answer is no. There is no way to duplicate the distinct, sweet flavor of scallop meat. Also, look at the structure of scallops. The meat fibers are horizontal while those of finfish are vertical.

Scallops are nutritious. They provide a good source of protein and are low in fat, calories and cholesterol.

Scallops are delicate and require short cooking times. When overcooked, they shrink and toughen. The same thing happens if they are left for any time after being cooked. They need to be served and eaten immediately.

Plus, scallops are versatile. They can be broiled, baked, sautéed, fried, poached, stewed, grilled and stir-fried. You can use them in casseroles or in combination with other seafoods such as our *Heavenly Seafood Casserole*, p. 144.

Swiss Baked Scallops

- 1 pound bay scallops (or sea scallops, quartered)
- 2 tablespoons margarine or butter
- 3/4 cup chopped onion
- 1/4 cup chopped green pepper
- 1 cup chopped celery
- 1 cup chopped fresh mushrooms
- 2 cups white sauce
- 1/2 cup fresh bread crumbs mixed with 1 tablespoon melted margarine or butter
- 1 cup freshly grated Swiss cheese

Prepare white sauce and set aside.

Melt 2 tablespoons margarine in medium skillet over medium heat. Sauté onion, green pepper, celery and mushrooms until tender. Add scallops and warm thoroughly over low heat. Pour in white sauce and mix gently.

Pour into greased, medium baking dish. Cover with crumb mixture and Swiss cheese. Bake at 350 F until golden brown, about 30 minutes. Serves 4 to 6.

White Sauce:
- 3 tablespoons margarine or butter
- 3 tablespoons flour
- 1 cup milk
- 1/4 teaspoon salt

Melt margarine in small saucepan over medium heat. Add flour and mix well. Gradually add milk, stirring constantly. Add salt. Cook until thick, continuing to stir. Remove from heat.

Rich Scallop Soup
- 1 pound scallops, finely chopped
- 2 cups milk
- 1 cup heavy cream
- 2 tablespoons margarine or butter
- 1 teaspoon salt
- 1/4 teaspoon freshly ground white pepper
- 1 teaspoon Worcestershire sauce
- paprika
- 3 tablespoons finely chopped fresh parsley

In top of double boiler, blend milk, cream, margarine, salt, pepper and Worcestershire. Place over boiling water and bring to simmer, stirring frequently.

Add scallops to mixture. Return to simmer and cook until tender, about 4 to 5 minutes. Pour into individual bowls. Sprinkle each with paprika and parsley. Serves 6.

Scallops with Green Onion Butter
- 1 pound bay scallops (or sea scallops, quartered)
- 1/4 cup margarine or butter, softened
- 1/3 cup minced green onion, including tops
- 1/4 teaspoon pressed garlic
- 2 tablespoons minced fresh parsley
- 1/4 teaspoon salt
- 1/4 teaspoon freshly ground white pepper

In small bowl, combine margarine, onion, garlic, parsley, salt and pepper. Place scallops in 4 individual shells or ramekins. Dot with margarine mixture.

Bake at 500 F until scallops are tender and opaque, about 10 minutes. Serves 4.

Baked Scallops
- 1 pound bay scallops (or sea scallops, quartered)
- 2 tablespoons dry white wine
- 1 tablespoon fresh lemon juice
- 1/4 teaspoon salt
- 1/4 teaspoon freshly ground white pepper
- 1/4 cup heavy cream
- 1/2 cup fresh bread crumbs mixed with 2 tablespoons melted margarine
  or butter

Mix wine, lemon juice, salt and pepper in medium bowl. Stir in scallops. Add cream and stir.

Place in a shallow, medium, greased baking dish. Sprinkle with crumb mixture. Bake at 400 F until scallops are done, mixture is bubbly and crumbs are browned, about 15 to 20 minutes. Serves 4.

Broiled Scallops
- 1 pound bay scallops (or sea scallops, quartered)
- 1/4 teaspoon garlic
- 1/4 teaspoon salt
- 2 tablespoons minced fresh parsley
- 1 tablespoon vegetable oil
- 1/4 cup dry vermouth
- 1/2 cup soft bread crumbs combined with 1/4 tablespoon melted margarine
- paprika

Combine garlic, salt, parsley, oil and vermouth in medium bowl. Stir in scallops.

Spoon scallop mixture into 4 shells or ramekins. Place on baking sheet. Broil about 4 inches from heat for 5 minutes. Sprinkle crumb mixture and paprika on top and broil until lightly browned, about 3 to 4 minutes. Serves 4.

Coquilles St. Jacques
- 1 pound bay scallops (or sea scallops, quartered)
- 1/2 cup dry white wine
- 1/2 cup water
- 4 tablespoons minced green onion, including tops
- 1 bay leaf
- 1 sprig parsley
- 1 teaspoon salt
- 2 tablespoons margarine or butter
- 1/2 cup fresh mushrooms, chopped
- 3 tablespoons flour
- 2/3 cup heavy cream
- 2 teaspoon fresh lemon juice
- 1/4 teaspoons freshly ground white pepper
- 1/3 cup freshly grated Swiss cheese combined with
- 1/4 cup soft bread crumbs

Place wine, water, onion, bay leaf, parsley and salt in large saucepan. Bring to boil, lower heat and simmer for 5 minutes. Add scallops. Return to simmer and cook until scallops are done, about 5 or 6 minutes. Remove scallops with slotted spoon and set aside. Remove bay leaf and parsley and reserve cooking liquid.

In small saucepan, melt margarine over medium heat. Sauté mushrooms until tender, about 5 minutes. Blend in flour. Add cream slowly, stirring constantly. Add cooking liquid and continue to cook until thickened and smooth. Stir in lemon juice and pepper. Thin with more cream, if needed.

Blend in scallops. Place in 4 individual shells or ramekins. Sprinkle with cheese/crumb mixture. Broil about 4 inches from heat until bubbly and lightly browned, about 5 minutes. Serves 4.

Scallop Cheese Bake
- 1 pound bay scallops (or sea scallops, quartered)
- 3 tablespoons margarine or butter
- 1 tablespoon chopped onion
- 3 tablespoons flour
- 1/4 teaspoon salt
- 1/8 teaspoon freshly ground white pepper
- 1/2 cup milk
- 1 4-ounce can chopped mushrooms, drained
- 2 tablespoons freshly grated Parmesan cheese
- 1 tablespoon chopped fresh parsley
- 1/2 cup freshly grated mild cheddar cheese
- 1/2 cup fresh cracker crumbs combined with 1 tablespoon melted margarine or butter

In large saucepan, melt margarine over medium heat. Cook onion until tender. Stir in flour, salt and pepper.

Add milk gradually, stirring constantly. Cook, continuing to stir, until thick. Remove from heat.

Stir in mushrooms, Parmesan, parsley and scallops. Turn into a greased, medium casserole dish and sprinkle with cheddar. Top with crumb mixture. Bake at 350 F until scallops are done, mixture is bubbly and crumbs are brown, about 25 minutes. Serves 4.

Fried Scallops
- 1 pound sea scallops
- 1 egg, beaten
- 1 tablespoon milk
- 1 teaspoon salt
- 1/4 teaspoon freshly ground black pepper
- 1/4 teaspoon paprika
- 1/2 cup flour
- 1/2 cup dry bread crumbs
- oil for frying

Rinse scallops and pat dry. Combine egg, milk, salt, pepper and paprika in small bowl. In shallow dish, combine flour and crumbs. Dip scallops in egg mixture, then roll in flour mixture.

Heat about 1/8 inch oil in large, heavy skillet. Cook scallops until golden brown on one side, about 2 to 3 minutes. Turn and repeat on other side. Drain on paper towels. Serves 4.

Farm-Raised
FISH

CHAPTER NINE RECIPES:

- Broiled Catfish
- Charcoal-Grilled Catfish
- Catfish Gumbo Supreme
- Savory Catfish with Lemon
- Fried Catfish
- Crispy Fried Catfish
- Spicy Fried Catfish
- Cajun Baked Catfish
- Baked Salmon with Sour Cream and Dill
- Baked Salmon with Wine Sauce
- Baked Salmon Steaks Provencal
- Poached Salmon Steaks with Dill Sauce
- Broiled Salmon Fillet with White Wine Sauce
- Broiled Salmon with Wine and Green Onion
- Grilled Salmon with Fennel
- Poached Salmon with Brandy Sauce
- Baked Hybrid Striped Bass with Wine
  and Tarragon Sauce
- Broiled Hybrid Striped Bass with Paprika and Herbs
- Oven-Fried Hybrid Striped Bass
- Hybrid Striped Bass with Lemon-Parsley Sauce

- Baked Hybrid Striped Bass in White Wine
- Simply Broiled Hybrid Striped Bass
- Pan-Fried Hybrid Striped Bass
- Broiled Tilapia with Dill Butter
- Pan-Fried Tilapia
- Broiled Tilapia with Hollandaise Sauce
- Poached Tilapia with Lemon-Tarragon Butter
- Sautéed Tilapia Fillets with Lime
- Pan-Fried Tilapia with Brown Butter Sauce
- Tilapia with Fine Herbs
- Tilapia Parmesan
- Crawfish Boil
- Golden-Fried Crawfish
- Crawfish Creole
- Crawfish Casserole
- Crawfish Étouffée
- Sautéed Crawfish
- Stewed Crawfish
- Crawfish Jambalaya
- Crawfish Gumbo

Farm-Raised

FISH

A NEW KIND OF CATFISH

The catfish, long relegated to the lowly position of an unglamourous scavenger, has now become a national favorite. Graduating from the river bottom to the farm, pond-raised catfish are making their appearance in white-cloth restaurants as well as in supermarkets.

Channel catfish are the most successful aquaculture species in the United States. Hundreds of millions of pounds are produced annually, mostly from 150,000 acres of catfish farms in Mississippi. Other states that produce smaller amounts of catfish include North Carolina, Texas and Alabama.

Once passed over because of their muddy, oily taste, today's mild-flavored catfish have a new image. The farm-raised fish are fed a grain diet. This ensures a mild, "nonfishy" flavor. They are so mild, in fact, that they need more seasonings than most other fish. A versatile fish, catfish can be prepared in a variety of ways. Try grilling, broiling, steaming, stir-frying or other favorite cooking methods. And, of course, there are always the traditional fried recipes we occasionally enjoy.

Flaky and moist, mild-flavored catfish can be substituted for most white-fleshed fish in recipes.

Because it is raised and harvested much like other farm crops, catfish supply is controlled. The fish are available year-round. We've seen them in supermarkets all across the state.

The tough skin of catfish is removed during processing. Since you buy the skinless, boneless fillets, there is no waste. Catfish are kept alive until processing to ensure freshness. If properly handled, those you find in the markets are a high-quality product.

A typical 3 1/2-ounce serving is low in calories, fat and cholesterol, and high in protein.

There's even a catfish fan club. The Loyal Order of Catfish Lovers has a few thousand members. Membership entitles you to a card, recipes and even a secret handshake. After trying a few of our catfish dishes, you may want to join.

Channel catfish are the most successful aquaculture species in the United States. Hundreds of millions of pounds are produced annually, mostly from 150,000 acres of catfish farms in Mississippi. Other states that produce smaller amounts of catfish include North Carolina, Texas and Alabama.

Broiled Catfish

- 6 medium catfish fillets
- 1/3 cup soy sauce
- 1/4 teaspoon Tabasco sauce
- 3 tablespoons vegetable oil
- 1 teaspoon pressed garlic
- 1/2 teaspoon ground ginger
- 1/2 teaspoon salt
- 1/4 teaspoon freshly ground black pepper
- lemon wedges

Combine soy sauce, Tabasco, oil, garlic, ginger, salt and pepper. Place fish in sauce and marinate in refrigerator for 30 minutes. Place fish on oiled broiler pan. Broil about 4 inches from heat, basting occasionally, for 8 to 10 minutes, or until fish flakes easily when tested with a fork. Serve with lemon wedges. Serves 6.

Charcoal-Grilled Catfish

- 6 medium catfish fillets
- 1/4 cup vegetable oil
- 1/2 teaspoon freshly ground white pepper
- 1/2 teaspoon garlic salt

Brush fillets with oil. Sprinkle one side with pepper and garlic salt. Place in well-oiled hinged grill. Place about 4 inches over moderate coals and grill until done on one side, about 5 minutes. Turn and repeat on other side until fish flakes easily when tested with a fork. Serves 6.

Catfish Gumbo Supreme
- 4 medium catfish fillets
- 1/4 cup vegetable oil
- 1 cup coarsely chopped celery
- 1/2 cup chopped green onion, including tops
- 3/4 cup chopped onion
- 4 teaspoons minced garlic
- 2 14 1/2-ounce cans chicken broth
- 2 14 1/2-ounce cans chopped tomatoes, undrained
- 1/2 teaspoon thyme
- 1 small bay leaf
- 1/2 teaspoon cayenne pepper
- 1/2 teaspoon oregano
- 1 teaspoon salt
- 2 boxes frozen sliced okra
- 4 ounces orzo (optional)

Cut fillets into 1-inch pieces and set aside.

Heat oil in large pot over medium heat. Lightly sauté celery, green onion, onion and garlic. Add broth, tomatoes, thyme, bay leaf, cayenne, oregano and salt. Bring to boil and add okra. Cover and simmer 15 minutes. Add orzo. Cover and continue simmering 15 minutes. Add catfish and simmer 10 minutes or until fish flakes easily. Remove bay leaf. Serves 8 to 10.

Savory Catfish with Lemon
- 4 medium catfish fillets
- 1/3 cup flour
- 1/2 teaspoon salt
- 1/4 teaspoon cayenne pepper
- 1/4 teaspoon freshly ground black pepper
- 2 tablespoons vegetable oil
- 3 tablespoons margarine or butter
- 2 tablespoons fresh lemon juice
- 2 tablespoons chopped fresh parsley
- 1/2 teaspoon Worcestershire sauce
- lemon wedges

Combine flour, salt, cayenne and pepper in a shallow bowl or pan. Dip fillets lightly in mixture.

Heat oil in large skillet over moderate heat. Add 2 tablespoons margarine and melt. Sauté fillets until golden brown on one side, about 4 to 5 minutes. Turn and repeat on other side. Remove from skillet.

Melt remaining margarine in skillet and brown slightly. Add lemon juice, parsley and Worcestershire sauce. Pour over fillets. Serve with lemon wedges. Serves 4.

Fried Catfish

- 6 medium catfish fillets
- 1 cup yellow cornmeal
- 1/4 cup flour
- 1 1/4 teaspoon salt
- 1/2 teaspoon cayenne pepper
- 1/2 teaspoon garlic powder
- vegetable oil for frying
- tartar sauce

Combine cornmeal, flour, salt, cayenne pepper and garlic powder. Roll fish in mixture. Heat about 1/8-inch oil in large skillet. Place fish in single layer in hot oil. Fry over medium heat 4 to 5 minutes or until golden brown. Turn and fry other side until fish are golden brown and flake easily when tested with a fork. Drain on paper towels. Serve with tartar sauce. Serves 6.

Crispy Fried Catfish

- 6 small catfish, pan dressed
- 1 2-ounce bottle of Tabasco sauce
- salt
- freshly ground black pepper
- 1 cup yellow cornmeal
- vegetable oil for frying

Marinate fish in Tabasco sauce for 30 minutes in refrigerator, turning once. Remove from sauce and lightly salt, then pepper. Roll in cornmeal to cover completely.

Heat oil in deep fat fryer or skillet to 375 F. Place fish in hot oil, and cook until golden brown on both sides. Drain on paper towels. Serve with tartar sauce. Serves 6.

(Note: It sounds as if the Tabasco will make the fish too hot, but it won't. It will add flavor only.)

Spicy Fried Catfish

- 6 small catfish fillets
- 1 cup yellow cornmeal
- 1 1/2 teaspoons paprika
- 1/2 teaspoon salt
- 1/2 teaspoon celery salt
- 1/2 teaspoon freshly ground black pepper
- 1/4 teaspoon dry mustard
- 1/2 teaspoon onion powder
- vegetable oil for frying
- tartar sauce

Prepare tartar sauce beforehand and allow flavors to blend, if possible.

Combine cornmeal and seasonings. Roll fish in seasoned cornmeal. Place fish in single layer in hot oil in large skillet. Fry over moderate heat for 4 to 5 minutes or until golden brown on one side. Turn and fry on other side until fish are golden brown and flake easily when tested with a fork. Drain on paper towels. Serve with tartar sauce. Serves 6.

Tartar Sauce:

- 3/4 cup mayonnaise
- 1 tablespoon minced onion
- 1/2 cup finely chopped dill pickle
- 1 tablespoon dill pickle juice
- 1 tablespoon fresh lemon juice
- chopped pulp from 1/2 lemon
- 1 tablespoon vinegar
- 1/4 cup finely chopped fresh parsley

Mix all ingredients together. Chill and allow flavors to blend. Store in refrigerator. Makes about 1 cup.

Cajun Baked Catfish
- 6 small catfish fillets
- 3 tablespoons margarine or butter, melted
- 1/2 teaspoon onion powder
- 1/2 teaspoon garlic powder
- 1/2 teaspoon salt
- 1/4 teaspoon freshly ground black pepper
- 1/4 teaspoon cayenne pepper
- 1/2 teaspoon dried thyme leaves

Brush tops of fish with melted margarine. In a flat dish or pan, mix onion powder, garlic powder, salt, black pepper, cayenne and thyme. Sprinkle tops of fish with seasoning mixture. Place in greased baking dish or pan. Bake at 400 F until fish flakes easily with a fork, about 8 to 10 minutes. Serves 6.

SALMON — AN OMEGA-3 CHAMP

It used to be that most salmon recipes began with "a can of salmon."

Now this has changed. In recent years, fresh salmon has become widely available. And instead of the usual cakes or casseroles, we can prepare a variety of dishes such as our *Baked Salmon with Wine Sauce*.

Salmon tastes delicious poached, steamed, baked, broiled, grilled and cooked in other favorite ways. And it makes a delectable and healthful entrée.

Salmon is an excellent source of omega-3 fatty acids. It is low in fat, cholesterol and calories.

It is interesting to note the history of salmon usage. As a food, it dates back at least to the Old Stone Age, 25,000 B.C. In the Middle Ages, it was served to the sounding of trumpets. In this country, Native Americans and early settlers dined on it. And now we have rediscovered it.

Farm-raised salmon have made the species more readily available. We no longer have to depend upon the seasonality of wild salmon. Most of the fresh salmon in supermarkets and seafood markets is farm-raised and available year-round.

Farmed salmon usually produces a high-quality product. They are raised under controlled conditions and processed quickly under ideal temperature and sanitation. Since wild salmon are not always handled as well, their quality is not always consistent.

The Atlantic salmon is the only species native to the Atlantic, while six Pacific species exist. Species vary in color, fat content and flavor.

The Atlantic salmon is the species most often farm-raised. Farmers raise it

Salmon tastes delicious

poached, steamed, baked,

broiled, grilled and cooked in

other favorite ways.

And it makes a delectable

and healthful entrée.

Salmon is an excellent source

of omega-3 fatty acids.

It is low in fat, cholesterol

and calories.

in countries around the world, including North America, Latin America and Europe. Often it's labeled by its country of origin, such as Norwegian salmon, instead of its true name, Atlantic salmon.

I have had frequent requests for information on fresh salmon preparation. As a result, we developed and evaluated recipes for this mouth-watering delicacy. We used farmed Atlantic salmon, as well as king and coho — two Pacific species. The fillets were about 1 1/2-inches thick and more than two feet long. We cut these into large pieces and specified a "2-pound fillet" in the recipe.

Many supermarket seafood sections have smaller fillets that you can cut into serving-size pieces. And most steaks make single servings. You can substitute small fillets for large ones or vice versa. Just remember to adjust your cooking time. Species and forms can be interchanged, too, such as using fillets instead of steaks. Our *Baked Salmon Steaks Provencal* tastes just as delicious with fillets.

Most instructions tell you that it's easier to skin salmon fillets after cooking. But, if you prefer, your seafood market's staff will skin them quickly and easily when you buy them. Handling and cooking the skinless fillets makes preparation and serving much simpler.

Before cooking, use needlenose pliers to remove the line of bones that go down into the fillet along the center. Feel along the fillet with your fingers to locate these bones.

We keep a pair of needlenose pliers with our fish-cleaning equipment. They make it easy to serve a beautiful, boneless salmon fillet. Although the pliers are not useful for all species, they are also good for removing the small bones from such fish as Spanish mackerel.

Try some fresh salmon recipes. Once you do, you'll be hooked!

Baked Salmon with Sour Cream and Dill

- 1 2-pound salmon fillet, skinless and boneless
- 2 tablespoons margarine or butter, melted
- 1 tablespoon fresh lemon juice
- 2 tablespoons minced onion
- salt
- 1 cup light sour cream
- 1 egg, beaten
- 1 tablespoon minced, fresh dill (or 1 teaspoon dried)
- 1/4 teaspoon freshly ground white pepper
- 1 teaspoon lemon zest

Place salmon in greased baking dish. Spread with margarine. Mix lemon juice and onion and spread over fish. Sprinkle with salt. Bake at 450 F for 20 minutes.

Mix sour cream with egg, dill and pepper. Spread on fish. Continue baking for 5 minutes, or until fish flakes easily when tested with a fork. Sprinkle with lemon zest. Cut into serving-size pieces. Serves 6 to 8.

Baked Salmon with Wine Sauce

- 1 2-pound salmon fillet, skinless and boneless
- 2 tablespoons margarine or butter, melted
- 2 tablespoons fresh lemon juice
- 1/4 teaspoon salt
- 1/4 teaspoon freshly ground black pepper
- lemon wedges (optional)

Brush fish with melted margarine. Pour lemon juice over fillet. Sprinkle with salt and pepper. Place in greased baking dish. Cover. Bake at 450 F for 20 minutes or until fish flakes easily when tested with a fork. Baste once during baking.

Place salmon on serving platter. Spoon margarine from baking dish into sauce and reheat. Spoon sauce over salmon. Cut into serving-size pieces. Garnish with lemon wedges. Serves 6 to 8.

Wine Sauce:

- 4 tablespoons margarine or butter
- 1 1/2 tablespoons dry white wine
- 1/2 teaspoon minced fresh tarragon (or 1/4 teaspoon dried)
- 1/4 teaspoon soy sauce

Melt 4 tablespoons margarine in small pan over medium heat. Stir in wine, tarragon and soy sauce. Bring to boil and remove from heat.

Baked Salmon Steaks Provencal

- 6 salmon steaks, 3/4 to 1 inch thick, small bones removed
- 3 tablespoons margarine or butter, melted
- salt
- freshly ground white pepper

Brush steaks with melted margarine. Sprinkle with salt and pepper. Place in lightly greased baking dish. Bake at 450 F about 10 minutes or until fish flakes easily with a fork. Baste once during baking. Serves 6.

Meanwhile, prepare Provencal Sauce.

Provencal Sauce:
- 6 tablespoons margarine or butter
- 1 cup finely chopped onion
- 1/2 cup finely chopped celery
- 1 teaspoon pressed garlic
- 2 tablespoons flour
- 1 cup canned chopped tomatoes, drained
- 1/2 cup dry white wine
- 1 teaspoon minced fresh tarragon or 1/2 teaspoon, dried
- 1/4 teaspoon salt
- 1 cup heavy cream

Melt margarine in medium saucepan over medium heat. Add onion, celery and garlic and sauté lightly. Blend in flour. Add tomatoes, wine and tarragon. Blend well. Heat until simmering. Add cream and continue to cook, stirring constantly, until thick and smooth.

Place steaks on serving platter and pour sauce over fish. Serves 6.

Poached Salmon Steaks with Dill Sauce
- 6 salmon steaks, 3/4 to 1 inch thick, small bones removed
- 5 cups water
- 1 cup dry white wine
- 1/3 cup chopped carrots
- 1/2 cup chopped onion
- 1/2 cup chopped celery
- 1/2 teaspoon salt
- 1/2 tablespoon black peppercorns

Combine water, wine, carrot, onion, celery, salt and peppercorns in fish poacher or large shallow pan. Bring to boil, reduce heat and simmer about 30 minutes. Place salmon in liquid and poach until it flakes easily with a fork, about 10 minutes. Place steaks on serving platter and pour Dill Sauce over them. Serves 6.

Meanwhile, prepare Dill Sauce.

Dill Sauce:
- 1 tablespoon margarine or butter
- 1 tablespoon flour
- 1/3 cup fish or chicken broth
- 1/3 cup light cream
- 1 tablespoon dry vermouth
- 1/4 cup finely chopped fresh parsley
- 1 tablespoon finely chopped fresh dill or 1 teaspoon dried
- 1/4 teaspoon salt
- 1/4 teaspoon freshly ground black pepper

In small skillet, melt margarine over low heat. Stir in flour; cook over low heat until roux is golden brown. Add broth, cream, vermouth, parsley, dill, salt and pepper. Cook until thick and smooth. Pour over steaks.

Broiled Salmon Fillet with White Wine Sauce
- 1 salmon fillet, about 1 pound, skinless, bones removed
- 4 tablespoons margarine or butter, melted
- 1/4 teaspoon salt

Brush salmon with melted margarine. Sprinkle with salt. Place on broiler pan and broil about 4 inches from heat. Cook 10 minutes or until fish flakes easily with a fork. Remove to serving platter and spoon warm sauce over top. Serves 3 to 4. May also be grilled. Meanwhile, prepare sauce.

White Wine Sauce:
- 3/4 cup fish or chicken broth
- 1/2 teaspoon dried thyme
- 1/3 cup finely chopped green onion, including tops
- 1/8 teaspoon nutmeg
- 1 cup dry white wine
- 1 cup heavy cream
- 2 tablespoons melted margarine or butter blended with 2 tablespoons cornstarch
- 1/4 teaspoon salt
- 1/4 teaspoon freshly ground white pepper

In medium saucepan, heat broth over medium heat. Mix in thyme, onion, nutmeg and wine. Bring to boil. Reduce heat to low and stir in cream. Bring to simmer and remove from heat. Add margarine and corn starch and blend well. Return to low heat and stir constantly until thick and smooth. Add salt and pepper. Serve warm.

Broiled Salmon with Wine and Green Onion
- 1 2-pound salmon fillet, skinless, small bones removed
- 4 tablespoons margarine or butter, melted
- 1/2 cup finely chopped green onion, including tops
- 1 1/2 cups dry white wine
- 2 cups heavy cream
- 1/4 teaspoon salt
- 1 teaspoon fresh lemon juice
- 2 1/2 tablespoons cornstarch

Put wine and onion in medium saucepan. Cook over medium heat 20 minutes to reduce. Add cream and continue to cook until thickened, about 20 minutes. Add salt and lemon juice.

Place small amount of sauce into a small bowl and gradually blend in cornstarch. Add back to sauce slowly. Stir constantly until thick and smooth.

Brush fillet with margarine. Broil about 4 inches from heat until fish flakes easily with a fork, about 15 to 20 minutes. During last few minutes of broiling fish, reheat sauce over low heat. Remove salmon to warm serving platter and cut into serving-size portions. Spoon sauce over fish. Serves 6 to 8.

Grilled Salmon with Fennel
- 4 salmon steaks, about 6 ounces each, small bones removed
- 2 tablespoons finely chopped fresh parsley
- 1/2 cup finely chopped green onion, including tops
- 1 teaspoon dried fennel seeds, ground
- freshly ground black pepper
- 1/4 cup vegetable oil
- 3 tablespoons fresh lime juice

Combine parsley, onion, fennel, pepper, oil and lime juice in shallow dish. Reserve 2 tablespoons for basting. Place steaks in remaining marinade for 30 minutes, turning once. Place in greased, hinged wire grill and cook about 4 inches over moderately hot coals until done on one side, about 6 to 8 minutes. Turn and cook on other side 6 to 8 minutes longer, or until fish flakes easily with a fork. Baste occasionally with remaining marinade while grilling. Serves 4. May also be broiled.

Poached Salmon with Brandy Sauce

- 2 pounds salmon fillets, skinless, bones removed
- 1 cup sliced carrots
- 1 cup sliced onion
- 3/4 cup sliced celery, including leaves
- 8 cups water
- 1 cup dry white wine
- 4 parsley sprigs
- 1 teaspoon salt
- 1 bay leaf
- 1 sprig fresh thyme or 1/2 teaspoon dried

Combine carrots, onion, celery, water, wine, parsley, salt, bay leaf and thyme in large shallow pan or poaching dish. Bring to boil. Reduce heat and simmer about 20 minutes.

Place salmon in poaching liquid and cook 15 to 20 minutes, or until fish flakes easily.

While fish is cooking, prepare Brandy Sauce.

When done, remove salmon from liquid to warm platter. Pour Brandy Sauce over fish. Cut into serving-size pieces. Serves 6 to 8.

Brandy Sauce:

- 2 tablespoons butter
- 2 tablespoons flour
- 1 cup light cream
- 1/8 teaspoon salt
- 1/8 teaspoon freshly ground white pepper
- 1/4 teaspoon paprika
- 1/2 tablespoon fresh dill or 1/2 teaspoon, dried
- 2 tablespoons brandy

Melt butter over low heat. Add flour slowly and blend well, about 3 to 4 minutes. Slowly add cream, stirring constantly until thickened. Add salt, pepper, paprika and dill. Stir in brandy. Pour over hot fish.

HYBRID STRIPED BASS — A NEW BREED

The hybrid striped bass is a latecomer to the seafood market. Raised primarily in aquaculture ponds and tanks, this species is the tasty result of university research.

By the late 1980s, scientists learned that crossing the striped bass with the white bass yielded a hybrid that was hardier, faster growing and more disease resistant than either of its parents. It became a perfect candidate for the aquaculture industry, filling a market niche left by declining East Coast catches of wild striped bass. Realizing the potential for the hybrid, the Sea Grant programs in North Carolina and South Carolina supported research to develop pond culture and hatchery techniques for the hybrid. The science proved successful and that commercial pond culture of hybrid striped bass could be successful and profitable on a large scale.

The rest is history. Today, almost all states in the South have some hybrid striped bass production, mostly in North Carolina, South Carolina, Florida, Louisiana and Texas.

While much of the hybrid harvest is shipped to the northeast where it is sold to restaurants and ethnic retail markets, the hybrid now appears on local menus and in seafood markets.

The hybrid striped bass has a silvery-black back and a white belly. Dark black stripes run along its sides. These stripes have a broken pattern as opposed to the wild striper's solid lines. Hybrid bass may grow to 20 pounds, but those harvested for food fish are 1 1/2 to 2 1/2 pounds.

As a result of being farm-raised, hybrid striped bass eat a high-protein, grain-based feed. They live in ponds and tanks where the water quality is constantly monitored and they receive continuous care from growers interested in delivering a top-quality product to market. And often, it's only a matter of hours between the time the farmer nets the fish to the time they are delivered to restaurants and seafood markets. The hybrid striped bass should be a quality catch for any consumer.

The meat of the striped bass is white and turns opaque when cooked. It has a delicate flavor and a firm, moist and flaky texture. Fillets can be broiled, grilled, steamed, sautéed or poached. Dressed whole fish can be baked. Striped bass can be substituted for any white-fleshed fish such as catfish or flounder.

This mild fish is low in calories, fat and cholesterol, and high in protein.

Hybrid striped bass is marketed year-round, but the greatest availability is from September through April. Fresh fish are sold whole, gutted or dressed, and on ice to assure high quality and extended shelf life.

The hybrid striped bass has a silvery-black back and a white belly. Dark black stripes run along its sides. These stripes have a broken pattern as opposed to the wild striper's solid lines. Hybrid bass may grow to 20 pounds, but those harvested for food fish are 1 1/2 to 2 1/2 pounds.

When buying farm-raised hybrid striped bass (or any other fish), be sure the eyes appear clear and not milky. The gills should be red, not brown, and the flesh resilient with a good sheen. The fish should have no smell.

Baked Hybrid Striped Bass with Wine and Tarragon Sauce

- 4 medium hybrid striped bass fillets
- 3 tablespoons margarine or butter, melted
- 2 tablespoons fresh lemon juice
- 1/8 teaspoon salt
- 1/8 teaspoon freshly ground black pepper
- parsley sprigs (optional)

Place fish in shallow greased baking pan. Brush with margarine. Dot with lemon juice. Sprinkle with salt and pepper. Bake at 450 F, basting once, until fish flakes easily with a fork, about 10 minutes. Garnish with parsley sprigs.

While fish is cooking, prepare Wine and Tarragon Sauce.

Garnish with parsley sprigs. Serves 8.

Wine and Tarragon Sauce:

- 2 tablespoons margarine or butter
- 1/2 tablespoon dry white wine
- 1/4 teaspoon finely chopped fresh tarragon
- 1/8 teaspoon soy sauce
- 1/8 teaspoon salt
- 1/8 teaspoon freshly ground black pepper

Prepare sauce while fish is baking. In small saucepan, melt margarine over medium heat. Add wine, tarragon, soy sauce, salt and pepper. Bring to boil and remove from heat. Spoon over fillets.

Broiled Hybrid Striped Bass with Paprika and Herbs

- 2 pounds hybrid striped bass fillets
- 1/2 cup margarine or butter, softened
- 1/2 teaspoon salt
- 1 teaspoon paprika
- 1/2 teaspoon freshly ground black pepper
- 2 tablespoons finely minced green onion
- 2 tablespoons finely minced fresh parsley
- 3/4 teaspoons dried tarragon
- 1 tablespoon fresh lemon juice

Cream margarine. Combine with salt, paprika, pepper, green onion, parsley, tarragon and lemon juice. Spread mixture on fish. Broil about 4 inches from heat, basting once or twice with pan juices, until fish is done, about 8 to 10 minutes. Transfer to platter and pour pan juices over fish. Serves 6 to 8.

Oven-Fried Hybrid Striped Bass
- 2 pounds hybrid striped bass fillets
- 1/2 cup milk
- salt
- freshly ground white pepper
- 1 cup fine dry bread crumbs
- 3 tablespoons margarine or butter, melted

In large shallow dish, combine milk and salt. Spread crumbs in another shallow dish or on wax paper. Dip fish in milk, then coat evenly with crumbs. Place fish in a single layer in greased baking dish. Drizzle with melted margarine. Bake at 500 F until crisp and golden brown, about 6 to 8 minutes, or until fish flakes easily with a fork. Serves 6 to 8.

Hybrid Striped Bass with Lemon-Parsley Sauce
- 1 pound hybrid striped bass fillets
- 2 tablespoons vegetable oil
- 2 tablespoons margarine or butter
- salt
- freshly ground black pepper
- flour

Heat oil in medium skillet over medium heat. Add margarine. Lightly salt and pepper fillets. Dredge in flour and shake off excess. Cook fillets over medium heat until golden brown on one side, about 4 minutes. Turn and repeat on other side. Remove from pan and drain on paper towels. Serves 3 to 4.

While fish is cooking, prepare Lemon-Parsley Sauce.

Lemon-Parsley Sauce:
- 6 tablespoons margarine or butter
- 2 tablespoons fresh lemon juice
- 1/8 teaspoon salt
- 2 tablespoons finely chopped fresh parsley

In small saucepan, melt margarine over medium heat. Add lemon juice and salt. Remove from heat. Add parsley and pour over cooked fish.

Baked Hybrid Striped Bass in White Wine
- 1 1/2 pounds hybrid striped bass fillets
- salt
- pepper
- 2 tablespoons fresh lemon juice
- 2 1/2 tablespoons margarine or butter
- 1/2 cup chopped onion
- 1/2 cup dry white wine
- 1/4 cup water
- 1/2 cup chopped fresh mushrooms
- 1 tablespoon chopped parsley
- 1 teaspoon minced garlic
- 1/8 teaspoon dried marjoram
- 1/8 teaspoon dried thyme
- 1/8 teaspoon cayenne pepper

Sprinkle fish with salt, pepper and 2 teaspoons lemon juice. Place chopped onion and wine in greased baking pan. Place fish on top and dot with small pats of margarine. Bake at 450 F for 12 to 15 minutes, or until fish flakes easily with a fork. Baste once or twice with pan juice.

While fish is baking, combine remaining lemon juice, water, mushrooms, parsley, garlic, marjoram, thyme and cayenne in small saucepan. Bring to a boil and reduce by half. When fish is done, add pan juice to mixture and continue cooking until sauce is thick and bubbly. Pour over fish. Serves 4 to 5.

Simply Broiled Hybrid Striped Bass
- 2 pounds hybrid striped bass fillets
- 1/4 cup margarine or butter, melted
- 1 tablespoon fresh lemon juice
- salt
- freshly ground white pepper
- paprika

Combine margarine and lemon juice. Brush over fillets. Sprinkle with salt, pepper and paprika. Broil about 4 inches from heat until golden and fish flakes easily with a fork, about 8 to 10 minutes. Serves 6 to 8.

Pan-Fried Hybrid Striped Bass
- 1 pound hybrid striped bass fillets
- salt
- freshly ground black pepper
- flour
- 2 tablespoons vegetable oil
- 2 tablespoons margarine or butter

Prepare Egg Wash and set aside.

Lightly salt and pepper fillets. Dredge in flour and shake off excess. Coat in egg wash.

Heat oil in medium skillet over medium heat. Add margarine. Cook fillets over medium heat until golden brown on one side, about 4 to 5 minutes. Turn and repeat on other side. Remove from pan and drain on paper towels. Serves 3 to 4.

Egg Wash:
- 1 egg
- 1/4 teaspoon salt
- 2 tablespoons freshly grated Parmesan cheese

Whisk egg. Stir in salt and Parmesan.

TILAPIA — A NEW "OLD" FISH

The mild, white-fleshed fish tilapia has been farm-raised and enjoyed in other parts of the world for centuries. Its origins can be traced back to the Nile River. Early records even show that Egyptian Pharaohs ate tilapia some 4,500 years ago.

Tilapia is reputed to be the fish that Jesus fed to the multitudes in the Biblical story. It is also supposedly the fish St. Peter caught when tested by Jesus and thus is frequently labeled "St. Peter's fish." Although you may see fish advertised this way, the name is not legally sanctioned by the U.S. Food and Drug Administration.

Once seen mostly in white-tablecloth restaurants, tilapia is now widely available in the seafood section of supermarkets nationwide.

Much of the tilapia sold in this country is raised in ponds or tanks in Latin America, Asia and the United States. A tropical fish, tilapia can thrive in either fresh or brackish water, but water temperatures must be higher than 55 F for it to survive.

The meat is white and firm, and the tender flakes have a sweet, mild flavor. Tilapia can be used in recipes calling for snapper, flounder, catfish or any other white-fleshed fish.

The mild, white-fleshed fish tilapia has been farm-raised and enjoyed in other parts of the world for centuries. Its origins can be traced back to the Nile River. Early records even show that Egyptian Pharaohs ate tilapia some 4,500 years ago.

Like farm-raised catfish, tilapia's mild flavor is enhanced by herbs and other seasonings. We tried it in some of our earlier recipes such as *Flounder with Fine Herbs in Parchment* (p. 188) and found it delightful. It also accepts sauces well. But, as with all seafood, do not allow sauces or seasonings to mask the true flavor of the fish.

Tilapia is versatile. You can broil, sauté, grill, bake, steam, fry, microwave or poach it.

Low in fat, a serving of tilapia is also low in calories and fat.

Broiled Tilapia with Dill Butter

- 8 small tilapia fillets
- 4 tablespoons margarine or butter, melted
- salt
- freshly ground black pepper

Prepare Dill Butter and set aside.

Brush fillets with melted margarine. Salt and pepper lightly. Broil about 4 inches from heat until done, about 8 to 10 minutes. Spread with Dill Butter. Serves 8.

Dill Butter:

- 1/2 stick margarine or butter, softened
- 2 tablespoons fresh dill or 2 teaspoons dried
- 1/2 teaspoon pressed garlic

Combine margarine, dill and garlic in small bowl. Spread over cooked fillets.

Pan-Fried Tilapia

- 1 pound tilapia fillets
- 2 tablespoons vegetable oil
- 2 tablespoons margarine or butter
- salt
- freshly ground white pepper
- flour

Prepare Egg Wash and set aside.

Heat oil in medium skillet to 375 F. Add margarine.

Lightly salt and pepper fillets. Dredge in flour. Shake off excess. Coat in egg wash. Place in skillet and cook at 375 F until golden brown on one side, about 4 minutes. Turn and repeat on other side. Remove and drain on paper towels. Serves 3 to 4.

Egg Wash:
- 2 eggs
- 2 tablespoons freshly grated Parmesan cheese
     Whisk eggs. Stir in Parmesan.

Broiled Tilapia with Hollandaise Sauce
- 1 pound tilapia fillets
- 4 tablespoons margarine or butter, melted
- salt
- freshly ground black pepper
- paprika
     Prepare Hollandaise Sauce and keep warm. Brush fillets with melted margarine. Lightly salt and pepper. Sprinkle with paprika. Broil about 4 inches from heat until done, about 8 to 10 minutes. Serve with Hollandaise Sauce. Serves 3 to 4.

Cooked Hollandaise Sauce:
- 3 egg yolks
- 1/4 cup water
- 2 tablespoons fresh lemon juice
- 1/2 cup firm, cold margarine or butter, cut into eighths
- 1/4 teaspoon salt
- 1/8 teaspoon paprika
- 1/16 teaspoon cayenne pepper
     In small saucepan, beat together egg yolks, water and lemon juice. Cook over very low heat, stirring constantly, until yolk mixture bubbles at edges. Stir in butter, one piece at a time, until melted and sauce is thickened. Stir in salt, paprika and cayenne. Keep warm over very low heat, stirring occasionally. (Cover and chill if not using immediately.) Makes about 3/4 cup.
     Note: Hollandaise sauce should not be prepared with raw eggs. This recipe is from the American Egg Board.

Poached Tilapia with Lemon-Tarragon Butter

* 1 pound tilapia fillets
* 4 cups water
* 1/2 cup chopped celery
* 1/4 cup sliced carrot
* 1/2 cup thinly sliced onion
* 1/2 teaspoon black peppercorns
* 1 teaspoon salt
* 1 bay leaf
* 2 sprigs fresh parsley
* 1 cup dry white wine

Prepare Lemon Tarragon Butter and set aside.

Mix poaching ingredients together. Simmer 15 to 20 minutes. Place fillets in liquid and poach until fish flakes easily with a fork, about 8 to 10 minutes. Remove immediately. Spread with Lemon Tarragon Butter. Serves 3 to 4.

Lemon-Tarragon Butter:

* 1/2 stick margarine or butter, softened
* 1/2 teaspoon dried tarragon
* 1/2 teaspoon fresh lemon juice

In small bowl, combine margarine, tarragon and lemon juice. Spread over warm fish.

Sautéed Tilapia Fillets with Lime

* 1 pound tilapia fillets
* salt
* freshly ground black pepper
* flour
* 2 tablespoons olive oil
* 1 tablespoon margarine or butter
* 1/2 teaspoon pressed garlic
* 1/2 cup dry white wine
* 1 tablespoon fresh lime juice
* 1/3 cup thinly sliced green onion

Lightly salt and pepper fillets. Dredge in flour.

Heat oil in medium skillet, then add margarine. Sauté fillets at 375 F until golden on one side, about 3 to 4 minutes. Turn and repeat on other side.

While fish is cooking, combine garlic, wine and lime juice.

Remove fillets to warm platter. Add wine mixture to pan, scraping bottom of pan. Cook until slightly reduced, about 2 minutes. Stir in onion and heat. Spoon over fish. Serves 3 to 4.

Pan-Fried Tilapia with Brown Butter Sauce

- 1 pound tilapia fillets
- salt
- freshly ground black pepper
- 2 tablespoons vegetable oil
- 6 tablespoons margarine or butter
- flour
- 2 tablespoons fresh lemon juice
- 1 tablespoon finely chopped fresh parsley

Sprinkle fish lightly with salt and pepper. Heat oil in medium skillet over medium heat. Add 2 tablespoons margarine and heat. Cook fillets at 375 F until golden brown on one side, about 3 to 4 minutes. Turn and repeat on other side. Remove to warm platter.

Wipe pan with paper towel. Heat remaining 4 tablespoons margarine over medium-high heat until it foams and begins to brown. Remove from heat and stir in lemon juice and parsley. Spoon over fillets. Serves 3 to 4.

Tilapia with Fine Herbs

- 1 pound tilapia fillets
- 1/4 cup margarine or butter
- 2 tablespoons fresh lemon juice
- 2 tablespoons chopped fresh parsley
- 2 tablespoons fresh snipped chives (or 1 tablespoons dried)
- 3 tablespoons fresh snipped dill (or 1 1/2 teaspoons dried)
- 1/16 teaspoon cayenne pepper
- 1/2 teaspoon salt
- paprika

In small saucepan, melt margarine over medium heat. Stir in lemon juice, parsley, chives, dill, cayenne and salt.

Place fillets in lightly greased baking dish. Pour margarine mixture over top. Sprinkle with paprika. Bake, uncovered, at 450 F until fish flakes easily with a fork, about 8 to 10 minutes. Transfer to warm platter.

Boil pan juices over high heat until reduced to about 1/4 cup. Pour over fish. Serves 3 to 4.

Tilapia Parmesan
- 6 small tilapia fillets
- 6 tablespoons margarine or butter, melted
- salt
- freshly ground black pepper
- 3/4 cup freshly ground Parmesan cheese
- paprika

Brush fillets on both sides with margarine. Lightly salt and pepper. Dredge in Parmesan.

Place on baking pan. Sprinkle tops with paprika. Bake at 450 F until done, about 8 to 10 minutes. Serves 6.

MUD BUGS FOR DINNER!

Crawfish. Crayfish. Crawdad. Swamp lobster. Mud bug. Whatever they are called, these little critters offer another food favorite among shellfish lovers.

Crawfish have been eaten in large quantities in Europe for centuries. And Scandinavian "krebfests" are as popular as Louisiana "crawfish boils."

In the United States, we have long associated crawfish with the bayous of Louisiana. But they are now gaining popularity in many other places, including more of the Southeast. Some coastal and inland restaurants serve them regularly.

Hardy crustaceans, crawfish are found on almost every continent. More than 400 species inhabit waters throughout the world, with 250 in the United States. The most important U.S. species is the red swamp crawfish. Though all species are edible, only a few grow large enough to be eaten. Most crawfish that are marketed are from 3 1/2 to 7 inches long.

The crawfish body is large compared to the tail. Since only the tail is eaten, it takes about six or seven pounds of whole crawfish to yield one pound of meat.

Louisiana harvests the most crawfish in America commercially, producing about 90 percent of the farmed and wild catch. A few other states, including Mississippi, Texas, Alabama and North Carolina, provide smaller amounts.

Whole crawfish are popular boiled. In this country, they have traditionally been hot and spicy. Most Europeans boil them with dill. You might want to try them this way, also.

These little shellfish have great versatility. The traditional "crawfish boil," in which the meat is eaten right from the shell, is a tribute to its true flavor. Like crabs and lobsters, crawfish must be alive when cooked.

In the United States, we have long associated crawfish with the bayous of Louisiana. But they are now gaining popularity in many other places, including more of the Southeast. Some coastal and inland restaurants serve them regularly.

Some crawfish are parboiled, dressed and frozen for sale. Most of these are imported from China, where they are farmed. These convenient, processed crawfish are delicious in etouffées, jambalayas, stews and casseroles. And of course they are tasty fried and sautéed. Since they have been slightly pre-cooked, be careful not to overcook them in the recipe. All our recipes except *Crawfish Boil* are prepared with cooked crawfish.

Crawfish tails resemble shrimp in appearance and texture, but many people say they taste like lobster. We decided that they have their own distinctive flavor. You can generally substitute crawfish for any dish that calls for cooked shrimp or crab meat.

Some recipes call for crawfish "fat" as well as the meat. This "fat" is really an organ, the hepatopancreas. It has a distinct flavor, and you may have to develop a taste for it.

Crawfish are high in protein, low in calories and fat. A serving contains about 135 mg. of cholesterol.

For the traditional crawfish boil, buy live crawfish. Be sure they are alive when you cook them. The tail should turn under and they should spread their claws when picked up. Allow 2 to 4 pounds per person, depending upon the other foods being served.

To boil crawfish, you need a little more than one quart of water for each pound of crawfish, plus more to cook the vegetables.

You can have a large group of people for an outdoor crawfish boil. Just use the same pots and cooking source that you use when having a shrimp boil. You need a pot with a lid and a basket that fits inside. Our recipe for *Crawfish Boil* is one that you can cook on the stove top. To use it for a larger group, just multiply the ingredients.

Crawfish Boil
- 10 pounds live crawfish
- 5 whole heads garlic, peeled
- 6 onions, halved
- 6 lemons, halved
- crawfish seasoning (Zatarain's is the traditional brand and is readily available. Use your favorite brand. Follow package directions.)
- 2 whole new potatoes per person
- 2 corn ears, halved, per person
  Fill pot halfway with water. Add garlic, onions and lemons. Bring to boil. Add seasoning. Add potatoes and boil 1 minute.

Add corn and crawfish. Cover and return to boil. Cook until done, about 15 minutes. Turn off heat and let stand from 10 to 25 minutes. (The longer it stands, the spicier it will be.) Remove basket, and turn contents onto paper lined table. Provide lots of napkins. Eat immediately. Serves 6 to 8.

Golden-Fried Crawfish
- 1 pound cooked, peeled crawfish tails
- 1 cup flour
- 1/2 cup yellow cornmeal
- 1 teaspoon salt
- 1/2 teaspoon freshly ground black pepper
- 1/2 teaspoon garlic powder
- 1/4 teaspoon cayenne pepper
- 1/2 teaspoon baking powder
- 2 eggs
- 1/2 cup light cream
- 1 tablespoon fresh lemon juice
- 1 tablespoon Worcestershire sauce
- 1/4 teaspoon Tabasco sauce
- vegetable oil for frying

In medium bowl, blend flour, cornmeal, salt, pepper, garlic powder, cayenne and baking powder.

In separate medium bowl, beat eggs. Add cream, lemon juice, Worcestershire and Tabasco. Mix well. Dip crawfish in liquid mixture, then dredge in dry ingredients. Deep fry in hot oil 375 F to 400 F, until golden brown, about 3 to 4 minutes. Drain on paper towels. Serve with cocktail or tartar sauce. Serves 3 to 4.

Crawfish Creole
- 1 1/2 pounds cooked, peeled crawfish tails
- 1/2 cup flour
- 1/2 cup vegetable oil
- 1 cup chopped onion
- 1/2 cup chopped celery
- 1/4 cup chopped green pepper
- 2 teaspoons crushed garlic
- 1 14 1/2-ounce can chopped tomatoes, undrained
- 1 6-ounce can tomato paste
- 1 1/2 cups water
- 1 1/2 teaspoons salt
- 1/4 teaspoon cayenne pepper
- 1/4 teaspoon freshly ground black pepper
- 1/2 teaspoon Worcestershire sauce
- 1/4 teaspoon Tabasco sauce
- 2 tablespoons chopped fresh parsley
- 1/4 cup chopped green onion, including tops
- cooked rice

Heat oil in large skillet over medium heat. Blend in flour gradually. Cook, stirring constantly, until roux is golden brown. Add onion, celery, green pepper and garlic. Sauté lightly. Add tomatoes and tomato paste. Blend well and simmer 5 minutes.

Add water, salt, cayenne, pepper, Worcestershire and Tabasco. Bring to boil, then reduce heat and simmer 20 to 30 minutes. Add crawfish and simmer 15 minutes longer. Add parsley and green onion and cook 5 minutes longer. Serve over rice. Serves 6 to 8.

Crawfish Casserole
- 1 1/2 pounds cooked, peeled crawfish tails
- 1 1/2 tablespoons butter or margarine
- 1/2 cup sliced fresh mushrooms
- 1/3 cup finely chopped onion
- 1/2 cup canned chopped tomatoes, drained
- 1 tablespoon flour
- 3/4 cup light cream
- 2 tablespoons dry sherry
- 1/2 teaspoon Worcestershire sauce
- 1/2 teaspoon Tabasco sauce
- 1 teaspoon salt
- 1/4 teaspoon freshly ground black pepper
- 1/2 cup dry bread crumbs
- 2 tablespoons margarine, melted

Melt 1 1/2 tablespoons margarine in large skillet over medium heat. Sauté mushrooms until tender. Add onion and tomatoes. Cook for 10 minutes. Stir in flour. Gradually add cream, stirring constantly. Add sherry, Worcestershire, Tabasco, salt and pepper. Mix well. Add crawfish tails and mix well. Place in lightly greased 2-quart casserole dish.

Mix bread crumbs with 2 tablespoons margarine and sprinkle over casserole. Baked uncovered at 350 F for 20 to 25 minutes or until bubbly and brown. Serves 6.

Crawfish Étouffée
- 1 pound cooked, peeled crawfish tails
- 1 teaspoon salt
- 1/4 teaspoon freshly ground black pepper
- 1/4 pound margarine or butter
- 2 tablespoons flour
- 1/4 teaspoon cayenne pepper
- 2/3 cup finely chopped celery
- 2 cups finely chopped onion
- 1/4 cup finely chopped green pepper
- 2 teaspoons finely chopped garlic
- 3/4 cup water
- 2 tablespoons finely chopped green onion tops
- 2 tablespoons finely chopped fresh parsley
- 1/4 cup dry white wine
- cooked rice

Season crawfish tails with salt and black pepper. Set aside. Melt margarine in heavy pot over medium heat. Add flour and cook until light brown. Add cayenne, celery, onion, green pepper and garlic. Cook, stirring often, until vegetables are tender, but not brown. Add crawfish tails and sauté until just tender, about 15 minutes. Add water and green onion. Bring to boil and simmer for 5 minutes more. Add parsley and wine and cook for 5 minutes. Allow to stand a few minutes. Serve over cooked rice. Serves 4 to 6.

Sautéed Crawfish
- 1 pound cooked, peeled crawfish tails
- 1/2 teaspoon white pepper
- 1/4 teaspoon salt
- 1/4 teaspoon cayenne pepper
- 1/4 teaspoon freshly ground black pepper
- 1/2 teaspoon dried basil leaves
- 1/4 teaspoon dry mustard
- 1/4 pound margarine or butter
- 1/2 cup finely chopped green onion tops
- 1 teaspoon minced garlic
- 1/2 teaspoon Tabasco sauce
- 1/2 cup fish or chicken broth
- cooked rice

In small bowl, combine white pepper, salt, cayenne, black pepper, basil and mustard. Set aside.

In medium skillet, melt half of margarine over medium heat. Lightly sauté onion and garlic. Add crawfish, Tabasco and seasoning mix. Sauté over high heat for 2 minutes, stirring occasionally. Add remaining margarine in pieces. Add broth gradually while moving pan back and forth to mix. Cook over high heat 3 to 4 minutes, shaking pan constantly. Serve over cooked rice. Serves 3 to 4.

Stewed Crawfish

* 1 pound cooked, peeled crawfish tails
* 1 1/2 teaspoons vegetable oil
* 3/4 cup chopped onion
* 1/2 cup chopped celery
* 1 1/2 teaspoons flour
* 1 cup canned chopped tomatoes, drained
* 3/4 teaspoon salt
* 1 teaspoon dried parsley
* 1/2 teaspoon minced garlic
* 1/16 teaspoon freshly ground black pepper
* 1 thin lemon slice
* 1/2 small bay leaf
* 1/8 teaspoon thyme
* 1/16 teaspoon cayenne pepper
* 1/8 teaspoon Tabasco sauce
* cooked rice

Heat oil in medium skillet over medium heat. Lightly sauté onion and celery. Stir in flour and cook until brown. Add tomatoes, salt, parsley, garlic, black pepper, lemon, bay leaf, thyme, cayenne and Tabasco. Simmer for 20 minutes. Add crawfish tails and simmer 15 to 20 minutes longer, or until tender. Remove bay leaf and lemon slice. Serve over rice. Serves 4 to 6.

Crawfish Jambalaya
- 1 pound cooked, peeled crawfish tails
- 2 tablespoons vegetable oil
- 1 tablespoon flour
- 1 cup chopped onion
- 1/2 cup finely chopped celery
- 1/2 cup finely chopped green pepper
- 4 teaspoons minced garlic
- 1 1/2 cups chicken broth
- 1/2 teaspoon salt
- 1/4 teaspoon freshly ground black pepper
- 1/4 teaspoon cayenne pepper
- 1/2 cup finely chopped green onion, including tops
- 1/2 cup finely chopped fresh parsley
- 2 cups cooked rice

Heat oil in large skillet over medium heat. Blend in flour gradually. Cook, stirring constantly, until roux is golden brown. Add onion, celery, green pepper and garlic. Sauté until tender. Add broth, salt, pepper and cayenne. Cook uncovered, about 20 minutes, stirring occasionally. Add crawfish tails and simmer until just tender, about 10 to 15 minutes. Add green onion and parsley. Cook 5 minutes longer. Mix with cooked rice. Serves 4 to 6.

Crawfish Gumbo
- 1 pound cooked, peeled crawfish tails
- 1/4 cup vegetable oil
- 3/4 cup finely chopped onion
- 2 teaspoons minced garlic
- 1 cup finely chopped celery
- 1/2 cup chopped green onion, including tops
- 1 cup chicken broth
- 1 14 1/2-ounce can chopped tomatoes, undrained
- 1/4 teaspoon thyme
- 1 small bay leaf
- 1/4 teaspoon cayenne pepper
- 1/4 teaspoon oregano
- 1/2 teaspoon salt
- 1 box frozen sliced okra
- 1 tablespoon finely chopped fresh parsley
- cooked rice (optional)

Heat oil in medium pot over medium heat. Lightly sauté onion, garlic, celery and green onion. Add broth, tomatoes, thyme, bay leaf, cayenne, oregano and salt. Bring to boil and simmer 10 minutes. Add okra and simmer 10 minutes. Add crawfish and simmer 20 minutes. Add parsley. Serve in bowls or over rice if desired. Serves 4 to 6.

RECIPES & MORE
Index

Grilled Tuna with Lime Butter.

Beer Batter Fried Oysters.

Shrimp au Gratin.

From simple to sophisticated,

this recipe collection created

by the Nutrition Leaders

offers the finest complements

to any fresh seafood.

IDEAS & NOTES

IDEAS & NOTES

IDEAS & NOTES

IDEAS & NOTES

IDEAS & NOTES

IDEAS & NOTES